Scots

Episcopalians

at Home and Abroad
1689-1800

By
David Dobson

CLEARFIELD

Printed for Clearfield Company by
Genealogical Publishing Company
Baltimore, Maryland
2011

ISBN 978-0-8063-5523-8

Made in the United States of America

INTRODUCTION

The Registers of the Church of Scotland represent the single most important source for family historians researching their ancestors prior to the introduction of statutory registration of births, marriages, and deaths in 1855. There are, however, other church registers which are difficult to access especially for the eighteenth century. The records of the Episcopal churches in Scotland are among such sources. The problem arises from a decision made in the late seventeenth century.

During the seventeenth century the Church of Scotland contained both Presbyterian and Episcopalian elements, the latter form of church government was favored by the Stuart kings. However in 1688 King James VII of Scotland, who was simultaneously King James II of England, fled to France enabling William and Mary to claim the thrones. The incoming King William, faced with the fact that the Scottish bishops had sworn allegiance to King James, decided that henceforth the Church of Scotland was to be Presbyterian. Episcopacy was therefore disestablished and replaced by a Presbyterian system of church government in Scotland. The contemporary population of Scotland was around one million people and according to recent research around 250,000 were Episcopalian. The majority of Episcopalians were found north of the River Tay, especially in the North East and in certain parts of the Highlands.

Under the Act of Toleration of 1712, during the reign of Queen Anne, Episcopalians who withdrew their allegiance to the House of Stuart were allowed to worship freely and were known as the Qualified Chapel. Many Episcopalians, however, could not accept the new regime in conscience and formed what were called Non-Juring churches. In 1719 under King George I the first Penal Act was passed which made it illegal for Episcopal ministers to preach to more than nine people at any one time, and were required to pray for King George while renouncing the exiled Stuarts. The Episcopal clergy supported the Jacobites in 1715 and in 1745. After the '45 the Government soldiers destroyed a number of Episcopal churches. Harsher Penal Laws were imposed – for example Episcopalians could not hold public office or go to university or college. Some Episcopalians chose to emigrate, notably the clergy who were recruited for service as Church of England ministers in the colonies. Others went abroad as Jacobite prisoners of war bound for service in the American plantations, some took refuge in Europe, and a number settled in the American colonies.

The Episcopal Church in Scotland was significantly reduced in power and influence by the late eighteenth century. The number of adherents was a fraction of that a century earlier, however the church continued to function. After the American Revolution, Samuel Seabury who had been elected Bishop of Connecticut sought consecration by the Archbishop of Canterbury in England but was unable to take the Oath of Royal Supremacy. Consequently he was consecrated by Scottish bishops in Aberdeen in 1784. On the death of Bonnie Prince Charlie, alias King Charles III, in 1788 the Scottish bishops agreed to pray for King George III which resulted in the Penal Laws being withdrawn in 1792. The Episcopalians in Scotland could then operate without restriction.

Because of the Penal Laws there are no registers comparable to those of the contemporary Church of Scotland. The records of baptism, marriage, and death, where they have survived are scattered. Many are in original manuscript form in churches or diocesan libraries, some are in typescript or manuscript in the National Archives of Scotland, a handful have been published in full or in part. This compilation is designed to alleviate the problems faced by researchers. The book is based on original research into surviving manuscripts together with selected extracts from published sources. It is in no way comprehensive but does illustrate the range of sources available to family historians with Scottish Episcopalian roots.

I should like to thank John W. Irvine FSA (Scot) for permission to include references to Perth Episcopalians based on a document in his possession.

David Dobson

Dundee, Scotland, 2010.

SOURCES

AER = Arbroath Episcopal Records

ANQ = Aberdeen Notes and Queries, series

AGB = Americans of Gentle Birth, Baltimore, 1770

AOB = Annals of Banff

APB = Aberdeen Propinqity Books

BNDBR Bishop Norie's Dundee Baptismal Register

CAG = Compendium of American Genealogy

CBER = Chapel at Bairnie, Episcopal Register

CCVC = Colonial Clergy of Virginia and the Carolinas

CFR = Cockburn Family Records, Edinburgh, 1913

CTB = Calendar of Treasury Books, series

CTER = Chapel at Tillydesk Episcopal Register

DAB = Dictionary of American Biography, London, 1928

DBR = Dundee Burgess Roll

DC = History of the Episcopal Church in the Diocese of Caithness

DUAS = Dundee University Archival Service

EBR = Edinburgh Burgh Records

ECG = Historical Account of the Settlement of the Episcopal
Congregation in Dundee in 1727, Dundee, 1744

EF = Episcopacy in Forfar, 1560-1910

EM = History of the Episcopal Church in the Diocese of Moray

EMA = Emigrant Ministers to America, 1690-1811, London, 1904

EV	=	Journals of Episcopal Visitations... 1762-1770, London, 1923
F	=	Fasti Ecclesiae Scoticanae, Edinburgh, 1915
F.Ab.	=	Fasti Aberdeonenses, Aberdeen, 1854
FPA	=	Fulham Papers, American, Oxford, 1965
GL	=	Guildhall Library, London
HEC	=	Haddington Episcopal Church Records
JCTP	=	Journal of the Committee for Trade and the Plantations, series
JSC	=	A Jacobite Stronghold of the Church, Edinburgh, 1907
JWI	=	John W. Irvine mss
KCA	=	Officers and Graduates of King's College, Aberdeen, 1893
KEITH	=	A Historical Catalogue of the Scottish Bishops, Edinburgh, 1824
LER	=	Leith Episcopal Records
LIS	=	List and Index Society
LPR	=	List of Prisoners Concerned in the Rebellion, 1745-46, Edinburgh, 1890
MCA	=	Fasti Academiae Mariscallanae Aberdonensis, Aberdeen, 1898
MRB	=	Register of Baptisms, Muthill, Perthshire, Edinburgh, 1887
MSA	=	Maryland State Archives
NA	=	National Archives, London
NAS	=	National Archives of Scotland, Edinburgh
NDER	=	New Deer Episcopal Register
NNQ	=	Northern Notes and Queries, series
OC	=	Old Churches, Minister and Families of Virginia

RAV	=	Register of Ancestors in Virginia, Richmond, 1979
SA	=	The Scots Antiquary, Edinburgh
SA1	=	Scotus Americanus, Edinburgh, 1982
SCHR	=	Scottish Church History Records, series
SCM	=	Stewart Clan Magazine
SER	=	St Andrews Episcopal Register
SEV	=	Some Emigrants to Virginia, Baltimore, 1953
SLIM	=	Calendar of Irregular Marriages in South Leith, 1697-1818,
SM	=	Scots Magazine, series
SPAER		St Pauls, Aberdeen, Episcopal Register, Aberdeen, 1908
SPAWI	=	Calendar of State Papers, America and the West Indies, series
SRS	=	Scottish Record Society
ST.ER	=	Stonehaven Episcopal Records
SUR	=	St Andrews University Register 1747-1897, St Andrews, 2004
TBD	=	The Three Bishops of Dunkeld, 1743-1808, Perth, 1915
TV	=	Tay Valley Family Historian, series
VG	=	Virginia Genealogies, Wilkes-Barre, 1891
WMQ	=	William and Mary Quarterly, series

ABBREVIATIONS

MI	=	Monumental Inscription

Scots Episcopalians at Home and Abroad, 1689-1800

ABERNETHY, WILLIAM, and his wife Anna Imrie, in Barrock, parish of New Deer, Aberdeenshire, parents of Mary baptised 2 April 1702. Witnesses : Robert Strachan and William Watson both in Barrock. Godmothers : Mary Gordon and Mary Strachan there. [NDER]

ABERNETHY, WILLIAM, ordained a deacon 1744, minister at Nairn from 1744 to 1746. [TBD#167]

ABBOT, DAVID, in Dundee, 1727. [ECD#26]

ADAM, ANNE, was confirmed in Forfar, Angus, in 1770. [EF#26]

ADAM, ELIZABETH, was confirmed in Forfar, Angus, in 1770. [EF#26]

ADAM, DAVID, in Seatown of Cowie, Kincardineshire, father of twins John and Robert, baptised in Stonehaven, 25 March 1761. [ST.ER]

ADAM, GEORGE, in Seatown of Cowie, Kincardineshire, father of John baptised in Stonehaven, on 9 May 1758, and William baptised in Stonehaven on 28 August 1760. [ST.ER]

ADAMSON, NELLIE, in Muirhouses, confirmed in Forfar in 1770. [EF#26]

ADDERTON, RICHARD, married Jean Urquhart, both in Newton Ayr, in Ayr, 13 December 1790. [NAS.CH12.26.1]

ADDISON, ..., a minister residing at the head of Chalmers' Close, Edinburgh, 1746. [JSC#63]

ADIE, ALEXANDER, son of the late John Adie, deacon convenor of Dunfermline, Fife, and Elizabeth Alexander, daughter of the late John Alexander minister at Kildrummy, Aberdeenshire, 14 May 1719; contract re John Adie, son of the said Alexander Adie and Elizabeth Alexander, 1729. [NAS.CH12.23.10/29]

AGNEW, ANDREW, a minister sent to Jamaica in 1706, later settled in Virginia. [EMA#10]

AGNEW, JOHN, born 1727 in Wigtownshire, a minister who emigrated to Virginia in 1751, settled as rector in Suffolk, Nansemond County, Virginia, father of Stair, a Loyalist in 1776, moved to New Brunswick, died 1812. [EMA#10][NA.AO13.27.7/10, etc][FPA#329]

AGNEW, STAIR, son of Reverend John Agnew, settled in Virginia before 1776, a Loyalist. [NA.AO13.27.171/5]

AITKEN, JOHN, born 1759, a wright, died 1845. [Montrose Episcopal MI]

AITKEN, WILLIAM, born 1727, a wright and guildsbrother of Montrose, Angus, died 1790, his wife Ann Petrie, born 1723, died 1790. [Montrose Episcopal MI]

AITKENHEAD, JOHN, in Brechin, Angus, buried 6 December 1800. [NNQ14.154]

AITKENHEAD, JOHN, father of a child baptised in Brechin, Angus, on 27 December 1799. [NNQ.14.153]

AITON, GEORGE, and his wife .... Stuart, parents of Mary Helen born and baptised in St Andrews, Fife, 8 July 1722; William born 20 November and baptised 21 November 1723 in St Andrews; Laurence born and baptised 19 July 1727 in St Andrews; Charles born 28 May and baptised in St Andrews on 29 May 1729. Sponsors : Mr M. Law, William Neish, and Mrs Wood. [SER]

ALEXANDER, AGNES, daughter of the late John Alexander minister at Kildrummy, Aberdeenshire, and James Cassie in Ribra, an antenuptial marriage contract, 1 September 1731. [NAS.CH12.23.33]

ALEXANDER, ANNA, fifth daughter of the late John Alexander minister at Kildrummy, Aberdeenshire, a deed, 11 July 1738. [NAS.CH12.23.35]

ALEXANDER, BARBARA, daughter of John Alexander minister at Kildrummy, Aberdeenshire, and William Reid of Auchmillan, an antenuptial marriage contract, 21 February 1721. [NAS.CH12.23.6]

ALEXANDER, ELIZABETH, daughter of the late John Alexander minister at Kildrummy, Aberdeenshire, and Alexander Adie, son of the late John Adie, deacon convenor of Dunfermline, Fife, an antenuptial marriage contract, 14 May 1719. [NAS.CH12.23.10]

Scots Episcopalians at Home and Abroad, 1689-1800

ALEXANDER, ISOBEL, daughter of John Alexander, daughter of John Alexander minister at Kildrummy, and Colin Petry, brother of George Petry of Newton of Prema, now at Miln of Gairth, Aberdeenshire, an antenuptial marriage contract, 3 April 1711. [NAS.CH12.23.5]

ALEXANDER, ISOBEL, confirmed in Forfar, Angus, in 1770. [EF#26]

ALEXANDER, JOHN, born 1665, educated at Baliol College, Oxford, a minister who settled in Virginia. [CCVC.5]

ALEXANDER, JOHN, educated at St Andrew's University, graduated MA in 1661, ordained 1668, minister at Creich, Sutherland, later in 1682 at Kildrummy, Aberdeenshire, husband of Anna Gordon, bonds, 1716; a memorandum, 1713, imprisoned as a Jacobite in Aberdeen and later Coupar Angus in 1716, deposed in 1717, died August 1717. Husband of Anna Gordon, parents of John, Isobel, Jean, and Agnes. [TBD#1/2] [NAS.CH12.16/30; 23/7]; testament, 24 July 1738, Comm. of Aberdeen. [NAS][F.6.133]

ALEXANDER, JOHN, born 1694 in Auchendore, Aberdeenshire, son of Reverend John Alexander, ordained 1724, Episcopal minister at Alloa, Clackmannanshire, Bishop of Dunkeld of the non-jurant Episcopal Church, 19 August 1743, died 24 April 1776. [St John's, Alloa, MI][TBD#1][F.6.133][Keith#540]

ALEXANDER, JOHN, son of the late John Alexander minister at Kildrummy, Aberdeenshire, discharge of tocher, 28 November 1719, minister at Clackmannan, 1739. [NAS.CH12.23.13/38/39]

ALEXANDER, JOHN, a minister who emigrated to Georgia, 1766. [EMA#10][FPA#325]

ALEXANDER, MARGARET, daughter of the late John Alexander minister at Kildrummy, Aberdeenshire, and Thomas Kirkwood schoolmaster at Cranstoun, Midlothian, an antenuptial marriage contract, 24 May 1719. [NAS.CH12.23.11]

ALEXANDER, SOPHIA, fourth daughter of the late John Alexander minister at Kildrummy, and John Gordon in Newton of Auchindore, Aberdeenshire, an antenuptial marriage contract, 7 and 31 August 1719. [NAS.CH12.23.12]

ALISON, ARCHIBALD, born 1758, minister at St Paul's, died 1839, husband of Dorothy Gregory, born 1754, died 1830. [St John's, Edinburgh, MI]

Scots Episcopalians at Home and Abroad, 1689-1800

ALLAN, ANDREW, a burgess and guildsbrother of Glasgow in 1723, a merchant in Charleston, South Carolina, 1727. [FPA#140]

ALLAN, HARRY, of Brignees, a writer, married Mary Drummond, relict of the late Thomas Cornwall of Bonhard, at the Citadel of Leith on 13 February 1738. Witnesses : Hugh Clerk a wine merchant in Edinburgh, Charles Allan brother of the bridegroom and a surgeon in Edinburgh, Robert Smith a wine merchant in Leith, Mrs Christian Main, and Mrs Rachel Houstoun. [LER][NNQ.8.125]; a writer in Leith, father of James confirmed in Leith on 7 December 1738; John confirmed in Leith on 5 March 1742; Elizabeth confirmed in Leith on 2 November 1743; Alexdrina, youngest daughter of Harry Allan a writer, was confirmed in Leith on 13 August 1747; and Robert confirmed in Leith on 8 October 1747. [SA.IX.13][LER]

ALLAN, WILLIAM, a mariner in Dundee, 1727, burgess of Dundee, 1735. [ECD#24][DBR]

ALLARDYCE, ALEXANDER, educated at Marischal College, Aberdeen, 1763-1767, graduated MA, minister at Old Deer, Aberdeenshire. [MCA#334]

ALLARDYCE, ..., daughter of James Ritchie of the West Islands(!?), was baptised in Brechin, Angus, on 22 October 1796. [NNQ.14.98]

ALVES, ALEXANDER, a shoemaker, father of John baptised at Plain Stone Square, Canongate, 25 February 1753. Witnesses : Mr Sutherland a brewer and .... Sime a writer.

ANDERSON, CHARLES, educated at King's College, Aberdeen, 1693, a minister, settled in Virginia 1700, died in Charles City on 7 April 1718. [Charles City MI]

ANDERSON, DAVID, minister at Perth from 1680, deprived in 1689, later a schoolmaster there, died 1697. [F.4.234]

ANDERSON, JAMES, and his wife Janet Wright in Cuilt, Muthill, Perthshire, : parents of Elspet born 29 January and baptised 31 January 1698. [MRB]

ANDERSON, JOHN, was confirmed in Fortrose, Easter Ross, 1770. [EV#327]

ANDERSON, JOHN, a minister, to the Leeward Islands in 1717, minister of Trinity parish, St Kitts, in 1719, minister of St George, Basseterre, St Kitts, 1723,

Scots Episcopalians at Home and Abroad, 1689-1800

also of Trinity, Palmeto Point, St Kitts, 1727, died in St Kitts 1734. [NAS.CH2.14.22; RD3.251.201; RD3.253.542; RD2.278.744][EMA#11][FPA#272] [SPAWI.1728.494.iii/iv; 1729.906]

ANDERSON, MARY, daughter of James Anderson and his wife Mary Miln in Coalhill of Waterton, Aberdeenshire, was baptised 11 May 1764. [CBER]

ANDERSON, SAMUEL, of Moredun, born 1756, a banker, died 1821, his wife Jane Hay, born 1766, died 1834. [St John's, Edinburgh, MI]

ANDERSON, THOMAS, was confirmed in Fortrose, Easter Ross, 1770. [EV#327]

ANDERSON, WILLIAM, a mariner from Virginia, married Mary Gist from London, in Haddington, East Lothian, on 24 January 1768. [NAS.CH12.2.18][HEC]

ANDREW, ANNE, was confirmed in Forfar, Angus, in 1770. [EF#26]

ANDREWS, JOHN, minister of Cameron parish, Fairfax County, Virginia, 1740 to 1767, missionary of the Society for the Propagation of the Gospel at Lewes, Delaware, 1767. [OC#272][FPA#193/305/330]

ANDREWS, WILLIAM, a minister by 1700, settled at Mohawk Castle, New York, as a missionary of the Society for the Propagation of the Gospel to the Six Nations in 1712, died 1728. [SCHR.14.148]

ANDREWS, WILLIAM, a minister in Portsmouth, Virginia, before 1764, to New York in 1770, an army chaplain in 1776, a Loyalist, returned to Scotland by 1778. [NA.AO13.27.234/44, etc][FPA#327]

ANDREWS, WILLIAM, late minister of the Episcopal Chapel in Glasgow, was buried in Ayr on 14 September 1791. [NAS.CH12.26.1]

ARBUTHNOTT, Dr ALEXANDER, burgess of Dundee 1685, in Dundee, 1727. [ECD#23][DBR]

ARBUTHNOTT, HELLEN, born 1760, died 1838, wife of Hugh James Patterson Rollo of Bannockburn. [St John's, Edinburgh, MI]

ARBUTHNOTT, JAMES, a cleric, emigrated to the Leeward Islands in 1705. [EMA#11]

5 |

ARBUTHNOT, Sir WILLIAM, born 1767, died 1829, his wife Lady Anne ......, born 1778, died 1846. [St John's, Edinburgh, MI]

ARCHIBALD, DAVID, in Glen Effock, father of William Archibald baptised 14 March 1731 at Lochlee, Angus. Witnesses: Thomas Jollie there and William Kinnear in Inchgrundle. Also of Jean Archibald baptised at Lochlee on 5 March 1733. Witnesses : Thomas Jollie there and James Campbell in Dalbreak. Also of David Archibald baptised 30 June 1735 at Lochlee. Witnesses: David Rose in Tillybirnie and Thomas Jollie in Glen Effock. [DUAS.BrMsDC3/174]

ARNOT, CHARLOTTE, daughter of James Arnot of Balkeithly and his wife Euphame Affleck, was born on 30 July 1728 and baptised at Balkeithly, Fife, on 3 August 1728. [SER]

ARNOTT, DAVID, a brewer in Arbroath, dead by 1749, husband of Jean Gavin, parents of John born 1733, residing on Shorehead, Arbroath, 1752. [SRS.13.76]

ARNOT, ELIZABETH, daughter of James Arnot of Balkeithly, Fife, and his wife Euphame Affleck, was born on 26 June 1726 and baptised at Balkeithly on 28 June 1726. [SER]

ARNOT, Mrs, of the Perth Episcopalian Congregation, 1742. [TV.77.21][JWI]

ATHY, WILLIAM, of the Royal Regiment of Artillery, married Margaret Thompson, in Ayr, 27 August 1797. [NAS.CH12.26.1]

ATKINSON, Sir GEORGE, MD, born 1762, died 1832. [St John's, Edinburgh, MI]

AUCHENLECK, ANDREW, a minister in Bermuda in 1706 and in Jamaica before 1710. [FPA#248][LIS.5.85/127]

AUCHENLECK, DAVID, a merchant in Dundee, 1727. [ECD#24]

AVEN, ARCHIBALD, from Banff, a minister who emigrated to Virginia in 1767 and settled in Norfolk, Virginia, before 1774. [NAS.CS16.1.157][EMA#11]

AYTON, WILLIAM, a goldsmith, married Thomasa, daughter of Thomas Wemyss an advocate, in Fife's Close, Edinburgh, 7 April 1741. [DUAS: BrMS3/Dc/12]

BADIOCHILL, WILLIAM, a minister in the Chapel of Seggat, a beneficiary under the will of Alexander Deuchar in Barbados, 1738 [NAS.CC8.8.100]

BAILIE, ANDREW, a cleric who emigrated to Barbados in 1709. [EMA#12]

BAILY, ..., a minister on the Western Shore of Maryland, dismissed in 1718. [FPA#29]

BAIN, EDWARD, and his wife Isobel McLeish, in Benebeg, Muthill, : parents of Lilias, born 11 November and baptised 12 November 1697. [MRB]

BAIN, JOHN, and his wife Margaret Keillar, in Ballohargie, Muthill, Perthshire, parents of William, born 6 December, baptised 19 December 1697. [MRB]

BAIN, JOHN, and his wife Elspet Harrower, : parents of Andrew born 8 January and baptised in Muthill, Perthshire, 10 January 1698. [MRB]

BAIN, MARGARET, was confirmed in Fortrose, Easter Ross, 1770. [EV#327]

BAIN, WILLIAM, was confirmed in Fortrose, Easter Ross, 1770. [EV#327]

BALFOUR, JAMES, born in Banchory Ternan on 15 August 1731, a missionary of the Society for the Propagation of the Gospel, to Trinity Bay, Newfoundland, in 1764 to 1774, at Harbour Grace and Carboneer, 1775-1792, died 1792. [EMA#12][FPA#299/327][LIS.5.3]

BALFOUR, JOHN, son of .... Balfour the younger of Forret, was baptised on 5 June 1723 in the house of the laird of Bandene in Dundee. [BNDBR]

BALFOUR, Mrs KATHERINE, an adult, niece of Lady Sinten, was baptised in Leith on 1 December 1762. [SA.IX.12][LER]

BALFOUR, ROBERT, of Balbirnie, married Anne, daughter of Sir Andrww Ramsay of Whitehill 2 June 1736, at Lady Ramsay's house, Edinburgh.[DUAS: BrMS3/Dc/12]

BALFOUR, WILLIAM, educated at Marischal College, Aberdeen, 1730, a minister who emigrated to Virginia in 1738. [EMA#12][WMQ.2.20/131]

BALMAINE, ALEXANDER, born 1740 in Edinburgh, educated at the Universities of St Andrews and of Edinburgh, 1757 to 1760, to America in 1772, assistant minister at Copley, Virginia, 1772, settled in Augusta and Frederick parishes, Virginia, married Lucy Taylor, died 1820. [Virginia Journal-23/11/1788] [EMA#12][FPA#310/330][OC#319]

BALNEAVIS, ALEXANDER, son of Alexander Balneavis of Carnbadie, graduated MA from St Andrews 1684, minister at Tibbermore, Perthshire, 1687-1689, deposed as a Jacobite, died before 6 January 1692. [F.4.168]

BALNEAVIS, WILLIAM, a minister who emigrated to Antigua in 1712. [EMA#12]

BAND, JOHN, and his wife Margaret Pride : parents of Isobel born 15 March 1724 and baptised 17 March 1724 in St Andrews, Fife; and John born on 28 April and baptised on 29 April 1726, in St Andrews. [SER]

BARCLAY, ADAM, graduated MA from King's College, Aberdeen, 1648, minister of Perth 1688, deprived in 1689. [F.4.231]

BARCLAY, ALEXANDER, graduated MA from King's College, Aberdeen, in 1668, minister of Auchterless in 1674, the from 1682 in Peterhead, deposed in 1695, intruded in 1708 but deposed in 1716 as a Jacobite, therafter an Episcopal preacher in Longate, Peterhead, husband of Margaret Burnet. [F.6.231]

BARCLAY, HENRY, a catechist in Albany, New York, 1735-1737, from London to to Virginia in 1737, a missionary of the Society for the Propagation of the Gospel at Albany and Fort Hunter 1738 -1746, later rector of Trinity, New York, died 1764. [EMA#12][LIS.5.85/127]

BARCLAY, JOHN, son of Reverend Adam Barclay, Episcopal minister in Peterhead, Aberdeenshire, 17... [F.4.231]

BARCLAY, JOHN, son of David and Christian Barclay in Kincardineshire, a minister who settled in St Peter's, Talbot County, Maryland, 17... [MSA.MHR]

BARCLAY, ROBERT, a tailor, father of Charles-John baptised in Advocate's Close, Edinburgh, on 6 January 1754. Witnesses: John Goodwillie, ... McGill, and Agnes Barclay. [DUAS: BrMS3/Dc/12]

BARCLAY, THOMAS, garrison chaplain at Albany, New York, and from 1709 a missionary of the Society for the Propagation of the Gospels among the iroquois, minister at Albany until his death in 1729. [SCHR.14.142][EMA#12]

BARCLAY, WILLIAM, a cleric who emigrated to New England in 1703. [EMA#12]

BARON, ALEXANDER, born in Aberdeen, educated at Marischal College 1745, to South Carolina in 1748, schoolmaster in Charleston, minister of St Paul's, South Carolina, 1753, died in St Helena's, SC, 1759. [FPA#306/329][CCVC]

BARON, ROBERT, a minister who emigrated to Bermuda in 1700 and later settled in Maryland. [EMA#13]

BARON, ROBERT, a missionary of the Society for the Propagation of the Gospel, emigrated to South Carolina in 1753, minister at St Bartholemew's, South Carolina, 1753. [FPA#306/329]

BAXTER, WILLIAM, a widower from Dundee, married Elizabeth Birnie or Donaldson, a widow, in Fraserburgh on 17 December 1797. [NAS.CH12.32.2]

BEAN, ALEXANDER, and his wife Rachael Duguid in the Mains of Dumbraik, Udny, Aberdeenshire, parents of James baptised 10 April 1764. [CBER]

BEAN, GEORGE, and his wife Janet Harper, parents of Christian baptised in Robinson's Close, Edinburgh, 5 July 1752. Witnesses: Christian Walker and James Harper. [DUAS.BrMsDC3/12]

BEARN, ALEXANDER, in Clochie, Lethnott, Angus, father of Janet baptised 14 May 1725. Witnesses: John Lowson and David Smart there. [DUAS.BrMS.DC3/174]

BEATON, ..., of Balfour, in Dundee, 1727. [ECD#24]

BEATTIE, HENRY, in Dundee, 1727. [ECD#26]

BEAVIS, GEORGE, of the 39th Regiment, married Catherine Stephenson, in Ayr, 18 February 1789. [NAS.CH12.26.1]

BELL, ANDREW, born 27 March 1753 in St Andrews, Fife, son of Alexander Bell and his wife Margaret Robertson, educated at St Andrews University 1768-1772, to Virginia as a minister and tutor in 1774, a Loyalist in 1776, later a chaplain HEICS, died 27 January 1832. [Westminster Abbey MI]

BELL, CHRISTOPHER BARKER, surgeon of the 65th Regiment, married Charlotte Montague Johnstone, daughter of Colonel Boulter Johnstone of the said regiment, on 30 September 1798 at St Andrew's Episcopal Church in Glasgow. Witnesses : Colonel Johnstone, his lady, and Mr Marshal the barrack master. [SA.X.23]

BELL, MARGARET PRIMROSE, a foundling, a child about a year old, laid down at the door of William Bell, wine merchant.... "discovered by Miss Peggy Rattray", was baptised in Leith on 25 May 1775. Mrs Janet and Margaret Rattray "taking the vows upon themselves". [SA.IX.12][LER]

BENNET, DUNCAN, and his wife Margaret McGregor, in Overardoch, Muthill: parents of Elspet born 5 January and baptised 9 January 1698. [MRB]

BETHUNE, DAVID, minister in Montserrat, 1715, of the parish of St Anne, Sandy Point, St Kitts, 1724, 1727. [FPA#270/274][SPAWI.1728.494i]

BETHUNE, HENRY, of Balfour, a trustee of the Carruber's Close congregation, Edinburgh, 1741. [JSC#83]

BIGGAR, MARGARET GRAHAM, daughter of Lieutenant Biggar of the 15th Regiment and his wife Mary Straton who married 3 March 1799, was baptised on 23 February 1800 in Brechin, Angus. [NNQ.14.154]

BINGO, JANE, daughter of James Bingo and his wife Mary Brown, was born and baptised in St Andrews, Fife, on 2 October 1728. [SER]

BINNY, ALEXANDER, was confirmed in Forfar, Angus, in 1770. [EF#26]

BINNY, BELL., was confirmed in Forfar, Angus, in 1770. [EF#26]

BINNY, WILLIAM, born Forfar 1728, died 1788, husband of Margaret Sturrock, born 1748, died 1843. [St John's, Forfar, MI]

BINON, Mrs, of the Perth Episcopalian Congregation, 1742. [TV.77.21][JWI]

BIRD, JOHN, a soldier of the Loyal Durham Fencible Cavalry, married Martha ..... from Irvine, in Ayr, 25 February 1795. [NAS.CH12.26.1]

BIRLS, JAMES, a mason in Montrose, Angus, husband of Jean Sangster, born 1741, died 1775. [Montrose Episcopal MI]

BIRNIE, ALEXANDER, a sergeant in Colonel Hay's Regiment, and Eleanor Milne, daughter of William Milne a mason at Philorth, : married in Fraserburgh, Aberdeenshire, on 20 November 1798. [NAS.CH12.32.2]

BIRREL, GEORGE, born 1750, died 1830, husband of Helen Pairman, born 1775, died 1834. [St John's, Edinburgh, MI]

BISSET, GEORGE, a missionary of the Society for the Propagation of the Gospel who emigrated to Rhode Island in 1767, master of Kay's Grammar School and assistant minister in Newport. [EMA#14][FPA#306/329]

BISSET, JAMES, Commissary of Dunkeld, married Abigail, daughter of the late William Mercer a writer in Edinburgh, in Carruber's Close, Edinburgh, 25 November 1740. [DUAS: BrMS3/Dc/12]

BISSET, ..., a child of James Bisset in Nether Carcary, Angus, was baptised on 10 August 1798. [NNQ.14.99]

BIZET, RORY, was confirmed in Arpafilie, Ross-shire, in 1770. [EV#327]

BLACK, ANDREW, son of John Black of the Royal Military Articifers, and his wife Janet, was born 9 April 1798 and baptised in St John the Evangelist, Edinburgh, on 22 April 1798. [NAS.CH12.3.26/3]

BLACK, WILLIAM, born 1679 in Dumfries, a minister who emigrated to New Jersey in 1706, settled in Accomack County, Virginia, in 1708, minister in Sussex County, Pennsylvania, 1709. [SCHR.XIV.149][EMA#14][FPA#173]

BLAIKIE, ANNA, daughter of John Blaikie and his wife Janet Kemp, was born 20 June and baptised 26 June 1768 in Haddington, East Lothian. Witnesses: John Blaikie and George Kemp. [NAS.CH12.2.13]

BLAIKIE, WILLIAM, a farmer in Netherton, and Margaret Cooper, daughter of Alexander Cooper in Broomhill: married at Broomhill of Pitsligo, Aberdeenshire, on 28 December 1799. [NAS.CH12.32.2]

BLAIR, GEORGE, late steward aboard the General Elliot, an East Indiaman, married Alison Sinclair from Oldhamstocks, East Lothian, in Haddington on 3 October 1786. Witnesses: John Clarke and Alexander Duncan. [NAS.CH12.2.2.18][HEC]

BLAIR, JAMES, born 1656 son of Reverend Robert Blair, educated at King's College, Aberdeen, 1670, emigrated to America in 1685, minister in Henrico, Virginia, James City, Va., and Bruton, Va., Commissary of Virginia from 1689 to 1741, founder of the College of William and Mary, died in 1743. [FPA#167/173] [NAS.RD2.59.439][GM.13.443][SM.5.343][KCA.2.234][SCHR.14.138]

BLAIR, JEAN, was baptised at Whiteloch, Blairgowrie, Perthshire, on 30 October 1753. [TBD#155]

BLAIR, JOHN, born 1668, a physician from Angus, emigrated via Darien to Jamaica in 1700, settled in St Catherine's, died 27 June 1728, probate 1728 PCC. [Spanish Town Cathedral, Jamaica, MI]

BLAIR, JOHN, a cleric who emigrated to the West Indies in 1702. [EMA#15]

BLAIR, JOHN, a cleric who emigrated to North Carolina in 1703. [EMA#15]

BLAIR, JOHN, of Bathyock, a trustee of the Carruber's Close congregation, 1741. [JSC#83]; married Patricia, daughter of Robert Stephen, in Edinburgh, 19 August 1762; parents of Christian baptised 17 August 1763, and David baptised 29 November 1764 in Milne's Square. [DUAS: BrMS3/Dc/12]

BLAIR, ROBERT, son of Reverend William Blair (1644-1716), assistant minister of Aberdeen Third Charge, later an Episcopal minister in Edinburgh. [F.6.15]

BLAIR, ROBERT, at Glamis Castle, was confirmed in Forfar in 1770. [EF#26]

BLAIR, WILLIAM, a minister who emigrated to Montserrat in 1750, in Antigua, 1751.[EMA#15][FPA#284]

BLAIR, WILLIAM, a weaver now a soldier in Colonel Halkett's Regiment in Holland, and his wife Jane McAlpine, parents of Jean baptised in Edinburgh on 18 February 1753. Witnesses: John Cameron, John Monro, and Jean Bryden. [DUAS.BrMsDC3/12]

BLAIR, Baillie, of the Perth Episcopalian Congregation, 1742. [TV.77.21][JWI]

BLAIR,......., a minister residing at The Skinner's Hall, Edinburgh, 1746. [JSC#63]

BLAKE, THOMAS, son of William Blake an Evangelical minister in Aberdeen, educated at Marischal College, Aberdeen, 1784, minister of Trinity and of St

James English Episcopal Chapel in Aberdeen also cleric of the Royal Infirmary 1779-1804. [MCA#362]

BLAW, Mrs BARBARA, of Kirkwall, Orkney, was baptised on 12 April 1759. [LER][SA.X.11]

BONHARD, Lady, of the Perth Episcopalian Congregation, 1742. [TV.77.21][JWI]

BOSWELL, GEORGE, a writer in Edinburgh and a trustee of the Carruber's Close congregation, 1741. [JSC#84]

BOWIE, JOHN, educated at Marischal College, Aberdeen, in 1770, a minister who emigrated in 1771, settled in St George's, Maryland. [FPA.21/302/326]

BOWMAN, ALEXANDER, and his wife Elspet Brown, in Mill of Broomfield, Aberdeenshire, parents of John baptised 10 March 1764; in Ulaw, Ellon, Aberdeenshire, parents of Jean baptised 16 March 1776. [CBER]

BOWMAN, DAVID, in Middlefoord, father of Janet Bowman baptised at Lochlee, Angus, on 6 July 1735. Witnesses : Alexander Robie there and James Campbell in Dalbreak. [DUAS.BrMsDC3/174]

BOWMAN, JOHN, in Achsallarie, father of Agnes Bowman baptised at Lochlee, Angus, on 4 March 1733. Witnesses : Walter Innes there and John Edward in Blackhills. [DUAS.BrMsDC3/174]

BOWMAN, THOMAS, in Drumcairn, Lethnot, Angus, father of a child baptised in September 1725. Witnesses : James Laing and John Lyall both there. [DUAS.BrMS.DC3/174]

BOWMAN, WILLIAM, in Tirrybuckle, baptised at Lochlee, Angus, in April 1735. [DUAS.BrMsDC3/174]

BOYD, ANDREW, educated at Glasgow University, a missionary of the Society for the Propagation of the Gospels, to Virginia in 1709. [SCHR.14.147][EMA#16]

BOYD, JOHN, a Society for the Propagation of the Gospel missionary in North Carolina, 1737, dead by 1739. [FPA#148][LIS.5.127]

BRACKENBURY, RICHARD, an Ensign of the 70th Infantry Regiment stationed at Edinburgh Castle, married Janetta Gunn, a spinster from Edinburgh, in Haddington, East Lothian, on 28 February 1777. [NAS.CH12.2.2.18][HEC]

BRAIDFOOT, WILLIAM JOHN, a minister emigrated to Virginia in 1772, settled in Portsmouth, Norfolk, Virginia, by 1774, died there in 1785. [EMA#16][FPA#310/330]

BRANDER, JOHN, a minister, to Virginia, 1759. [FPA#330]

BREACK, JOHN, a merchant in Edinburgh, married Catherine Naughton, in Edinburgh, 25 June 1746. [DUAS: BrMS3/Dc/12]

BRECHIN, JAMES, a minister who emigrated to Virginia in 1702, a minister there from 1705 to 1719. [EMA#16][SNQ.1.153]

BRECHIN, SUSAN, daughter of George Brechin in Sheathin, Aberdeenshire, was baptised 9 April 1776. [CTER]

BRIMMER, WILLIAM, son of John Brimmer and his wife Margaret Moffat, was baptised in Ayr, 24 November 1776. [NAS.CH12.26.1]

BROADBENT, THOMAS, an iron-refiner, and Agnes Fallows, married in St Andrew's Episcopal Church in Glasgow on 11 July 1763, witnesses Joab and Thomas Fallows, iron-refiners in Partick. [SA.X.21]

BRODIE, JAMES, a merchant in West Kirk parish, Edinburgh, married Ann Gough, a widow from Coldingham, Berwickshire, in Haddington, East Lothian, on 29 June 1776. Witnesses : George Lawers and Elizabeth Buchanan. [NAS.CH12.2.2.18][HEC]

BRODIE, JANET WALKER, born 1789, died 1874. [St John's, Edinburgh, MI]

BROWN, AGNES, was confirmed in Forfar, Angus, in 1770. [EF#26]

BROWN, ALEXANDER, in Milntown, father of John Brown baptised in September 1731 at Lochlee, Angus. Witnesses : Thomas Kinnear there and John Edward in Blackhills. [DUAS.BrMsDC3/174]

BROWN, ALEXANDER, in Achronie, father of Alexander Brown baptised at Lochlee, Angus, on 17 October 1735. Witnesses : Alexander Mitchell in Droustie and Robert Will in Wester Achronie. [DUAS.BrMsDC3/174]

BROWN, GEORGE, of Horn, burgess of Dundee, 1725, in Dundee, 1727. [ECD#24][DBR]; father of Grisel, baptised in Horn's house in Dundee on 16 August 1723; Margaret, baptised in Horn's house in Dundee on 28 January 1725; Helen, baptised in his house in Dundee on 26 July 1726. [BNDBR]

BROWN, JAMES, educated at St Andrews University 1762-1766, emigrated to Virginia as a tutor in 1769, ordained in 1774, settled in Georgia from 1776, later a minister in Pensacola, West Florida, a Loyalist, returned to Georgia, a chaplain to the British Army in New York, moved to England. [NA.AO12.99.296, etc][SUR#109]

BROWN, JOHN, burgess of Dundee 1725, a merchant in Dundee, 1727. [ECD#23][DBR]

BROWN, JOHN, burgess of Dundee 1703, a brewer in Dundee, 1727. [ECD#23][DBR]

BROWN, Mrs MARY, of the Perth Episcopalian Congregation, 1742. [TV.77.21][JWI]

BROWN, ROBERT, in Dundee, 1727. [ECD#26]

BROWN, SIMON, a surgeon in the Royal Navy, married Ann Campbell, a spinster from Haddington, East Lothian, there on 16 September 1775. Witnesses Elizabeth McCall and Janet Durham. [NAS.CH12.2.2.18][HEC]

BROWN, WILLIAM, a minister in Auchindoir, Aberdeenshire, a beneficiary under the will of Alexander Deuchar in Barbados, 1738 [NAS.CC8.8.100]

BRUCE, ANDREW, son of the Commissary of St Andrews, Archdeacon of St Andrews, Bishop of Dunkeld from 1679 to 1686, Bishop of Orkney from 1686 to 1688, died March 1700. [Keith#229]

BRUCE, JOHN, educated at Marischal College, Aberdeen, to America as a schoolmaster before 1774, returned to Virginia from London 1775, settled in Norfolk, Virginia. [EMA#17][FUL.23][FPA#304/331]

BRUCE, JOSEPH, a merchant in Fraserburgh, and Margaret Murdoch, : married in Fraserburgh, Aberdeenshire, on 15 September 1796. [NAS.CH12.32.2]

BRUCE, MARGARET, daughter of Patrick Bruce in Seagate, Dundee, was baptised on 27 March 1723. [BNDBR]

BRUCE, WILLIAM, was married in Brechin on 22 January 1797. [NNQ.14.98]

BRUCE, ..., child of James Bruce, a candlemaker in Brechin, Angus, was baptised on 15 January 1797, and another on 18 March 1798, one was buried on 2 January 1800. [NNQ.14.98/99]

BRUIN, WILLIAM, son of William Bruin a soldier in the 35th Regiment, was buried in Ayr on 17 August 1790. [NAS.CH12.26.1]

BUCHAN, ALEXANDER, a merchant in Fraserburgh, a widower, and Margaret Davidson, : married there on 7 October 1804. [NAS.CH12.32.2]

BUCHAN, HUGH, son of David Buchan in Aberdeen, educated at Marishcal College, Aberdeen, 1778-1780, minister in Elgin, Morayshire. [MCA#353]

BUCHAN, JAMES, in Milntown, was father of John baptised 8 September 1729 at Lochlee, Angus. Witnesses : John Edward in Milntown and John Crockat in Balie; James baptised at Lochlee on 4 Februart 1732. Witnesses : Thomas Kinnear and Alexander Brown there. [DUAS.BrMsDC3/174]

BUCHAN, JOHN, son of David Buchan in Huntly, Aberdeenshire educated at Marischal College, Aberdeen, 1784, minister in Kirriemuir, Angus. [MCA#362]

BUCHAN, JOHN, a carpenter from North Berwick, married Ann Douglas of the same parish, in Dirleton, East Lothian, on 19 March 1787. Witnesses : James Hasswell and Leslie Douglass. [NAS.CH12.2.2.18][HEC]

BUCHAN, ROBERT, educated at Edinburgh University in 1770, emigrated to Virginia as a minister in 1772. [EMA#17][FPA#310/330]

BUCHAN, ROBERT, son of John Buchan in Arthrochy, Logie, Aberdeenshire, was baptised 22 June 1776. [CTER]

BUCHANAN, DAVID, a flesher, and his wife Susan Callander, parents of John baptised in the Herb Mercat, Edinburgh, 27 October 1762. Witness Deacon Wemyss. [DUAS.BrMsDC3/12]

BUCHANAN, JOHN, born 1743, from Dumfries-shire, educated at Edinburgh University in 1774, assistant minister in Henrico, Virginia, 1774, returned to Virginia from London in 1775, a minister in Lexington and Henrico parishes, died in Richmond 1822. [FPA#311/331][EMA#17]

BUCHANAN, JOHN, minister of Haddington Episcopal Church, East Lothian, 1775. [NAS.CH12.2.13]

BUCHANAN, MATHEW, emigrated to New York in 1704, and possibly to Carolina in 1710. [EMA#17]

BURN, JOHN, MD, married Elizabeth Alder, a widow, both from Berwick on Tweed, in Haddington, East Lothian, on 16 August 1769. [NAS.CH12.2.18][HEC]

BURGESS, COLIN, born 1749, son of John Burgess in Dingwall, Easter Ross, a minister in St Anne's parish, Jamaica, 1795. [FPA#316]

BURNET, MARGARET, daughter of George Burnet a wig-maker in Dundee, was baptised on 24 March 1726 in Dundee. [BNDBR]

BURNETT, ..., a minister who emigrated to Virginia in 1700. [EMA#18]

BURNSIDE, AMBROSE, a soldier of the Princess of Wales Light Dragoons, and Marion Lason (?) from Ayr, : married there2 April 1798. [NAS.CH12.26.1]

BUTLER, MAY, daughter of Thomas Butler, was born 1 September and baptised 10 September 1768. Witnesses : Richard Hemes and Bartholemew Bower. [NAS.CH12.2.13]

BUTTER, CHARLES, a merchant, married Mary Butter a mantua maker, in Writer's Court, Edinburgh, 28 April 1744. [DUAS: BrMS3/Dc/12]

CADDELL, HENRY, a minister who emigrated to Barbados in 1798. [EMA#18]

CAIRNCROSS, ALEXANDER, a minister in Dumfries, Bishop of Brechin, Bishop of Glasgow from 1684 to 1686, Bishop of Raphoe in Ireland from 1693 to his death in 1701. [Keith#168/270]

CALDER, ANNA, was confirmed in Fortrose, Easter Ross, 1770. [EV#327]

CAMERON, ALLAN, an adult from Lochaber, was baptised in South Leith on 4 February 1767. [SA.IX.12][LER]

CAMERON, DONALD, was confirmed in Fortrose, Easter Ross, 1770. [EV#327]

CAMERON, DONALD, a practitioner of physic and surgery in the parish of St Thomas in the East, Jamaica, married Ann Cornwall Gunn, a spinster of the same parish, at the house of Robert Paterson there on 27 December 1784 by M. Howard the rector, according to the rites of the Church of England, witnesses being David Bryce and Robert Aikman. [StAUL.ms]

CAMERON, JAMES, was confirmed in Kinlochleven in 1770. [EV#350]

CAMERON, JANET, was confirmed in Kinlochleven in 1770. [EV#350]

CAMERON, JOHN, was confirmed in Kinlochleven in 1770. [EV#350]

CAMERON, MARY, was confirmed in Kinlochleven in 1770. [EV#350]

CAMERON, UNNA, was confirmed in Fortrose, 1770. [EV#327]

CAMPBELL, AGNES, daughter of Archibald Campbell of Clathick, an advocate, and Mary Anne his wife, was born 15 December 1798 and baptised in St John the Evangelist, Edinburgh, on 1 January 1799. [NAS.CH12.3.26/5]

CAMPBELL, ALEXANDER, in Auququinaminc, Pennsylvania, 1727. [FPA#102]

CAMPBELL, ALEXANDER, born 12 April 1778 in Creich, educated at Edinburgh and Glasgow Universities, a minister who emigrated to Jamaica in 1803, settled in St Andrew's, Jamaica, died 8 December 1858. [EMA#18][FPA#316][St Andrew's, Jamaica, MI]

CAMPBELL, ARCHIBALD, Bishop of Aberdeen, 1721 to 1724. [Keith#530]

CAMPBELL, ARCHIBALD, son of Alexander Campbell and his wife Margaret Stewart in Kirnan, Kilmichael, Argyll, educated at Marischal College, Aberdeen, from 1739 to 1745, a minister to Virginia, settled in Washington County, Va., from 1754 to 1774. [EMA#18][SCM.12.9][SEV.20] [OC#2/159]

CAMPBELL, COLIN, in Balie, was father of Sylvester baptised at Lochlee, Angus, on 12 April 1730. Witnesses : James Campbell in Dalbreak and Sylvester Campbell in Ardoch; James baptised at Lochlee 13 May 1732. Witnesses : John Christison in Balie and James Gordon in Glen Catt. [DUAS.BrMsDC3/174]

CAMPBELL, COLIN, MA, missionary of the Society for the Propagation of the Gospel in Burlington, New Jersey, from 1738 until his death in August 1766. [FPA#109][LIS.5.86]

CAMPBELL, COLIN, a minister who emigrated to Jamaica in 1751, rector of St Andrew's parish, Jamaica, by 1792. [FPA][MAGU#168]

CAMPBELL, DUNCAN, of the Perth Episcopalian Congregation, 1742. [TV.77.21][JWI]

CAMPBELL, DUNCAN, son of ..... Campbell in Nungate, was born 16 May and baptised in Haddington, East Lothian. Witnesses : Mr Mitchell and Mr Ainslie. [NAS.CH12.2.13]

CAMPBELL, ELIZABETH, adult daughter of James Campbell of Lochend, was baptised and confirmed at Lochend, Caithness, on 10 August 1762, in the presence of her parents. [LER][SA.X.12][DC#277]

CAMPBELL, HELEN, daughter of Archibald Campbell of Clathick, an advocate, and his wife Mary Anne, was born on 20 December 1797 and baptised in St John the Evangelist, Edinburgh, on 3 January 1798. [NAS.CH12.3.26/3]

CAMPBELL, HUGO, brother to James Campbell of Lochend, father of Isabella, Janet and Margaret who : baptised at Wick, Caithness, on 12 August 1762. [DC#277]

CAMPBELL, ISAAC, born 1720, educated at Glasgow University in 1734, a minister who emigrated to America by 1747, settled in Trinity, Newport, Charles County, Maryland, husband of Jean Brown, parents of William, Jean, Gustavus, James, John, and Cecilia, died in Newport 30 July 1784. [EMA#18][VG#165]

CAMPBELL, JAMES, a minister who emigrated to Virginia in 1721. [EMA#18]

CAMPBELL, JAMES, in Dallbreak, was father of Mary Campbell, baptised at Lochlee, Angus, on 11 April 1728. Witnesses : Sylvester and Charles Campbell in Ardoch. [DUAS.BrMsDC3/174]

CAMPBELL, JAMES, son of Alexander Campbell, a joiner then in London, and his wife Anna Maxwell, was baptised in Leith on 21 June 1734. [SA.IX.13][LER]

CAMPBELL, JAMES, of Lochend, and his wife .... Sinclair, : confirmed at Thurso, Caithness, on 8 August 1762. [DC#277]

CAMPBELL, JOHN, in Ardoch, Cairncross, was father of a son baptised at Lochlee on 31 January 1728. Witnesses : Charles and Sylvester Campbell in Ardoch; John baptised 3 January 1731 at Lochlee, Angus. Witnesses : John Christison in Cairncross and James Campbell in Dalbreak. [DUAS.BrMsDC3/174]

CAMPBELL, JOHN, educated at King's College, Aberdeen, 1771, in Stratton Major, Virginia, 1772, returned to Virginia from London in 1773, a Loyalist who settled in Jamaica, rector of St Andrew's, Jamaica, 1792. [EMA#18][FPA#262/310/330]

CAMPBELL, JOHN, of Strachur, married Helen Campbell, daughter of Mungo Campbell of Grenada in the West Indies, at Park, near Fushinnan, Renfrewshire, on 1 November 1787. Witnesses : Mr and Mrs Campbell of Park, their two daughters, Captain James Campbell of the 4th [?] Regiment. Alexander Campbell the bride's brother, her father the said Mungo Campbell, and others. [SA.X.22]

CAMPBELL, SOPHIA, daughter of Hugh Campbell at Millrig, Ayrshire, and his wife Sophia ...., was baptised in Ayr on 27 September 1798. [NAS.CH12.26.1]

CAMPBELL, WILLIAM, adult son of James Campbell of Lochend, was baptised and confirmed at Lochend, Caithness, on 10 August 1762, in the presence of his parents. [LER][SA.X.12][DC#277]

CANT, ANDREW, an Episcopal preacher in Edinburgh, 1723, later Bishop of Glasgow. [NAS.B66.25.766][Keith#553]

CANT, ..., a minister who emigrated to the Leeward Islands in 1692. [EMA#19]

CAR, ISOBEL, daughter of John Car a baker in Murraygate, Dundee, was baptised on 24 June 1723. [BNDBR]

CARDNO, JOHN, son of William Cardno in Fraserburgh, educated at Marischal College, Aberdeen, 1792-1795, minister in Portsoy, Banff. [MCA#375]

CARDNO, WILLIAM, a square-wright in Fraserburgh, Aberdeenshire, and Elizabeth Cummine, : married there on 21 April 1793. [NAS.CH12.32.2]

CARGILL, JAMES, a merchant, and his wife Catherine Auchenleck, parents of James baptised in the Old Posthouse Close, Edinburgh, on 19 May 1754. Witnesses : Lady Woodcokdale, Mr and Mrs Pringle, also David Berry's son and daughter; James baptised in Edinburgh 21 September 1760. Witnesses : Lady Woodcockdale, Mrs James Hay, Mr Berry, and Robert Pringle; Katherine baptised in Edinburgh on 26 November 1761. Witnesses : Lady Woodcockdale, Katherine Berry, and Mrs Pringle. [DUAS.BrMsDC3/12]

CARGILL, JOHN, a minister who emigrated to the Leeward Islands in 1708. [EMA#19]; possibly later in Southwark, Surry County, Virginia. [FPA#174]

CARGILL, JOHN, born 1745, a merchant, died in September 1780. [Kingston Church MI, Jamaica]

CARGILL, RICHARD, born 1744, an Assemblyman and Colonel of the St Thomas Regiment of Foot Militia, settled in St Thomas in the East parish, Jamaica, died in March 1781. [Kingston parish MI, Jamaica]

CARMICHAEL, Dr. & Mrs, of the Perth Episcopalian Congregation, 1742. [TV.77.21][JWI]

CARMICHAEL, REBEKAH, niece to Lady Stewart, was confirmed in Leith on 28 August 1751. [SA.IX.13][LER]

CARMICHAEL, STEWARTINA-CATHERINE, daughter of Stewart Carmichael, was posthumously baptised at Bonnyhaugh on 4 January 1756. Bishop Keith, her grandfather, was godfather, Mrs Keith, her grandmother, was godmother, as was Mrs Forbes. [LER][SA.X.10]

CARNBADYR, Lady, daughters, of the Perth Episcopalian Congregation, 1742. [TV.77.21][JWI]

CARNEGIE, JOHN, a graduate of Glasgow University, emigrated to Virginia 1700, minister of St Stephen's parish, Virginia, from 1702 until 1709. [SCHR.14.142][EMA#39]

CARNEGY, ISOBEL, daughter of Patrick Carnegy of Lour, Angus, was baptised in St John's, Forfar, 6 February 1756. [EF#33]

CARNEGY, JOHN, a stabler in Dundee, 1727, burgess of Dundee, 1735. [ECD#24][DBR]

CARSE, THOMAS, a miller in Berwick on Tweed, married Elizabeth Scot, from Berwick on Tweed, in Haddington on 25 June 1769. [NAS.CH12.2.18][HEC]

CARSTAIRS ROBERT, and his wife Margaret Corstorphin, parents of John born and baptised on 12 January 1723 in St Andrews, Fife; and James, born and baptised on 6 March 1726 in St Andrews, Fife. [SER]

CARSTAIRS, WILLIAM, of Radernie, Fife, and his wife Catherine Carstairs, parents of Archibald born on 25 July and baptised on 28 July 1723 in St Andrews; Helen born 8 July and baptised 9 July 1725 in St Andrews, Fife. [SER]

CARSTAIRS, WILLIAM, a minister residing at the Head of Niddry's Wynd, Edinburgh, 1746. [JSC#63]

CARTER, Dr WILFRED, minister of the Protestant Episcopal Church in Ayr, 1787-1800. [NAS.CH12.26.1]

CASSIE, ISOBEL, daughter of Andrew Cassie a writer in Aberdeen, was baptised 30 November 1720. Witnesses : Alexander Mill cleric-depute and William Forbes a merchant. [SPAER]

CASSIE, JAMES, in Ribra, and Agnes Alexander, daughter of the late John Alexander minister at Kildrummy, an antenuptial marriage contract, 1 September 1731. [NAS.CH2.23.33]

CATTO, ALEXANDER, son of Alexander Catto a merchant in Aberdeen, was baptised 24 September 1720. Witnesses : Alexander Strachan and Alexander Gordon in Clumy, merchants. [SPAER]

CAY, JANE, daughter of Robert Hodshon Cay, an advocate, and his wife Elisabeth, was born 1 August 1797 and baptised in St John the Evangelist, Edinburgh, on 11 September 1797. [NAS.CH12.3.26/2]

CHALMERS, Ensign JOHN, and Margaret Layng, daughter of Edward Layng a skipper in Leith, : married on 15 November 1703. Witnesses : Captain George Foules and Archibald Foules a merchant in Edinburgh. [SLIM#60]

CHALMERS, WILLIAM, a founder in Glasgow, married Margaret Dick, a resident of Glasgow, widow of Mr Belton, at St Andrew's Episcopal Church, Glasgow, on 11 June 1778. [SA.X.21]

CHALMERS, WILLIAM, from New Deer, Aberdeenshire, married Jean Mitchel, in Fraserburgh, Aberdeenshire, on 10 July 1790. [NAS.CH12.32.2]

CHAPMAN, JOHN, a surgeon in Blairgowrie, Perthshire, was baptised on 13 July 1759. [TBD#164]

CHAPMAN, ROBERT, a printer in Glasgow, married Elizabeth Rachell Porter, daughter of John George Porter a portrait painter, on 16 December 1789, in St Andrew's Episcopal Church, Glasgow. Witnesses : Alexander Duncan a printer, and David Thomas a portrait painter. [SA.X.22]

CHEYNE, CHARLES ALEXANDER, eldest son of Reverend George Cheyne, was confirmed in Alloa, Clackmannanshire, on 20 June 1764. [SA.IX.14][LER]

CHEYNE, Reverend GEORGE, father of Hugh, Ninian Richard, and Thomas Rede, who : confirmed at Torbrex on 19 June 1764. [LER][SA.IX.14]

CHISHOLM, Lady, was conformed in Fortrose, Easter Ross, in 1770. [EV#327]

CHRISTIE, ALEXANDER, a writer in Edinburgh and a trustee of the Carruber's Close congregation, 1741. [JSC#84]

CHRISTIE, ALEXANDER, son of James Christie a farmer in Montquhitter, educated at Marischal College, Aberdeen, 1779, a minister in Keith. [MCA#354]

CHRISTIE, ANDREW, son of Captain Alexander Christie of Baberton, was born 7 July 1798 and baptised in St John the Evangelist, Edinburgh, on 9 July 1798. [NAS.CH12.3.26/5]

Scots Episcopalians at Home and Abroad, 1689-1800

CHRISTISON, JOHN, in Shairhead, father of John baptised at Lochlee, Angus, on 30 April 1732. Witnesses : John Christison in Berryhill and John Christison in Cairncross; James baptised 25 September 1735 at Lochlee. Witnesses : James Campbell in Dalbreak and James Christison in Cairncross. [DUAS.BrMsDC3/174]

CHRISTISON, JOHN, in Cairncross, father of Margaret Christison baptised 27 April 1735 at Lochlee, Angus. Witnesses : John Nicoll in Sheulie and James Campbell in Dalbreak. [DUAS.BrMsDC3/174]

CLAPPERTON, ALEXANDER, a writer in Edinburgh, married Jean Black of Whittinghame, in Haddington on 19 February 1772. [NAS.CH12.2.18][HEC]

CLARK, HUGH, a merchant in Edinburgh and a trustee of the Carruber's Close congregation, 1741. [JSC#83]

CLARK, HUGH, son of Alexander Clark of the West Lothian Cavalry and his wife Catherine, was born 28 March 1798 and baptised in St John the Evangelist, Edinburgh, on 29 April 1798. [NAS.CH12.3.26/3]

CLARK, JOHN, a weaver in Montrose, Angus, husband of Emilia Brown, parents of Mary born 1795, died 1805. [Montrose Episcopal MI]

CLARK, THOMAS, born 1755, Captain of the 63rd Regiment and of the Forfar and Kincardineshire militia, died 1842. [Montrose Episcopal MI]

CLARK, WILLIAM, a Captain of the Royal Navy, married Jane Tod, a spinster in Dunbar, East Lothian, there on 19 May 1790. Witnesses : Thomas Tod and Alexander Tod. [NAS.CH12.2.2.18][HEC]

CLARK, WILLIAM, married Margaret Bauld, both of Hamilton, Lanarkshire, on 14 March 1792. [SA.X.23]

CLARK, WILLIAM, Captain of the 35th Regiment, was buried at Ayr on 19 August 1790. [NAS.CH12.26.1]

CLARKE, ANNE, was baptised at Whiteloch, Blairgowrie, Perthshire, on 30 October 1753. [TBD#155]

CLEPHANE, DAVID, educated at St Andrews University 1694-1703, a minister who emigrated to Virginia in 1710. [EMA#20]

CLERK, ANDREW, a schoolmaster who emigrated to New York in 1705. [EMA#20]

CLERKSON, JOHN, a wine merchant, and spouse Barbara Taylor, parents of Marion baptised in Monteith's Close, Edinburgh, on 1 October 1752. Witnesses : Dr Taylor, Lady Pitcairlies; James and Charles, twins, baptised in Kinloch's Close, on 7 October 1753. Witnesses : Dr Taylor, Mrs James Stewart treasurer of the Widows' Fund, and Lady Pitcairlie; John baptised in Leith Wynd on 1 September 1757. Witnesses : Alexander Cunningham a writer, Peter Adie a surgeon, and Miss Campbell; William baptised 24 May 1761. Witnesses : William Taylor a merchant, Miss Taylor, Captain James Cathcart of Inverleith; William baptised in World's End Close on 23 September 1764. Witnesses : uncles William and James Taylor, also R. Taylor. [DUAS.BrMsDC3/12]

COAL, ANNA, was baptised at Glasclune near Blairgowrie, Perthshire, on 20 March 1742. [TBD#41]

COBB, ..., a child of ...Cobb, near Newton Mill, Brechin, Angus, was baptised on 11 May 1800. [NNQ.14.154]

COCKBURN, ALEXANDER or ARCHIBALD, a minister who emigrated to the Leeward Islands in 1710, minister of St Mary's Cayon, St Kitts, and of Christchurch, Nicholas Town, St John's Cape, St Kitts, 1711, a minister in St Kitts from 1722 to 1737. [EMA#20][FPA#275][CFR#260][SPAWI.1728.494.i/ii]

COCKBURN, PATRICK, a minister in Aberdeen, a beneficiary under the will of Alexander Deuchar in Barbados, 1738 [NAS.CC8.8.100];

COLIN, ARTHUR, and his wife Isabella Cheapland, parents of Arthur born on ..... March and baptised in Leuchars, Fife, on 5 March 1723, Jane born 2 May and baptised 3 May 1725 in St Andrews; James born 1 March and baptised 2 March 1727 in Leuchars; and Thomas born 29 May and baptised 30 May 1728 in Leuchars. [SER]

COLLINS, JOHN, a soldier of the Fifeshire Light Dragoons, and Agnes Murray from Ayr, : married there 15 February 1796. [NAS.CH12.26.1]

COLQUHOUN, DUNCAN, was confirmed in Ballachulish, Argyll, on 7 July 1770. [EV#311/344]

COLQUHOUN, EFFIE, was confirmed in Ballachulish, Argyll, in 1770. [EV#344]

COLQUHOUN, Captain WILLIAM, of Garscadden, married Betty Stewart, Blantyre, in Edinburgh, 15 April 1760. [DUAS: BrMS3/Dc/12]

COLVILLE, WILLIAM, husband of Katherine Guthrie, parents of William, Ann, Nicolas, and Isobel, in Applegate Arbroath, Angus, 1752. [SRS.13.60]

COMIN, JAMES, a schoolmaster who emigrated to the Leeward Islands in 1695. [EMA#21]

CONN, HUGH, a minister who died in Bladenburg, Prince George County, Maryland, on 28 June 1752. [SM.14.510]

CONN, WILLIAM, a tailor in Canongate, father of Elizabeth baptised in Edinburgh on 16 February 1753. Witnesses : Elizabeth Conn, Isabel Crawford, William Reid, and Henry Tait. [DUAS.BrMsDC3/12]

CONNELL, ELIZABETH, daughter of Robert Connell in Nethertonholm, and his wife Agnes ..., was baptised in Ayr on 27 November 1799. [NAS.CH12.26.1]

CONQUEROR, DAVID, of the Perth Episcopalian Congregation, 1742. [TV.77.21][JWI]

CONQUEROR, PATRICK, and family, of the Perth Episcopalian Congregation, 1742. [TV.77.21][JWI]

CONQUEROR, Mrs REBECCA, of the Perth Episcopalian Congregation, 1742. [TV.77.21][JWI]

CONSTABLE, JOHN, a flesher burgess of Dundee, 1723, in Dundee, 1727. [ECD#26][DBR]

COOK, DAVID, son of James Cook a dyer in Dundee, was baptised in James Cook's house in the Murraygate of Dundee on 4 March 1725. [BNDBR]

COOK, HELEN, was confirmed in Ballachulish, Argyll, in 1770. [EV#344]

COOK, JAMES, minister of Lanbryde, died 1714. [EM#153]

COOK, JEAN, was confirmed in Ballachulish, Argyll, in 1770. [EV#344]

COOPER, ELIZABETH, daughter of James Cooper and his wife Helen Bowman, was baptised 13 December 1768. [CBER]

COOPER, GEORGE, a shipmaster, married Jean Cooper, relict of John Steuart a gardener, in Edinburgh on 25 January 1738. Witnesses : George Dalling and his wife, John Goodbraun, and Murdoch Smith.[LER][NNQ.8.125]

COOPER, WILLIAM, a Lieutenant of the Fraserburgh Volunteers, and Margaret Reid, daughter of James Reid a shipmaster in Fraserburgh, Aberdeenshire, : married on 16 January 1802. [NAS.CH12.32.2]

CORBET, WALTER, late of St Vincent, West Indies, now at Toll Cross, married Janet Cunningham, daughter of Colonel John Cunningham on 28 March 1774 at St Andrew's Episcopal Church, Glasgow. Witnesses : James and Cunningham Corbet. [SA.X.21]

CORDINER, CHARLES, an Episcopalian minister in Banff, a letter, 1780. [NAS.GD26.13.284; GD44.43.253/56]

CORDINER, WILLIAM, a cleric who emigrated to New England in 1706. [EMA#21]

CORMACH, JAMES, son of Robert Cormach and his wife Jean Burgess in the Mains of Turnerhall, Aberdeenshire, was baptised 5 February 1764. [CBER]

CORNWALL, WALTER, son to Bonhard, was confirmed on 4 October 1736. [SA.IX.13][LER]

CORSAR, FREDERICK, a merchant burgess in Dundee,1700, father of Elizabeth baptised in the house of the laird of Invergowrie, on 12 March 1725. Godfather was the laird of Invergowrie, while his wife and his daughter, Mrs Margaret Clayhills, : godmothers; and Anne baptised in his house in Dundee, on 18 July 1726. Godfather was the laird of Invergowrie, while his wife and his daughter, Mrs Margaret Clayhills, : godmothers. [BNDBR][DBR]

CORSTORPHINE, JOHN, of Nydie, Fife, and his wife Margaret Bethune, parents of Margaret born on 12 November, and baptised at Nydie on 14 November

1722; Anne born on 26 August, and baptised on 28 August 1726, at Nydie; and George born 1 June and baptised 5 June 1728 at Nydie. [SER]

COULL, JAMES, a minister who emigrated to Antigua in 1773. [EMA#22]

COUPER, HENRY, son of James Couper in Cotterton of Craigie, was baptised in Dundee on 28 February 1725. [BNDBR]

COUPAR, JAMES, in Dundee, 1727. [ECD#26]

COUPAR, JEAN, aged about 80, was confirmed in Leith on 11 November 1761. [SA.IX.14][LER]

COUPAR, PATRICK, in Dundee, 1727. [ECD#26]

COUTTS, WILLIAM, a minister in Virginia, 1767. [FPA#309]

COWPAR, ELSPET, daughter of James Cowpar and his wife Helen Bowman in Ellon, Aberdeenshire, was baptised 5 July 1764. [CBER]

CRABB, ..., daughter of deacon Crabb, was baptised in Brechin, Angus, on 23 June 1799. [NNQ.14.153]

CRAIG, ELIZABETH, daughter of William Craig in Toull, was baptised in Stonehaven, Kincardineshire, on 6 February 1761. [ST.ER]

CRAIG, GEORGE, a missionary of the Society for the Propagation of the Gospel who emigrated to Pennsylvania in 1750. [EMA#22][FPA#305]

CRAIG, JAMES, an assistant minister at Copley, Westmoreland County, Virginia, 1754, returned to Virginia from England in 1758. [EMA#22][FPA#307/330]

CRAIG, JAMES, born 1 November 1748, son of Archibald Craig and his wife Christian Innes in Elgin, Morayshire, educated at Marischal College, Aberdeen, 1763-1767, a minister who settled in Cumberland parish, Lunenburg County, and St John's, Baltimore County, Maryland, died 1795. [FPA.21.302]

CRAIG, JEAN, daughter of William Craig in Cottontrae, was baptised in Stonehaven, Kincardineshire, on 24 January 1758. [ST.ER]

CRAIG, WILLIAM, was baptised in Stonehaven on 8 July 1759. [ST.ER]

CRAIGHEAD, JAMES, son of James Craighead in the parish of Mains, was baptised in Dundee on 15 October 1725. [BNDBR]

CRAIGHEAD, JAMES, in Dundee, 1727. [ECD#26]

CRAIGIE, JOHN, of Dunbarnie, married Mrs Christian Smith, daughter of Patrick Craigie of Meffin, in the Old Bank, Edinburgh, 8 November 1738. [DUAS: BrMS3/Dc/12]

CRAMOND, JAMES, an Episcopalian in Keam of Duffus, Moray, a letter, 1778. [NAS.CH12.24.267]

CRAW, Mrs CLEMENTINA, daughter of John Craw of East Renton, was confirmed on 23 October 1740. [SA.IX.13][LER]

CRAW, DANIEL, son of .....Craw, a writer, was born 14 April and baptised 18 April 1768 in Haddington, East Lothian. Witnesses : David Moffat and James Tait. [NAS.CH12.2.13]

CRAWFORD, JAMES, a minister who emigrated to Maryland in 1711. [EMA#22]

CRAWFORD, JOHN, of West Kirk parish, Edinburgh, married Betty Crawford of Tron Church parish, Edinburgh, in Haddington on 25 April 1772. Witnesses : James Fairbairn and Bartholemew Bower. [NAS.CH12.2.18][NEC]

CRAWFORD, THOMAS, a minister who emigrated to Maryland and Virginia in 1703, minister at Dover, Delaware, in 1709. [EMA#22][SPG.11.153] [SCHR.14.146]

CRAWFORD,........, of Monorgan, father of James baptised in Monorgan's house in Dundee on 12 July 1723. Godfathers : James Paton minister of 'Catnes' [Kettins?], and Thomas Crichton an apothecary in Dundee, and the godmother was Mr Paton's wife; David baptised in the house of James Paton, minister of 'Catness' in Dundee on 19 August 1724. Godfathers : Mr Paton and Thomas Crichton a surgeon apothecary in Dundee, while the wife of Mr Paton was godmother; John baptised in the house of James Paton minister of 'Catness' in Dundee on 3 February 1726. Godfathers : Dr John Blair and the laird of Milnhill, and the wife of Thomas Crichton a surgeon apothecary in Dundee as godmother. [BNDBR]

CREE, JOHN, born 1746, a surgeon in the Royal Navy, died at sea in 1788, his wife Margaret Robertson, born 1747, died in Montrose, Angus, in 1839. [Montrose Episcopal MI]

CREIGHTON, ALEXANDER, a burgess of Dundee, 1727. [ECD#23]

CRICHTON, DAVID, son of Alexander Crichton in Seagate, Dundee, was baptised on 9 April 1723. [BNDBR]

CRICHTON, JAMES, a mason in Fisherrow, married Mrs Margaret, daughter of .... Christian in Fisherrow, in South Leith on 2 May 1751. Witnesses : John Smith, David Ramsay, Anne and Margaret Stewart. [LER][NNQ.8.127]

CRICHTON, PATRICK, son of Patrick Crichton of Crunan, was baptised in his house in Seagate, Dundee, on 20 November 1725. Godfathers : Dr David Fotheringham and Dr Kinloch, with Mrs Landels as godmother. [BNDBR]

CRICHTON, PATRICK, in Dundee, 1727. [ECD#26]

CRICHTON, THOMAS, a surgeon apothecary in Dundee, father of Henry baptised in Dundee on 7 December 1722. Godfathers : James Kinloch of that Ilk and Henry Crawford of Monorgan, while the godmothers : Lady .... and Thomas Crichton's sister; Clementina Anna Margerita baptised in Mr Crichton's house in Dundee on 18 November 1723. Godfather was the laird of Monorgan, and godmothers : Mr Crichton's mother, and the wife of Dr Fotheringham; Elizabeth baptised in his house on 3 February 1725. Godfather was the laird of Monorgan, and the godmothers : Lady Kinloch and Mr Crichton's mother; Anna baptised in his house on 5 May 1726. Godfather was the laird of Monorgan, while the godmothers : the mother of Thomas Crichton's wife, and Mrs Ogilvy, relict of Ogilvy of Newhall the younger. [BNDBR]

CRIDLAND, SIMONIDES, Lieutenant of the 17th Infantry Regiment, married Mary Syme a spinster of West Kirk parish, Edinburgh, in Haddington on 9 July 1772. Witnesses : Richard Aylmer and Bartholemew Bower. [NAS.CH12.2.2.18][HEC]

CROKAT, Reverend JAMES, minister at Meigle, Perthshire, around 1743. [TBD#46]

CROKAT, JOHN, in Migvie, was father of a son baptised at Lochlee, Angus, on 17 September 1727. Witnesses : John Edward and John Crofts in Milntown. Also of Harrie, baptised at Lochlee on 17 April 1729. Witnesses : James Webster and John Kinnear both there. Also of Lilias baptised at Lochlee on 14 March 1731. Witnesses : Sylvester Crockat in Cairncross and Thomas Kinnear in Milntown. [DUAS.BrMsDC3/174]

CROKAT, JOHN, in Dalbreak, father of Agnes Crockat baptised at Lochlee, Angus, 24 September 1735. Witnesses : James Campbell there and David Kinnear in Achlochie. [DUAS.BrMsDC3/174]

CROCKAT, JOHN, a merchant in Dundee, 1727. [ECD#24]

CROCKAT, WILLIAM, in Kirn, was father of Margaret Crockat baptised on 11 October 1729 at Lochlee, Angus. Witnesses : James Campbell in Dalbreak and Thomas Jollie in Glen Effock. Also of James Crockat baptised at Lochlee on 22 March 1732. Witnesses : James Campbell in Dalbreak and James Thomson in Whigingtown. [DUAS.BrMsDC3/174]

CROMBIE, FRANCIS, minister at Alyth, Perthshire, by 1732. [TBD#37]

CROW, FRANCIS, born 1627, son of Patrick Crow of Heughhead and his wife Elizabeth Clapperton, minister of Chirnside, Berwickshire, from 1653 to 1658, emigrated to Jamaica in 1686, died in Essex, England, in 1692. [F.2.33]

CRUDEN, ALEXANDER, born 1721, son of Alexander Cruden and his wife Giles Walker in Aberdeen, educated at Marischal College, Aberdeen, a minister who emigrated to Virginia in 1750 and settled in South Farnham, Virginia, by 1752, a Loyalist in 1776, died in Aberdeen, probate June 1792 PCC. [KCA.2.312][NA.AO1328.191][EMA#22][FPA#329]

CRUDEN, GEORGE, a widower, and Isabel Crombie, : married in Fraserburgh, Aberdeenshire, on 28 November 1801. [NAS.CH12.32.2]

CRUICKSHANK, ALEXANDER, born October 1752, minister at Muthill, Perthshire. [TBD#252]

CRUICKSHANK, JAMES, a chaplain bound for the Leeward Islands in 1694, minister of St George's, and St Peter's, Montserrat, from 1694 to 1724;

Councillor of Montserrat, 1734.
[CTB.X.1.514][FPA#270/273/274][SPAWI.1734.140;1737.55iii]

CULBERT, EUPHAM, was confirmed in Forfar, Angus, in 1770. [EF#26]

CULBERT, Mrs, of the Perth Episcopalian Congregation, 1742. [TV.77.21][JWI]

CUMINE, ALEXANDER, a schoolmaster at Port Royal, South Carolina, a Loyalist in 1776, a minister in Kingston, Jamaica, 1777. [FPA][NA.AO12.49.422]

CUMINE, JOHN, son of Alexander Cumine in Langside, Aberdeenshire, educated at Marischal College, Aberdeen, 1786-1787, minister in Langside. [MCA#366]

CUMING, JOHN, a minister who emigrated to the Grenades in 1770. [EMA#22]

CUMING, ROBERT, a graduate of Glasgow University, emigrated to North Carolina in 1749, a missionary of the Society for the Propagation of the Gospels at St Johns from 1749. [EMA#22][SCHR.14.149][FPA#327]

CUMMING, GEORGE, a cleric who emigrated to the Leeward Islands in 1709. [EMA#22]

CUMMING, GEORGE, minister of Essil, Morayshire, died 20 September 1723. [EM#153]

CUMMING, ROBERT, born 1664, graduated MA from King's College, Aberdeen, 1680, minister of Urquhart and Glenmoriston, Inverness-shire, from 1686 until his death in 1730. Husband of (1) Helen Kinnaird, (2) Isobel Chisholm. [F.6.482]

CUMMING, ROBERT, of Logie, Moray, his widow Leslie Ballie born Mayville, Ayrshire, 1768, died 1843. [St John's, Edinburgh, MI]

CUMMINGS, ARCHIBALD, a minister who emigrated to Pennsylvania in 1726, the Bishop of London's Commissary at Philadelphia, 1729. [EMA#22][FPA#102][LIS.5.69/86/128]

CUNNINGHAM, CHARLES, a minister who emigrated to Jamaica in 1707, in Barbados by 1717. [EMA#22][FPA#223]

CUNNINGHAM, ..., a cleric who emigrated to Jamaica in 1700. [EMA#22]

CUNINS, ROBERT, and his wife Margaret Beveridge, parents of David born and baptised in St Andrews, Fife, on 14 July 1722; Jane born 5 September and baptised 6 September 1724 in St Andrews; and Robert born 19 June and baptised 29 June 1727 in St Andrews, Fife. [SER]

CURRIE, DAVID, a minister from Edinburgh, who emigrated to Virginia in 1730, minister of Christchurch and St Mary's parishes 1743 to 1792, died 1792. [OC#128]

CURRIE, WILLIAM, a minister who returned to Pennsylvania in 1736, in Philadelphia by 1741, minister at Radnor and at Periomen from 1743 to 1783. [EMA#23][FPA#109/111][LIS.5.4/69/]

CUSHNIE, PATRICK, son of Patrick Cushnie in Stonehaven, Kincardineshire, educated at Marischal College, Aberdeen, 1795-1799, graduated MA, minister in Montrose. [MCA#379]

CUTHBERT, ELISABETH, daughter of Thomas Cuthbert and his wife Jane .... in Girvan, Ayrshire, was baptised in Ayr on 13 December 1799. [NAS.CH12.26.1]

CUTHBERTSON, PETER, a goldsmith, and Margaret Caw, parents of Christian baptised in Libberton's Wynd, Edinburgh, 22 May 1752. Witnesses Katherine Beatt and ...Caw; Margaret baptised in Lower Baxter's Close on 16 January 1754. Witnesses : Mrs Caw and David Beatt; William baptised in Canongate Head, Edinburgh, on 3 March 1755. Witnesses : David Beatt, ...Polson, and Chris. Caw. [DUAS: BrMS3/Dc/12]

DALGARDNO, GEORGE, and his wife Marjory Castle in Coothill, parish of New Deer, Aberdeenshire, parents of Agnes born 14 May and baptised 16 May 1698. Godmother was Agnes Fordyce, daughter of George Fordyce in Bruxie. Witnesses : Alexander Rickart in Coothill, also George and John Henderson in Deed. [NDER]

DALGETTY, JEAN, in New Milne, was confirmed in Forfar, Angus, in 1770. [EF#26]

DALLAS, GEORGE, from London, a merchant, married Henrietta Dallas, widow of William Morison of Craigleith, at Multer's Hill, Edinburgh, 10 November 1763. [DUAS: BrMS3/Dc/12]

DALLAS, Dr ROBERT, a physician from Jamaica, father of Elizabeth Christiana baptised 29 March 1765 in the Old Assembly Close, Edinburgh. Witnesses : Mrs Gibb, Mrs Betty Dallas, Mr Harper jr, and William Dallas. [DUAS: BrMS3/Dc/12]

DALLAS, WILLIAM, of Newton, a wright, married Davidonnia, daughter of George Haliburton late Provost of Edinburgh, in Fish Mercat Close, Edinburgh, 16 April 1754; parents of James baptised 1 April 1755 in Anchor Close, Edinburgh. Witnesses : Lady Craigleith, Thomas Haliburton, and Mr Dallas; Thomas baptised 4 January 1758 in Anchor Close, Edinburgh. Witnesses : Miss Reg. Haliburton, Mrs Gibb, John Mansfield a banker, and Lady Craigleith; William baptised in Anchor Close on 25 January 1759. Witnesses : Mrs William Harper jr., Mr Dallas, and Margaret Haliburton; Margaret baptised in Ship Tavern Close on 8 April 1759. Witnesses : Margaret Haliburton, Lady Craigleith, and Mrs Harper jr.; David baptised in Ship Close on 28 June 1761. Witnesses : Misses Haliburton and Scott, Mrs Harper; Peter baptised 18 June 1762. Witness Mrs Harper jr..[DUAS: BrMS3/Dc/12]

DALNOON, ALEXANDER, a widower from New Pitsligo, Aberdeenshire, and Barbara Macdonald in Fraserburgh, : married there on 28 March 1799. [NAS.CH12.32.2]

DALRYMPLE, INGRAM WILLIAM, son of Martin Dalrymple and his wife Frances Ingram, was born 16 May 1799 and baptised in St John the Evangelist, Edinburgh, on 7 June 1799. [NAS.CH12.3.26/7]

DANIEL, THOMAS, and Alice Nash, both of Auchencruive, St Quivox parish, : married in Ayr, 24 December 1793. [NAS.CH12.26.1]

DARLING, GEORGE, educated at Edinburgh University, a minister in Virginia from 1735 to 1738. [WMQ.2.20.130][FPA#189]

DAUNEY, FRANCIS, educated at Marischal College, Aberdeen, in 1737, emigrated to Jamaica in 1785, rector of St David's there. [EMA#23][FPA#316]

DAVIDSON, ALEXANDER, educated at King's College, Aberdeen, 1693, a minister who emigrated to Maryland in 1710. [EMA#23]

DAVIDSON, ALEXANDER, an Episcopal minister in Brechin and in Menmuir, Angus, died 1782, his wife Margaret Stewart died 1820. [Brechin Cathedral MI]

DAVIDSON, CHRISTIAN, daughter of William Davidson and his wife Margaret Cumine in Boat of Logie, Aberdeenshire, was baptised 2 December 1763. [CBER]

DAVIDSON, JOHN, in Drumvcairn, Lethnott, Angus, was father of a child baptised 29 March 1724. Witnesses : James Laing and John Lyell in Drumcairn. [DUAS.BrMS.DC3/174]

DAVIDSON, JOHN, from Jamaica, and his wife Elisabeth Wallas, parents of Elizabeth baptised in Aberdeen on 7 June 1788. [SPAER]

DAVIDSON, ROBERT, a minister of St Paul's, Cabaccaterre, St Kitts, 1734, minister of St Paul's, Falmouth, Antigua, 1742. [FPA#280/282][SPAWI.1735.602vii]

DAVIDSON, Mrs, of the Perth Episcopalian Congregation, 1742. [TV.77.21]JWI]

DAWSON, Reverend WILLIAM, son of John Dawson a cleric in Staffordshire, graduated BA in 1764, formerly an Episcopalian minister in Perth, emigrated to and settled in Pensacola, Florida, 1764, testament confirmed 17 April 1770, Comm. Edinburgh. [NAS.CC8.8.121-2][EMA#24][FPA#325]

DEMPSTER, GEORGE, born 1678, son of Reverend John Dempster, a merchant in Dundee, 1727, later of Dunnichen, died 2 June 1753, husband of Margaret Rait. [ECD#21/23][F.5.362/365]

DEMPSTER, JOHN, born around 1643, son of George Dempster, MA St Andrews 1662, schoolmaster in Brechin, minister of Monifieth, Angus, from 1676 to his death in August 1708, husband of Anna Maule or Erskine, parents of George, John, Charles, James, Henry, Mary, and Jean. [F.5.362]

DEUCHAR, ALEXANDER, son of William Deuchar in Kemnay, Aberdeenshire, emigrated to Barbados in 1718, rector of St Thomas, Barbados, died 1732, testament confirmed 19 April 1738, Comm. Edinburgh. [EMA#24][FPA#226][NAS.CC8.8.100][APB.3.28]

DEUCHAR, ALEXANDER, a writer in Edinburgh and a trustee of the Carruber's Close congregation, 1741. [JSC#84]

DEVERAL, WILLIAM, a soldier of the North Fencible Highlanders, and Isabel Mitchell, : married in Ayr, 7 March 1798. [NAS.CH12.26.1]

DEWAR, JOHN, an Ensign of the 1st Foot Guards Regiment, married Caroline Vernon of Middlesex, in Haddington on 7 July 1766. [NAS.CH12.2.18][HEC]

DIACK, ALEXANDER, in Norfolk, Virginia, letters, 1764/ 1775. [NAS.CH12.24.17/203]

DICK, ARCHIBALD, assistant at St Margaret's, Caroline County, Virginia, 1761, returned to Virginia from England in 1762. [EMA#24][FPA#308/330]

DICK, JAMES, a journeyman wright in Leith, and Jean Forbes daughter of Alexander Forbes a brewer in Montrose, Angus, : married by Alexander McKenzie in Edinburgh on 30 March 1743. Witnesses : David Grey and Cecil King. [SLIM#627]

DICKIE, ADAM, a minister who emigrated to Virginia in 1731, settled in Drysdale parish, King and Queen County, Va., by 1732. [EMA#24][FPA#184]

DICKSON, JAMES, was confirmed in Forfar, Angus, in 1770. [EF#26]

DICKSON, WALTER, a Writer to the Signet, born 1776, died 1855, husband of Margaret Goldie, born 1788, died 1876. [St John's, Edinburgh, MI]

DICKSON, WILLIAM, died 1798, his wife Christian Gordon, born 1781, died 1807. [Montrose Episcopal MI]

DOCTOR, ROBERT, son of James Doctor a merchant in Coupar Angus and his wife Margaret Swan, was baptised at Blairgowrie, Perthshire, on 20 January 1744. [TBD#105]

DODD, JAMES, in Tolbooth parish, Edinburgh, late an Ensign of the 102nd Infantry Regiment, married Christian Smeaton of the same parish, in Haddington on 11 January 1777. [NAS.CH12.2.2.18][HEC]

DODS, ALEXANDER, a farmer in Athelstaneford, East Lothian, married Katherine Dudgeon of the same parish, in Haddington on 27 December 1786. Witnesses : Katherine Maitland and James Nisbet. [NAS.CH12.2.2.18][HEC]

DOLLRIE, ..., and family, of the Perth Episcopalian Congregation, 1742. [TV.77.21][JWI]

DON, WILLIAM, of the Episcopal Congregation of Forfar, Angus, 1797. [EF#36]

DONALD, GEORGE, a gardener, married Margaret Angus, servant to Mrs Laing, at the Yardheads of Leith on 20 December 1744. Witnesses : Stewart Carmichael, John Miller and his wife, Mrs Barbara White, and Mrs Jean Turnbull. [LER][NNQ.8.125]

DONALDSON, COLIN, a minister who emigrated to Jamaica, 1801. [EMA#24]

DONALDSON, JAMES, of Broughton Hall, born 1751, founder of Donaldson's Hospital, died 1830, husband of Jane Gillespie, born 1770, died 1828. [St John's, Edinburgh, MI]

DONALDSON, JEAN, daughter of William Donaldson a merchant in Dundee, was baptised in the house of Walter Grahame a merchant there on 26 May 1723. [BNDBR]

DONALDSON, JOHN, educated at King's College, Aberdeen, 1700, a minister who emigrated to Maryland in 1711, served in Somerset, Westminster, and King and Queen parishes, Maryland, died in Maryland in 1747. [EMA#24][FPA#32/34]

DONALDSON, THOMAS, son of Hay Donaldson was born 29 August and baptised 6 September 1768 in Haddington, East Lothian. Witnesses : Mr Denham and Mr Kellie. [NAS.CH12.2.13]

DONALDSON, WILLIAM, burgess of Dundee in 1699, a merchant in Dundee, 1727. [ECD#23][DBR]

DORWARD, GEORGE, born 1717, a master weaver in Barngreen, Arbroath, Angus, 1752. [SRS.13.45]

DOUGAL, THOMAS, born 1761, died 1826, his wife Mary Ann Guise, born 1769, died 1840. [Montrose Episcopal MI]

DOUGLAS, ALEXANDER, educated at Edinburgh University, a minister who emigrated to South Carolina in 1750, settled at St James', Santee. [EMA#24][FPA#306/329]

DOUGLAS, ANDREW, a merchant and druggist in Edinburgh, married Christian, sister of Cheape of Rossie, in Edinburgh, 28 June 1750; parents of Christian-Henrietta. Witnesses : Margaret and .... Cheap, and Mrs Fleming. [DUAS: BrMS3/Dc/12]

DOUGLAS, CAMPBELL, married Agnes Marshall, daughter of Robert Marshall a saddler in Glasgow, on 1 July 1793 in Hamilton. Witnesses : Colin Douglas of Mairn, and Robert Marshall. [SA.X.23]

DOUGLAS, HUGH, of Garrall and Virginia married Catherine Nasmith in Ayr, 9 March 1790. [NAS.CH12.26.1]

DOUGLAS, JOHN, a minister who emigrated to Antigua, 1732, minister of St George's, Antigua, to Nevis, 1751. [EMA#24][FPA#280/284]

DOUGLAS, ROBERT, born 1624, son of Robert Douglas of Kilmonth, educated in Aberdeen, minister in Laurencekirk and in Lanarkshire, Bishop of Brechin 1682 to 1684, Bishop of Dunblane 1684 to 1688 when he was deposed, died in Dundee on 22 September 1716. [Keith#183]

DOUGLAS, ROBERT, brother to Sir William Douglas, and Mrs Anne Hay, relict of Patrick Craigie, : married in St Andrews, Fife, on 1 September 1754. [SER]

DOUGLAS, WILLIAM, born 1708, son of .... Douglas and his wife Griselda McKeand in Penningham, Galloway, educated at Glasgow University, a minister and tutor who emigrated to Virginia 1749, assistant minister of William and Mary, Charles County, Maryland,1749, settled in St James parish, Northam, Goochland County, Virginia.
[EMA#25][WMQ.2.1.158][SNQ.1.154][FPA#301/329]

DOULL, ELIZABETH, was confirmed at Thurso, Caithness, on 8 August 1762. [DC#277]

Scots Episcopalians at Home and Abroad, 1689-1800

DOW, JOHN, a minister who emigrated to Jamaica in 1729. [EMA#25]

DOWIE, WILLIAM, a minister who emigrated to Maryland in 1762. [EMA#25][FPA#301/326]

DOWNIE, ..., a journeyman watchmaker, and his wife Sara Morison, parents of John baptised in the West Bow of Edinburgh on 19 February 1753. Witnesses : Mrs Dickson and Deacon Barclay. baptised 16 March 1776.

DOWNIE, ..., daughter of .... Downie was baptised in Brechin, Angus, on 26 May 1799. [NNQ.14.152]

DRIVER, WILLIAM, born 1724, a vintner in Montrose, Angus, died 1780, husband of Elizabeth Driver, born 1738, died 1796. [Montrose Episcopal MI]

DRUMMOND, Mrs CHRISTIAN, of the Perth Episcopalian Congregation, 1742. [TV.77.21][JWI]

DRUMMOND, GEORGE, of the Perth Episcopalian Congregation, 1742. [TV.77.21][JWI]

DRUMMOND, JAMES, born 1629, son of James Drummond minister of Foulis Wester, was minister of Auchterarder and later Muthill, Perthshire, appointed Bishop of Brechin in 1684, deposed in 1689, died in Slains Castle, Aberdeenshire, 1695. [F.6.188][Keith#169]

DRUMMOND, JAMES, and his wife Christian Cook, in Muthill, Perthshire, : parents of Emilia baptised 15 May 1775. [MRB]

DRUMMOND, JOHN, and his wife Margaret Sharp in Dahurley, Muthill, Perthshire, : parents of Janet, born 5 January and baptised 8 January 1698. [MRB]

DRUMMOND, JOHN, of Kelty, Dunning, Perthshire, and his wife Euphemia Aytone, : parents of Robert born there 27 March and baptised 4 April 1775. [MRB]

DRUMMOND, Dr WILLIAM ABERNETHY, Bishop of Brechin in 1787, Bishop of Edinburgh from 1787 to 1805, died 27 August 1809. [Keith#529/545]

DRUMSAY, Lady, of the Perth Episcopalian Congregation, 1742. [TV.77.21][JWI]

DUFF, ALEXANDER, of the Perth Episcopalian Congregation, 1742. [TV.77.21][JWI]

DUGUID, WILLIAM, educated at Marishcal College, Aberdeen, 1702-1706, ordained by the Bishop of Carlisle. [MCA#282]

DUMBRECK, PATRICK, in Aberdeen, 1711. [NAS.CH1.2.31/273-280]

DUNBAR, DAVID, a minister in Portsmouth, New Hampshire, 1734. [FPA#82]

DUNBAR, Sir GEORGE, of Mochrum, his widow Dame Jane, born 1751, died 1830. [St John's, Edinburgh, MI]

DUNBAR, HANCOCK, a minister who emigrated to Virginia in 1725, settled in St Stephen's parish, King and Queen County, died 1778. [EMA#25][WMQ.2.22.532][VaGaz.4.12.1778]

DUNBAR, JOHN, a glover, married Janet Drummond a shopkeeper, at the house of Murdoch Smith in South Leith on 28 October 1740. Witnesses : Murdoch Smith, James Donaldson, and Helen Drummond sister of the bride. [LER][NNQ.8.125]

DUNBAR, WILLIAM, born 1661 in Moray, educated at King's College, Aberdeen, MA 1681, minister of Cruden from 1691 until 1718 when he was deposed as a Jacobite, Bishop of Moray and Ross 1727, Bishop of Aberdeen 1733 to 1745, died December 1745 or early 1746, husband of Isobel Moir widow of Thomas Jaffrey of Dilspro; he died in 1746. [F.6.188][TBD#25] [Keith#532/541]; a beneficiary under the will of Alexander Deuchar in Barbados, 1738 [NAS.CC8.8.100]

DUNBAR, Sir WILLIAM ROWE, 6th baronet of Mochrum, born 1780, died 1841. [St John's, Edinburgh, MI]

DUNCAN, AGNES, was confirmed in Forfar, Angus, in 1770. [EF#26]

DUNCAN, ALEXANDER, a minister who emigrated to Carolina in 1717. [EMA#25]

DUNCAN, ALEXANDER, minister at Kilpatrick-Easter, Dunbartonshire, pre-1689, Bishop of Glasgow, 1731 to his death in 1733. [Keith#552]

DUNCAN, ALEXANDER, a house-carpenter in Fraserburgh, and Margaret Mackie, : married there on 21 September 1806. [NAS.CH12.32.2]

DUNCAN, DAVID, a minister who emigrated to the Leeward Islands in 1712. [EMA#25]

DUNCAN, JAMES, a merchant in Dundee, 1727. [ECD#24]

DUNCAN, JAMES, in Newbigging, Lethnott, Angus, was father of James baptised 24 February 1724. Witnesses : John Lyell in Drumcairn and David Campbell in Ardoch. [DUAS.BrMS.DC3/174]

DUNCAN, WILLIAM, assistant minister of St Michael's, Maryland, 1773, returned from London to Maryland in 1774, rector of Newport, Isle of Wight County, Virginia, a Loyalist, in London by 1784. [FPA#1773/326][NA.AO12.56.220, etc]

DUNCAN, ..., of Ardownie, in Dundee, 1727. [ECD#23]

DUNCANSON, WILLIAM, though appointed as a minister in the Bahamas he was unable to take up his duties, consequently he moved via Charleston to Savannah, Georgia , dismissed in 1762. [FPA#19/132][LIS.5.4]

DUNDAS, JOHN, a minister who emigrated to South Carolina, settled in Prince Frederick parish, 1772. [EMA#25][FPA#307/329]

DUNLOP, GEORGE, born 1776, died 1852, husband of Isabella Simpson, born 1786, died 1837. [St John's, Edinburgh, MI]

DUNLOP, W., rector of Stratton Major Parsonage, Virginia, in 1769. [FPA#211]

DUNN, ROBERT, a private of the Regiment of the Isles, and Elizabeth Dickson from St Quivox parish, : married in Ayr, 14 August 1798. [NAS.CH12.26.1]

DUNN, WILLIAM, son of William Dunn a shipmaster in Aberdeen, was baptised on 13 October 1720. Witnesses : William Forbes senior and William Strachan merchants. [SPAER]

DUNOON, WILLIAM, an Episcopal preacher, 1691. [NAS.CH1.2.1/90]

DUTHIE, WILLIAM, born before 1692, a notary public in Arbroath, Angus, 1752. [SRS.13.62]

DYCE, JANET, daughter of James Dyce a merchant in Aberdeen, was baptised 29 October 1720. Witnesses : James Brebner and William Strachan merchants. [SPAER]

EDGAR, HENRY, born at Keithock, Brechin, Angus, in 1698, son of David Edgar of Keithock and his wife Elizabeth Guthrie, educated at Marischal College, Aberdeen, 1711-1715, Episcopal minister in Arbroath, residing in High Street, Arbroath in 1752, husband of Barbara Raitt, Bishop in 1759, he died 22 August 1766, and she died 21 May 1774 aged 81. [F.5.365] [MCA#293][TBD#188][SRS.13.66][Keith#549]

ELLIOT, WILLIAM, a writer, married Agnes, daughter of James Dallas of St Martin's, at Craig Leith, 27 April 1748; parents of Henrietta, baptised at Lauriston on 29 September 1753. Witnesses : Lady Carigleith, William Dallas of Newton, Miss Jane Shaw and Miss Elliot; William posthumously baptised at Hallyards near Kirkliston on 21 March 1755. Witnesses : granduncle William Elliot a writer, William Dallas, Lady Craigleith, Cornelius Elliot, and Christopher Dallas. [DUAS: BrMS3/Dc/12]

ELPHINSTON, JOHN, son of Harry Elphinston a tide-surveyor in Aberdeen, was baptised 14 August 1720. Witnesses : Dr John Gordon and John Rickert of Auchnacant. [SPAER]

ELPHINSTONE, WILLIAM, minister at Longforgan, Perthshire, 1715-1716. [F.5.353]

ERSKINE, GEORGE, a cleric who emigrated to Jamaica in 1711. [EMA#26]

ERSKINE, HELEN, daughter of William Erskine, minister of Muthill, Perthshire, and his wife Helen Drummond, was born 22 October and baptised by Bishop Rose on 30 October 1774. [MRB]

ERSKINE, JOHN, a minister in Pennsylvania, 1749. [FPA#305]

ERSKINE, JOHN JAMES, son of Reverend William Erskine and his wife Helen Drummond in Muthill, was baptised at Doune on 18 July 1771, a civil servant in India, died in Edinburgh 1833, buried in Muthill, Perthshire. [TBD#244]

ERSKINE, MARGARET, wife of Archibald Stirling of Keir, was "hypothetically baptised" at Inveresk on 3 August 1761. Witness was Mrs Magdalene Stirling. [DUAS.BrMsDC3/12]

ERSKINE, MARY ANN, daughter of Reverend William Erskine and his wife Helen Drummond in Muthill, was baptised in Doune on 12 March 1772. [TBD#244]

ERSKINE, THOMAS, son of Reverend William Erskine, was baptised at Muthill on 27 November 1754. [TBD#171]

ERSKINE, WILLIAM, was confirmed on 24 June 1736. [SA.IX.13][LER]

ERSKINE, WILLIAM, son of Reverend William Erskine was baptised in Muthill, Perthshire, on 29 August 1768. Laurence Oliphant of Gask and Captain William Drummond : godfathers and Mrs Oliphant of Gask was godmother. [SA.IX.12][LER]

ERSKINE, WILLIAM, born 1773, died 1852, husband of Maitland Mackintosh, born 1792, died 1861. [St John's, Edinburgh, MI]

ESPLIN, CHARLES, and his wife Patricia ......, parents of Charles baptised near the Cross of Edinburgh on 19 December 1753. Witnesses : Mrs Preston and John Esplin; and of Janet baptised in Edinburgh on 8 November 1756. [DUAS.BrMsDC3/12]

EUAN, JAMES, in Glen Tennate, was father of Charles Euan baptised at Lochlee, Angus, in July 1729. Witnesses : David Watt, James Watt, and Alexander Coutts there. [DUAS.BrMsDC3/174]

EWART, DAVID, born 1755, of the Chancery Office, died 1826, husband of Janet Fell, born 1772, died 1827. [St John's, Edinburgh, MI]

EWING, ALEXANDER, educated at Edinburgh University, a minister who emigrated to Bermuda in 1787; once a Presbyterian later an Anglican, son of Alexander Ewing, a mathematician in Edinburgh, died in Bermuda on 15 October 1822. [EMA#26][SM.86.255][FPA#246]

FAIRBAIRN, JAMES, son of James Fairbairn, a sergeant of the 90th Regiment of Foot, was born 10 December 1798 and baptised in St John the Evangelist, Edinburgh, on 16 December 1798. [NAS.CH12.3.26/5]

FALCONER, DAVID, of Balmashanner, and his wife Isabel MacGill, parents of Jane born on 1 December and baptised on 2 December 1726 in St Andrews; Magdalene born on 18 January, and baptised on 19 January 1728; Margaret and Agnes born and baptised in St Andrews on 21 May 1729.[SER]

FALCONER, ELIZABETH, daughter of William Falconer in Stonehaven, Kincardineshire, was baptised there on 22 January 1758.[ST.ER]

FALCONER, JAMES, from Moray, a minister who emigrated to Virginia in 1718, settled in Charles parish, York County, probate 1728, York, Virginia. [EMA#27][FPA#168/174]

FALCONER, JAMES, minister of Ayr, 1742. [EV#358]

FALCONER, JOHN, son of Lord Halkerton, was baptised on 4 October 1736. [SA.IX.13][LER]

FALCONER, PATRICK, a cleric who emigrated to Virginia in 1710. [EMA#27]

FALCONER, WILLIAM, born in Elgin, Moray, son of Alexander Falconer a merchant and his wife Jean King, ordained a deacon in 1728, minister in Forres, 1741, Bishop of Caithness and Orkney, 1741, Bishop of Moray, 1742, died in 1784. [TBD#35][Keith#528/550]

FARQUHAR, GEORGE, a minister in Aberdeen, a beneficiary under the will of Alexander Deuchar in Barbados, 1738 [NAS.CC8.8.100];

FARQUHARSON, ALEXANDER, a cleric who emigrated to New Jersey in 1717. [EMA#27]

FARQUHARSON, JAMES, a cleric who emigrated to Pennsylvania in 1712. [EMA#27]

FARQUHARSON, JOHN, and his wife Bathia Michie, parents of a daughter baptised in Edinburgh on 9 August 1753. baptised 16 March 1776.

FERGUSON, JOHN, a tailor, father of Isabell baptised in Todderick's Wynd, Edinburgh, on 24 August 1757. [DUAS.Br.MS3.DC/12]

FERGUSON, MARGARET, was confirmed in Forfar, Angus, in 1770. [EF#26]

FERRIER, ANNY, daughter of .... Ferrier in Kinnaird's Mill, Angus, married Captain Carnegie from Montrose, at Kinnaird's Mill on 21 May 1796. [NNQ.14.97]

FERRIER, CECILIA, daughter of Thomas Ferrier and his wife Anne Venison, was born 14 December and baptised in St Andrews on 15 December 1729. [SER]

FIDDLER, ERNEST, son of John Fiddler and his wife Elizabeth Kid in Bomakessie, Aberdeenshire, was baptised 16 June 1776. [CTER]

FIFE, DAVID, a merchant in Dundee, father of James baptised in Dundee on 7 November 1722; Alexander baptised in David Fife's house in Dundee on 14 April 1724; and John was baptised in his house on 13 January 1726. [BNDBR]

FIFE, JOHN, a clerk, father of Colquhoun baptised at Clamshell Turnpike, Edinburgh, on 19 February 1764. [DUAS.BrMsDC3/12]

FIFE, WILLIAM, junior, a merchant in Banff, married An McLachlan, daughter of John McLachlan a merchant in Glasgow, on 12 August 1790, at St Andrew's Episcopal Church, in Glasgow. They : married by James Franks. [SA.X.22]

FINDAL, Lady, of the Perth Episcopalian Congregation, 1742. [TV.77.21][JWI]

FINDLATOR, GEORGE, from Peterhead, Aberdeenshire, and Rebecca Durham, daughter of Reverend Mr Durham, : married in Fraserburgh, Aberdeenshire, on 23 February 1800. [NAS.CH12.32.2]

FINDLATOR, JOHN, a minister who emigrated to the Grenades in 1771. [EMA#27]

FINLASON, EDWARD, surgeon of the Queen's Dragoons, married Dorothea Peach from Derby, in Haddington, East Lothian, on 11 November 1771. Witnesses : Abram Cormack and Bartholemew Bower. [NAS.CH12.2.18][HEC]

FINDLATOR, ..., a minister in St Vincent's, 1796. [FPA#292]

Scots Episcopalians at Home and Abroad, 1689-1800

FINDLAY, ALEXANDER, born St Stephen's parish, South Carolina, in August 1740, a minister returned from London to Georgia, 1770. [EMA#27][FPA#300/325]

FINNEY, WILLIAM, educated at King's College, Aberdeen, and Glasgow University, a minister who emigrated to Virginia in 1710, settled in Henrico parish, died in 1727, probate 5 June 1727, Henrico, Virginia. [SCHR.14.149][FPA#175]; possibly the William Finney minister at Brandon, Virginia, son of William Finney a merchant in Aberdeen who died by 1755. [NAS.SH.1755]

FINNIE, ALEXANDER, a minister who emigrated to Virginia in 1724. [EMA#27]

FITCHET, MARGARET, was confirmed in Forfar, Angus, in 1770. [EF#26]

FITZSIMMONS, WILLIAM, minister of the Protestant Episcopal Church in Ayr, pre 1776. [NAS.CH12.26.1]

FLEMING, GILBERT, a minister in Antigua, 1751. [FPA#284]

FORBES, ALEXANDER, educated at King's College, Aberdeen, 1706, a minister who emigrated to Virginia in 1709, minister in Upper Parish, Isle of Wight county, Va. [EMA#27][FPA#168/175]

FORBES, HELEN, daughter of Reverend William Forbes, was baptised in Fisherraw, Leith, on 20 November 1755. Reverend William Forbes was godfather, Mrs Colt and Mrs Margaret Forbes (daughter of the said William Forbes) : godmothers. [LER][SA.X.10]

FORBES, JANE, daughter of William Forbes, a banker, and his wife Wilhelmina, was born 25 May 1798 and baptised in St John the Evangelist, Edinburgh, on 2 June 1798. [NAS.CH12.3.26/5]

FORBES, JOHN, a minister who emigrated to East New Jersey in 1733. [EMA#28]; died and buried there in 1736. [JCTP.1737.37]

FORBES, JOHN, educated at King's College, Aberdeen, graduated MA, a minister who emigrated to St Augustine, East Florida in 1764. [EMA#28][FPA#300/325]

FORBES, MARGARET, daughter of Thomas Forbes and his wife ..... Urquhart, was born on 15 June and baptised on 17 June 1726 in St Andrews, Fife. [SER]

FORBES, MARION, daughter of Reverend William Forbes, was baptised at Fisherraw, Leith, on 26 April 1754. Witnesses : Mrs Dalrymple (grandmother of the child), James Forbes, Mrs Forbes, Mrs Cassils, Janet Forbes, Janet and Margaret Rattray. [LER][SA.X.11]

FORBES, PATRICK, a minister in South Leith, 1746. [JSC#63]

FORBES, ROBERT, a cleric who emigrated to Carolina in 1708. [EMA#27]

FORBES, ROBERT, son of Charles Forbes schoolmaster of Rayne, Aberdeenshire, minister of the Episcopal congregation in Leith, a Jacobite in 1745; a marriage contract with Ann Garioch, 1749; appointed Bishop of Ross in 1762; died 18 November 1775. [NAS.RD4.176/1.281][SHS.2.202][Keith#551]

FORBES, WILLIAM, a minister in Musselburgh, Midlothian, 1746; married Mrs Grissel Dalrymple at the house of Mrs Dalrymple in Fisherrow, Leith, on 10 May 1753. Witnesses : Rev. William Abernethie, Mrs Dalrymple, and Mrs Fullarton alias Lady Carberry. [JSC#63][LER][NNQ.8.125];

FORBES, WILLIAM, son of James Forbes and his wife Rachel Williamson in Aquharnie, Cruden, Aberdeenshire, was baptised 18 April 1777. [CTER]

FORDYCE, JOHN, MA, a minister who was ordained in 1730 and sent to Jamaica in 1730, possibly in Newfoundland, died in Prince Frederic parish, South Carolina, 1751. [EMA#28][FPA#5/153][LIS.5.86/128]

FORREST, MARGARET OSWALD, daughter of John Forrest and Wilhelmina his wife was born on 27 November 1797 and baptised in St John the Evangelist, Edinburgh, on 24 December 1797. [NAS.CH12.3.26/2]

FORRESTER, GABRIEL, an Ensign of the 60th [Royal American] Regiment, married Jean Hamilton, daughter of the late Robert Hamilton of Hamilton Hill, on 28 September 1778. Witnesses : Robert Graham of Garbraid, Benjamin Batton, Commissary Cleric of Glasgow, James Shields, and John Shanks, merchants in Glasgow. [SA.X.22]

FORSYTH, ANN, daughter of William Forsyth and his wife Elizabeth Cassie in Tilliefaar, Udny, Aberdeenshire, was baptised 4 December 1763. [CBER]

FORSYTH, MARGARET, was confirmed in Fortrose, 1770. [EV#327]

FOTHERINGHAM, DAVID, son of James Fotheringham a merchant in Dundee, was baptised in his house in Dundee on 15 February 1725. Godfathers : Archibald Fotheringham of Drumlochie and John Strachan a merchant in Dundee, while Mrs Helen Miln daughter of the laird of Milnfield was godmother. [BNDBR]

FOTHERINGHAM, ROBERT, son of James Fotheringham a merchant in Dundee, was baptised in Mr Fotheringham's house on 19 January 1724. Godfathers : Robert Graham, eldest son of the laird of Fintry, and James Clephan, son of Colonel Clephan, and Lady Balinshaw was godmother.

FOTHERINGHAM, WILLIAM, a missionary of the Society for the Propagation of the Gospel, to Trinity Bay, Newfoundland in 1762, died on arrival at St John's, Newfoundland. [EMA#28][FPA#299/327][LIS.5.4]

FOTHERINGHAM, Mrs, of the Perth Episcopalian Congregation, 1742. [TV.77.21][JWI]

FOULIS, JAMES, a minister who emigrated to Virginia 1750, an assistant in Norfolk, 1750. [EMA#28][FPA#307/329]

FRASER, GEORGE, a minister who emigrated to Pennsylvania in 1733. [EMA#28]

FRASER, GEORGE, a minister who emigrated to Virginia in 1738. [EMA#28]

FRASER, HUGH, born 1643, son of Reverend Alexander Fraser in Petty, Inverness, graduated MA from King's College, Aberdeen, 1662, minister at Kiltarlity and Glen Convinth, Inverness-shire, from 1667 until his death in 1612. Husband of Anna Murray. [F.6.469]

FRASER, HUGH, son of William Fraser of Fraserfield, educated at Marischal College, Aberdeen, 1777-1781, later rector of Woolwich. [MCA#352]

FRASER, JAMES, a minister who emigrated to Virginia before 1775, settled in Hartford, Orange County, North Carolina, a Loyalist in 1776, moved to Annapolis, Nova Scotia, by 1786. [NA.AO.13.24.172/182]

FRASER, JOHN, a minister who emigrated to Virginia in 1701, curate in Northumberland, and later in King George's parish, died in Pitscataway, Maryland, November 1742. [EMA#28][FPA#35]

FRASER, JOHN, educated at Edinburgh University, a minister who emigrated to Virginia or Florida in 1769, later settled in East Florida, died in New Smyrna during 1772. [EMA#28][FPA.308/309/325/330]

FRASER, PATRICK, a minister who emigrated to the Bahamas in 1792. [EMA#28]{possibly the Patrick Fraser from Perth who settled on Long Island, the Bahamas, probate 1795 PCC}

FRASER, WILLIAM, a minister who emigrated to New Jersey in 1766. [FPA#327] [EMA#28]

FREEBAIRN, DAVID, formerly minister of Dunning, Perthshire, Bishop of Edinburgh from 1733 until his death in 1739. [Keith#527]

FULLARTON, DAVID, a minister who emigrated to Dominica in 1767. [EMA#28][FPA#327]

FULLARTON, JOHN, Bishop of Edinburgh from 1720 until his death in May 1727. [Keith#524]

FULLARTON, JOHN, minister at Christ Church parish, South Carolina, died in 1735. [FPA#147]

FULLER, AGNES, daughter of Thomas Fuller of the Scotch Brigade and his wife Agnes Peacock, was baptised in Ayr 30 June 1799. [NAS.CH12.26.1]

FYFFE, BEATRIX, servant to Lady Balmerino, relict of Lord Arthur, was confirmed in Leith on 31 March 1748. [SA.IX.13][LER]

FYFE, DAVID, minister at Glamis and Glenboy, Angus, was deposed for conducting an illegal marriage in Dundee, 1743. [ECD#61]

FYFFE, JOHN, born 1760, Captain in the Royal Navy, died 1835, husband of Elizabeth Hunter, born 1776, died 1861. [St John's, Edinburgh, MI]

FYFFE, WILLIAM, a minister who emigrated to Virginia in 1729. [EMA#29]

FYVIE, ELSPET, daughter of William Fyvie and his wife Jean Watson in Kinmuck, Ellon, Aberdeenshire, was baptised 8 June 1777. [CTER]

GADDERAR, JAMES, minister at Kilmaurs, Ayrshire, before 1689, Bishop of Aberdeen from 1724 until his death in February 1733. [Keith#532]

GAIRDEN, JOHN, son of James Gairden and his wife Jean Keith in Milne of Bairnie, Aberdeenshire, was baptised on 28 November 1763. [CBER]

GAIRDNER, DAVID, of Kirktonhill, born 1723, died 1794, husband of Elizabeth Christie, born 1741, died 1825. [Montrose Episcopal MI]

GALL, EUPHAN, of the Perth Episcopalian Congregation, 1742. [TV.77.21][JWI]

GALL, JOHN, of Kinloch, married Mary Graeme, relict of Adam Mercer a writer in Edinburgh, in Fowlis's Close, Edinburgh, 26 April 1744. [DUAS: BrMS3/Dc/12]

GALLOWAY, JAMES, of Craighall, was confirmed at Whiteloch, Blairgowrie, Perthshire, on 2 September 1750. [TBD#155]

GAMMOCK, WILLIAM, in Glamis, Angus, 1743. [ECD#69]

GARDEN, ALEXANDER, born 1685 in Edinburgh, rector of St Philip's, Charleston, South Carolina, from 1719 to 1753, from London to SC 1743, Bishop's Commissary there from 1726 to 1748, died 21 September 1756. [CCVC][FPA#137][LIS.5.87][EMA#29]

GARDEN, GEORGE, born 1649, son of Alexander Garden minister at Forgue, educated at King's College, Aberdeen, minister in the Presbytery of Aberdeen from 1677 until he was deposed in 1692, died 31 January 1733. [F.6.2]

GARDEN, JAMES, son of Alexander Garden, educated at Marischal College, Aberdeen, a minister who emigrated to Virginia in 1754, minister of St Patrick's parish, Prince Edward County, Virginia, 1758 to 1773. [EMA#29][FPA#307/329] [OC#2/24]

GARDEN, WILLIAM, a minister, emigrated to Virginia, 1775. [FPA#331]

GARDYNE, JAMES, and his wife Mary Wallace, in Arbroath, 1752. [SRS.13.65]

GARRINGTON, THOMAS, a drummer of the 44th Regiment, married Elizabeth Dunlop, in Ayr, 8 February 1790. [NAS.CH12.26.1]

GAVIN, ANTHONY, a chaplain in Gibraltar, a minister who emigrated to Virginia in 1735, settled in St James's parish, Goochland, Va., by 1738. [EMA#29][FPA#185/187/190]

GEDD, JAMES, son of William Gedd in Edinburgh, a printer and a Jacobite who settled in Jamaica, 1746. [P.2.222]

GEDD, WILLIAM, a jeweller in Edinburgh and a trustee of the Carruber's Close congregation, 1741. [JSC#84]

GEDD, WILLIAM, son of William Gedd in Edinburgh, a merchant and a Jacobite, who died in St James parish, Jamaica, on 4 January 1767. [SM.29.389]

GEIKIE, ..., a child of John Geikie, was baptised at Provost Smith's in Brechin, Angus, on 5 October 1798, and a son at Mrs Smith's on 20 January 1800. [NNQ.14.100/153]

GENTLE, JAMES, and his wife Elizabeth Drummond, in Muthill, Perthshire, parents of Mary born 27 February and baptised 4 March 1774, also of Margaret born 9 May baptised 14 May 1775. [MRB]

GERARD, ANDREW, a minister in Aberdeen, 1731, husband of Mrs Burnet, relict of Robert Burnet son of John Burnett minister of Monymusk, Aberdeenshire, Bishop of Aberdeen from 1747 until his death on October 1767. [TBD#5][NAS.CH12.23.44][Keith#533]

GERARD, GORDON, in Aberdour, Fife, and Barbara Martin a servant at Ladysford, : married at Ladysford, on 6 December 1798. [NAS.CH12.32.2]

GIB, BARBARA, daughter of Robert Gib a tailor in Dundee, was baptised in Dundee on 17 July 1726. [BNDBR]

GIB, DAVID, in Glencairn, Lethnott, Angus, father of Elizabeth baptised 17 January 1724. Witnessses : David ..... and John Lowson; also of Isaac baptised

22 March 1725. Witnesses : John Lyell and James Laing, both in Drumcairn. [DUAS.BrMS.DC3/174]

GIB, JOHN, son of Robert Gib a tailor in Nethergate, Dundee, was baptised on 13 July 1723 in the house of Thomas Davidson in Nethergate. [BNDBR]

GIB, ROBERT, in Dundee, 1727. [ECD#26]

GIBBON, JOHN, son of John Gibbon in the Miln of Acqhurrie, was baptised in Stonehaven, Kincardineshire, on 20 March 1760. [ST.ER]

GIBSON, Sir ANDREW, of Pentland, a trustee of the Carruber's Close congregation, Edinburgh1741. [JSC#83]

GIBSON, DAVID, married Elspet Carrie in Arbirlot, Angus, 1739, parents of Marjory born 1751, residing in Marketgate, Arbroath, 1752. [SRS.13.85]

GIBSON, ELIZABETH, in Drumgley, was confirmed in Forfar in 1770. [EF#26]

GIBSON, ISABEL, daughter of John Gibson and his wife Euphemia Richard, was born on 7 February and baptised on 28 February 1726 in St Andrews. [SER]

GIBSON, ISABEL, in Drumgley, was confirmed in Forfar in 1770. [EF#26]

GIBSON, JOHN, and Ann Wilson, in Crieff, Perthshire, : parents of Nelly born 19 February and baptised 24 February 1775. [MRB]

GIBSON, THOMAS, and his wife Barbara Barnet, in Lentibbert, Muthill, : parents of Grizal born 5 February and baptised 7 February 1698. [MRB]

GIBSON, THOMAS, of Cliftonhall, an under-clerk of Session, a trustee of the Carruber's Close congregation, Edinburgh, 1741. [JSC#83]

GILLAN, JOHN, once a bookseller, then minister of Carrubers Close Chapel in Edinburgh, Bishop of Dunblane, from 1727 until his death in January 1735. [TBD#8][Keith#547]

GILLESPIE, ALEXANDER, son of William Gillespie in Aberdeen, was baptised 17 November 1720. Witnesses : Alexander Scott a shipmaster and Alexander Fraser a glover. [SPAER]

GILLIAM, WILLIAM, minister of Camden parish, Virginia, 1774. [OC.2.14]

GILLIES, ROBERT, a mason in Berwick on Tweed, married Margaret Clark, also from there, in Haddington, East Lothian, on 4 June 1778. [NAS.CH12.2.2.18][HEC]

GLASGOW, JOHN, a minister who emigrated to Antigua in 1708. [EMA#30]

GLEGG, JAMES, born 1762, a surgeon in the Royal Navy, died 1807. [Montrose Episcopal MI]

GLEN, WILLIAM, a minister who emigrated to Virginia in 1708. [EMA#30]

GOLD, DAVID, in Achin, father of Helen Gold baptised 25 November 1732 at Lochlee, Angus. Witnesses : John Edward in Blackhills and David Malcolm in Blackcraig. [DUAS.BrMsDC3/174]

GOLDIE, GEORGE, born 1741, a minister who emigrated to Virginia in 1766, settled in Frederick County, Virginia, and in St Mary's County, Maryland, died 1791. [EMA#30][VG#183][FPA#330]

GOLDIE, GEORGE, a merchant in Edinburgh, married Mrs Sophia McDowall alias Osborne, widow of Captain Osborne, late of the Honorable East India Company Service, at St Andrew's Episcopal Church in Glasgow on 12 July 1779. Witnesses : Patrick Heron of Heron, and William Campbell, a Writer to the Signet. [SA.X.22]

GOLDMAN, BARBARA, daughter of James Goldman a minister in Dundee, was baptised on 13 August 1723 in Mr Goldman's house in Dundee. Godfather was George Rait MD in Dundee, and godmothers : Barbara Rait, daughter to William Rait minister of Monikie, and Barbara Goldman, daughter of Alexander Goldman in Dundee. [BNDBR]

GOLDMAN, Reverend JAMES, 1712, [Keith#545]; a pastor in Dundee, 1727, [ECD#25]; of the Seagate Chapel, Dundee, 1743. [TBD#49]; father of James baptised at home on 1 April 1725. Godfathers : George Rait MD and George Dempster a merchant in Dundee, with Dr Rait's wife as godmother. [BNDBR]

GOODHOUR, JOHN, and his wife Isobel Smith, in Burnhill, New Deer, Aberdeenshire, parents of Alexander born 14 May and baptised 15 May 1705. Witnesses : Alexander Walker in Burnhill and Alexander Smith in Coothill. [NDER]

GOODWILLIE, JOHN, a writer, and his wife ....Corstorphine, parents of Anne baptised in the Lawn Mercat of Edinburgh on 5 September 1753. Witnesses : William Lumdsden, Robert Barclay, and B. McGill; Magdalen baptised in the Lawn Mercat, Edinburgh, on 3 February 1757. [DUAS.Br.MS3.DC/12]

GOOLD, JOHN, and his wife Margaret Miller, in Muthill, Perthshire, : parents of Janet baptised 19 June 1774. [MRB]

GORDON, ALEXANDER, from Glasserton, Galloway, settled as a minister in Virginia and Maryland, 1763 to 1775, at Antrim parish, Virginia, 1763. [NAS.CS16.1.143][OC#2/10][FPA#308]

GORDON, ALEXANDER, minister of Antrim parish, Virginia, from 1790 to 1819, died 1819. [OC#2/10]

GORDON, ANNA, relict of John Alexander late minister at Kildrummy, Aberdeenshire, and her son in law Colin Petrie in Mill of Gartly, receipts for church records, 1718. [NAS.CH12.23.8]

GORDON, CHRISTIAN, daughter of Robert Gordon and his wife Isobel Gordon in Backhill of Dudwick, Aberdeenshire, was baptised 29 February 1764. [CBER]

GORDON, DAVID, minister of the Episcopal Congregation in Pittenweem, Fife, testament, 28 April 1756, Comm. St Andrews. [NAS]

GORDON, GEORGE, of Gordonbank, a writer, and his wife ....Muirhead, parents of James baptised in Kinloch's Close, Edinburgh, 21 May 1752. Witnesses: Mrs Muirhead and ....Gordon of Avochie. [DUAS.BrMsDC3/12]

GORDON, JAMES, son of John Gordon of Kinnellar a merchant in Aberdeen, was baptised 27 August 1720. Witnesses : James Gordon of Barns and James Cattenach merchant. [SPAER]

GORDON, JANE, daughter of Charles Gordon of Ruthlan, was baptised 5 December 1720. Witnesses : John Gordon of Kineler and John Gordon doctor of physick. [SPAER]

GORDON, JOHN, HM Chaplain in New York, Bishop of Galloway 1688, in 1689 he moved to Ireland and later to France, chaplain at the Jacobite court at St Germains. [Keith#283]

GORDON, JOHN, in Newtown of Achindore, Aberdeenshire, and Sophia Alexander fourth daughter of the late John Alexander minister at Kildrummy, an antenuptial marriage contract, August 1719. [NAS.CH12.23.12]

GORDON, JOHN, born 1717, son of Dr John Gordon and his wife Margaret Duell, educated at King's College, Aberdeen, 1734, then at Oxford University, 1737, minister in White Clay Creek Hundred, Delaware, 1738-1743, settled in Anne Arundel County, Maryland, died at St Michael's, Talbot County, Maryland, in 1790. [Talbot Wills.VJ.P6/341]

GORDON, JOHN, a merchant in Edinburgh and trustee of the Carruber's Close congregation, 1741. [JSC#83]

GORDON, LUDOVICK, graduated MA from King's College, Aberdeen, 1669, minister at Huntly 1692-1716, deposed as a Jacobite. [F.5.317]

GORDON, PATRICK, a cleric who emigrated to New York in 1702, possibly in Philadelphia by 1726. [EMA#30][FPA#102]

GORDON, PATRICK, a minister residing in Old Assembly Close, Edinburgh, 1746. [JSC#63]

GORDON, PATRICK, and Margaret Connor, both from St Quivox, : married in Ayr, 19 September 1798. [NAS.CH12.26.1]

GORDON, ROBERT, son of George Gordon in Kinmundy, minister of Abercorn 1683, deposed in 1689, an Episcopal preacher in Cluny from 1691, died there 13 January 1713. [F.4.151]

GORDON, WILLIAM, a cleric who emigrated to Barbados in 1699, a minister there in 1703, Commissary of Barbados, 1716, minister of St Michael's from 1701; 1726. [EMA#30][FPA#221/222/226][SPAWI.1726.333]

GORDON, WILLIAM, a cleric who emigrated to North Carolina in 1707. [EMA#30]

GORDON, WILLIAM, a minister who emigrated to West Florida in 1767, later in Virginia by 1775, and Exuma, the Bahamas, from 1786. [EMA#30][FPA#220/300/311/325]

GOURDIE, Lady, and daughter, of the Perth Episcopalian Congregation, 1742. [TV.77.21][JWI]

GOURDON, JOHN, a cleric and schoolmaster who emigrated to Maryland in 1695. [EMA#30]

GOURDON, WILLIAM, a cleric who emigrated to Barbados in 1701. [EMA#30]

GRAEME, DAVID, the younger of Garvock and his wife Mary Nisbet, : parents of Moray born in Kippon, Dunning, Perthshire, on 13 October and baptised there 18 October 1774. [MRB]

GRAHAM, ALEXANDER, married Clementina Garden in 1752, a merchant in Marketgate, Arbroath, Angus, 1752. [SRS.13.84]

GRAHAME, ALEXANDER, son of Walter Grahame a merchant in Dundee, was baptised in Dundee on 11 December 1722. Walter Grahame's two brothers Alexander and John Grahame : godfathers, and Christian Grahame their sister, was godmother. [BNDBR]

GRAHAM, ARCHIBALD, minister in Rothesay, Bute, Bishop of the Isles 1680 to 1688. [Keith#310]

GRAHAM, ANNA, daughter of David Grahame in Duntrune, was baptised there on 28 June 1726. Godfather was James Ramsay a merchant in Dundee, while the godmothers : the Dowager Lady Dundee and Lady Fintry. [BNDBR]

GRAHAME, Mrs ANNE, of the Perth Episcopalian Congregation, 1742. [TV.77.21][JWI]

GRAHAME, CHARLES DAVID, son of David Grahame in Duntrune, was baptised there on 27 March 1723. Godfathers : the Master of Gray and John Grahame a merchant in Dundee, and godmother was the Mistress of Gray. [BNDBR]

GRAHAM, DAVID, of the Episcopal congregation in Seagate, Dundee, 1743. [ECD#61]

GRAHAME, ELIZABETH, daughter of Walter Grahame a merchant in Dundee, was baptised in his house on 25 February 1724. Godfather was John Grahame the youngest brother of Walter Grahame, and the godmothers : Mrs White and her daughter the wife of Provost Guthrie. [BNDBR]

GRAHAME, ELIZABETH, daughter of John Graham a merchant in Dundee, was baptised in his house in Dundee on 30 July 1725. Godfather was his brother John Grahame and godmothers : the lady of Wallace of Craigie and the lady of Milnhill. [BNDBR]

GRAHAME, GEORGE, an Episcopal minister in Glasgow, sermons, 1730-1740. [NAS.NRAS.2704.43.60]

GRAHAME, GEORGE, son of Walter Grahame a merchant in Dundee, was baptised in his house in Dundee on 19 December 1725. Godfathers : George Dempster and George Ramsay merchants in Dundee, with Mrs Grisel Grahame, sister german to Walter Grahame, as godmother. [BNDBR]

GRAHAME, JOAN, of the Perth Episcopalian Congregation, 1742. [TV.77.21][JWI]

GRAHAME, JOHN, and ROBERT, twin sons of David Grahame a vintner in Couttie's Wynd, Dundee, : baptised 24 June 1722. Witnesses : Westhall and James Young a surgeon apothecary. [BNDBR]

GRAHAM, MATHEW, a farmer in Stirling, married Esther Mayo a resident of Glasgow or Alloa, on 13 August 1799 in St Andrew's Episcopal Church, Glasgow. Witnesses : Henry Fleming and Elizabeth Falconer. [SA.X.23]

GRAHAM, ROBERT, in Dundee, 1727. [ECD#21]

GRAHAM, ROBERT, of Fintry, in Dundee, 1727. [ECD#27]

GRAHAM, ROBERT, a minister who emigrated to Maryland in 1773, assistant at St Paul's, Baltimore County. [EMA#30][FPA#302/326]

GRAHAM, WILLIAM, of Airth, Stirlingshire, and his wife Ann Stirling, : parents of Wilmina Graham born in Airth on 13 December 1773, baptised there on 12 January 1774. [MRB]

GRAHAM, WILLIAM, from Aberdeen, married Isabella Abernethy, also from Aberdeen, in Haddington, East Lothian, on 11 February 1778. Witnesses : James Fairbairn and Patrick Thomson. [NAS.CH12.2.2.18][HEC]

GRANGER, WILLIAM, of Wariston House, married Mrs Agnes, daughter of Robert Barclay a merchant tailor, at Avenue Head, on 19 June 1760. Witnesses : Robert Barclay, William Barclay, Baillie Macgill, Mrs Crafurd, and Mrs Macgill. [LER][NNQ.8.127]

GRANT, ALEXANDER, a teacher in Antigua who converted to Anglicanism, from London to Antigua in 1749, settled in Tortula, dead by 1750. [EMA#30][FPA#284/289]

GRANT, ANDREW, a minister in Aberdeen, a beneficiary under the will of Alexander Deuchar in Barbados, 1738 [NAS.CC8.8.100];

GRANT, LUDOVICK, a minister at Fortrose, Easter Ross, 1761. [EV#360]

GRANT, ROBERT, in Tarfside, was father of a daughter baptised at Lochlee, Angus, on 14 October 1729. Witnesses : John Christison and William Crockat both in Cairncross.[DUAS.BrMsDC3/174]

GRAY, ALEXANDER, born 1660, son of Provost Thomas Gray of Aberdeen, educated at Marischal College, Aberdeen, minister of St Clement's, Aberdeen, 1688 to 1716 when he was deposed as a Jacobite. [F.6.27]

GRAY, ANDREW, burgess of Dundee 1705, a brewer in Dundee, 1727. [ECD#24][DBR]

GRAY, JAMES, son of James Gray in Cottarton of Craigie, was baptised in Dundee on 27 June 1725. [BNDBR]

GRAY, JAMES, in Dundee, 1727. [ECD#26]

GRAY, SAMUEL, a cleric who emigrated to Maryland in 1705, and to Antigua in 1710. [EMA#31]

GRAY, WILLIAM, a farmer in Pitblae, and Helen Still in Middleburgh, : married in Fraserburgh, Aberdeenshire, on 20 July 1793. [NAS.CH12.32.2]

GREEN, WILLIAM, factor for Mr Charteris, and his wife ....Macintosh, parents of Katherine baptised near New Milne, Edinburgh, on 16 June 1757. Witnesses : Mr and Mrs Robertson, ... Craig, ...Grant, four servants at New Milns. [DUAS.Br.MS3.DC/12]

GREEN, Reverend, from England, married Jean Allardice from Brechin, Angus, there on 21 October 1798. [NNQ.14.100]

GREENHILL, GEORGE, son of Patrick Greenhill in Dundee, was baptised there on 19 December 1722. [BNDBR]

GREENHILL, HELEN, daughter of Patrick Greenhill of Banchrie, was baptised in his house in Dundee on 25 February 1724. [BNDBR]

GREENHILL, HUGH, at Whiteloch, was confirmed at Whiteloch, Blairgowrie, Perthshire, on 2 September 1750. [TBD#155]

GREGG, JAMES, a cleric who emigrated to St Kitts in 1711. [EMA#31]

GREIG, ANN, wife of Robert Kid, and their children Ann and James, in Berryfauld, Arbroath, Angus, 1752. [SRS.13.43]

GREIG, JOHN, a sailor, then in Greenland, and his wife Jean Brown, parents of John baptised in Edinburgh on 24 May 1754. Witnesses : John Archibald a hairdresser, Margaret Falconer, and James Ramsay. [DUAS: BrMS3/Dc/12]

GRIEVE, NATHANIEL, son of John Grieve in Turreff, Aberdeenshire, educated at Marischal College, Aberdeen, 1798-1802, graduated MA, minister in Ellon, Aberdeenshire. [MCA#386]

GRIGGS, WILLIAM, a soldier of the 44th Regiment, married Mary Green, in Ayr, 15 October 1791. [NAS.CH12.26.1]

GUILD, JAMES, a writer in Edinburgh and a trustee of the Carruber's Close congregation, 1741. [JSC#84]

GUISE, JOHN, born 1729, late a Lieutenant of the 6th Regiment of Foot, died 1786, husband of Mary Forbes, born 1730, died 1803. [Montrose Episcopal MI]

GUISE, SAMUEL, born 1752, late a surgeon HEICS in Bombay, died 1811. [Montrose Episcopal MI]

GULEN, AGNES, daughter of John Gulen and his wife Mary Bruse, was born and baptised on 22 September 1723 in St Andrews, Fife. [SER]

GUTHRIE, ALEXANDER, in Dundee, 1727. [ECD#26]

GUTHRIE, DAVID, minister at Carsebank, near Forfar, around 1735. [TBD#41]

GUTHRIE, GEORGE, son of John Guthrie a merchant in Dundee, was

GUTHRIE, GIDEON, an Episcopal preacher in Brechin, a Jacobite in 1745. [NAS.CH2.575.1]

GUTHRIE, HARRY, a writer, and his wife Elizabeth Tytler, parents of Harry baptised in Newington, Edinburgh, on 30 November 1752. Witnesses : William Tytler a writer, George Lindsay a clerk, and Euphane Guthrie; Anne baptised in Newington, on 20 December 1754. Witnesses : George Lindsay a clerk, Mrs Lindsay, Mrs William and Jean Tytler. [DUAS: BrMS3/Dc/12]

GUTHRIE, JOHN, a merchant in Dundee, 1727. [ECD#24]; father of James baptised in Dundee on 3 February 1723; Christian baptised in John Guthrie's house on 7 January 1724; George baptised on 25 January 1725

GUTHRIE, JOHN, of Guthrie, born 1763, died 1845, wife Ann Douglas, born 1770, died 1845. [St John's, Forfar, MI]

GUTHRIE, ROBERT, a merchant in Dundee, 1727. [ECD#23]

GUTHRIE, THOMAS, an apothecary in Dundee, 1727. [ECD#24]

GUTHRIE, WILLIAM, a cleric who emigrated to Jamaica in 1709. [EMA#31]

GUTHRIE, WILLIAM, of Clepington, Dundee, 1727. [ECD#21/23]

HACKET, PETER, and Elizabeth Rennie, in Rosehearty, Aberdeenshire, : married on 9 September 1790. [NAS.CH12.32.2]

HADDEN, JAMES, born 1754, died 1808, husband of Mary Johnston, born 1760, died 1833 , husband of Mary Johnston, born 1760, died 1833. [Montrose Episcopal MI]

HALIBURTON, ALEXANDER, from Crail, Fife, and Helen, daughter of Robert Milne, : married in St Andrews on 29 April 1779. [SER]

HALIBURTON, GEORGE, born 1638, son of the minister at Collace, graduated MA from St Andrews 1646, DD 1673, minister at Coupar Angus, Bishop of Brechin, burgess of Dundee 1678, Bishop of Aberdeen from 1682 until 1688, died at Denhead, Coupar Angus on 29 September 1715. [Keith#134][DBR]

HALIBURTON, JOHN, a merchant in Edinburgh and a trustee of the Carruber's Close congregation, 1741. [JSC#83]

HALIBURTON, WILLIAM, a minister to Virginia, 1766. [FPA#330][EMA#32]

HALL, Lieutenant ANTHONY, married Catherine Hay, in Ayr, 23 July 1797. [NAS.CH12.26.1]

HALL, JOHN, a weaver, and his wife .... Horseburgh, parents of Janet baptised at the Meadows, Edinburgh, on 22 April 1756. Witness was Chris. Hall; Robert baptised near Hope Park on 11 April 1758. Witnesses : .... Horsburgh and James Hall; Charles baptised in Canongate 15 April 1760. Witnesses : James Hall and William Brown. [DUAS.BrMsDC3/12]

HALL, WILLIAM, of the Perth Episcopalian Congregation, 1742. [TV.77.21][JWI]

HAMILTON, ANNE, wife of Austin Leigh a minister in Dominica, 1772. [NAS.RS27.199.181]

HAMILTON, ANNE, daughter of Hamilton of Kilibrachment, was confirmed in Leith on 17 December 1772. [SA.IX.14][LER]

HAMILTON, ARTHUR, a minister in Virginia, 1767, returned to Virginia from London, 1768. [FPA#309/330]

HAMILTON, BELL, a minister who emigrated to Maryland in 1747. [EMA#32]

HAMILTON, JAMES, a musician in Edinburgh, married Katherine Dewar from Edinburgh, in Haddington, East Lothian, on 6 February 1771. Witnesses : Robert Scott, William Garner, and Georgina Dallas. [NAS.CH12.2.18][HEC]

HAMILTON, JAMES, of Barns, married Eleanora Dunn, eldest daughter of John Dunn of Tannochside, there in 1785. Witnesses : John Dunn, Lieutenant A. Stewart of the 1st [Royal Scots] Regiment, Mrs Margaret Joblin, Miss Judith Dunn, and Miss Mary Leitch. [SA.X.22]

HAMILTON, JOHN, son of John Hamilton of Blair and his wife Barbra Elphinstone, Bishop of Dunkeld, 1686. [Keith#100]

HAMILTON, JOHN, married Miss Isabella Stirling, at the house of Lady Stirling in South Leith, on 15 June 1762. Witnesses : Sir William Stirling of Ardoch, Hamilton of Wishee, James Lindsay, Mrs Campbell, and Miss Menzies. [LER][NNQ.8.127]

HAMILTON, WILLIAM, late an Ensign of the 88th Regiment, married Mary Brown, daughter of Thomas Brown a resident of Glasgow, at St Andrew's Episcopal Church, Glasgow, on 17 November 1783. [SA.X.22]

HAMILTON, ..., a cleric and schoolmaster who emigrated to the Leeward Islands in 1701, in Nevis, 1716. [EMA#32][FPA#270]

HANDYSIDE, GEORGE, a writer in Edinburgh and a trustee of the Carruber's Close congregation, 1741. [JSC#84]

HANNA, WILLIAM, in Broomfield, Virginia, 1771, returned to Virginia from London in 1772. [EMA#32][FPA#310/330]

HAPPELL, ADOLPHUS, a sugar boiler in South Leith, father of Rachel baptised in South Leith on 10 July 1762. Witnesses : Mrs Midcaf and Mrs Trotter; and John baptised in South Leith on 5 May 1765. [SA.IX.12][LER]

HARDIE, PATRICK, smith at the Bridge of Braid, married Anne Scott, for 13 years a servant to Mr Ruddiman, at Thomas Ruddiman's house in Edinburgh, 28 April 1738. [DUAS: BrMS3/Dc/12]

HARLAW, ANDREW, a minister who emigrated to Virginia in 1722. [EMA#32]

HARPER, JAMES, and Katherine Dickson, : married in Gray's Close, Edinburgh, 1 July 1747. [DUAS: BrMS3/Dc/12]

HARPER, WILLIAM, an Episcopal minister in Bothkennar, Stirlingshire, a Jacobite in 1745. [LPR#316]; residing on the East Side of Carruber's Close, Edinburgh, 1746. [JSC#63]

HARRIS, WILLIAM, a shoemaker in Fraserburgh, Aberdeenshire, and Agnes Murdoch, : married there on 10 January 1793. [NAS.CH12.32.2]

HARRUER, JOHN, and his wife Janet Alexander, : parents of Janet born 20 January and baptised in Muthill, Perthshire, on 24 January 1698. [MRB]

HAY, GEORGE, an Episcopal preacher, 1717. [NAS.CH1.2.37.4/255]; a minister in Portsoy, a beneficiary under the will of Alexander Deuchar in Barbados, 1738 [NAS.CC8.8.100]

HAY, GEORGE, printer, father of Thomas baptised "on the back stairs from the Meal Market" in Edinburgh on 30 June 1752. Witnesses: Walter Ruddiman, James McKenzie and T. Traill writers. Alexdrina, youngest daughter of Harry Allan a writer, was confirmed in Leith on 13 August 1747.

HAY, JAMES, a Writer to the Signet, a trustee of the Carruber's Close congregation, 1741. [JSC#83]; married Margaret, daughter of the late Archibald Campbell a Writer to the Signet, in Bull's Land, Edinburgh, 30 October 1741. [DUAS: BrMS3/Dc/12]

HAY, JAMES, son of John Hay in Restalrig, was born on 21 January 1738 and baptised in Leith on 22 January 1738. Witnesses : Alexander Hay, Mrs Allan, and Mrs Watson. [SA.IX.13][LER]

HAY, JAMES, a writer in Edinburgh and a trustee of the Carruber's Close congregation, 1741. [JSC#84]

HAY, JAMES, was born in the East Indies in December 1795 and baptised in St John the Evangelist, Edinburgh, on 29 January 1799. [NAS.CH12.3.26/5]

HAY, THOMAS, son of John Hay in Restalrig, was born on 14 May 1739 and baptised on 15 May 1739 in Leith. Witnesses : Sheriff Hay the grandfather and Mrs Craigy the aunt. [SA.IX.13][LER]

HEMPSEED, ALEXANDER, married Barbara Rob, in Edinburgh, 15 October 1763. [DUAS: BrMS3/Dc/12]

HENDERSON, ALEXANDER, born 1737, son of Reverend Richard Henderson in Blantyre, Lanarkshire, educated at Glasgow University, emigrated to Virginia in 1756, a merchant and tobacco factor in Colchester, Occoquan, and Dumfries there, Vestryman of Pohick church, Truro parish, Fairfax County, 1774, died 1815 in Dumfries, Virginia. [Alexandria Library, Va: Letterbook] [MAGU#36][F.3.228][SRA.T.MJ][OC#226/233][Lake Mont Clair MI]

HENDERSON, DONALD, a workman or chairman, and his wife Ann Henderson, parents of Christian baptised in Edinburgh on 7 March 1754. Witnesses : John Hyslop and Elizabeth Stewart; of Donald baptised in Bailie's Close, Canongate, on 4 October 1755; Daniel baptised in the Herb Mercat, Edinburgh, on 20 September 1759. [DUAS.Br.MS3.DC/12]

HENDERSON, JANET, was confirmed in Fortrose, Easter Ross,1770. [EV#327]

HENDERSON, DUNCAN, and family, of the Perth Episcopalian Congregation, 1742. [TV.77.21][JWI]

HENDERSON, JOHN, son of Thomas Henderson a merchant in Dundee, was baptised in his house in Dundee on 17 August 1726. [BNDBR]

HENDERSON, JOHN, son of John Henderson and his wife Margaret Somerville, was born 7 August and baptised 14 August 1768 in Haddington, East Lothian. Witnesses : Patrick Somerville and John Henderson. [NAS.CH12.2.13]

HENDERSON, JOHN, late of Jamaica, married Helen Leslie on 4 October 1789 in Mrs Leslie's house. Witnesses : Dr Irvine and Mr Alexander. [SPAER]

HENDERSON, THOMAS, a merchant in Dundee, 1727. [ECD#24]

HENDERSON, WILLIAM, in Newbigging, Scotland, 1742; settled on Colonel Armistead Churchill's plantation on the Rappahannock River, Virginia, 1743, letters. [NAS.CH12.23.315/358/410][TBD#23]

HENDRIE, WILLIAM, a writer, married Margaret, daughter of the late James Gray a writer in Edinburgh, at Mr Semple's house, Edinburgh, 22 September 1747; parents of Agnes baptised in Grass Mercat, Edinburgh, 1 June 1752. Witnesses: John Callendar and Mrs Streephill. [DUAS: BrMS3/Dc/12]

HENNING, WILLIAM, son of William Henning and his wife Margaret, was born 24 April 1798 and baptised in St John the Evangelist, Edinburgh, on 9 May 1798. [NAS.CH12.3.26/3]

HENRY, PATRICK, son of Alexander Henry and his wife Jean Robertson in Aberdeenshire, emigrated to Virginia in 1731, minister of St George's parish, Spotsylvania County 1733 to 1734, then of Hanover County, 1737-1777, died

1777, probate Hanover County, 1777.
[EMA#33][WMQ.2.21/64][OC.2.69][FPA#187/214]

HEPBURN, ALEXANDER, a minister in Peterhead, Aberdeenshire, a beneficiary under the will of Alexander Deuchar in Barbados, 1738 [NAS.CC8.8.100];

HEPBURN, JOHN, son of John Hepburn the younger, was baptised in St John's, Forfar, Angus, on 5 April 1754. [EF#33]

HERDMAN, JAMES, born 12 May 1746, son of William Herdman in Dunnottar, Kincardineshire, educated at King's College, Aberdeen, 1763, a minister who emigrated to Virginia in 1770 and settled in Henrico County, Virginia. [EMA#33][FPA#309/330]

HERIOT, JAMES, a goldsmith, and his wife Janet, parents of James baptised in Fowlis's Close head, Edinburgh, on 1 October 1752. Witness was James McDouall a merchant; Margaret baptised near Bowhead, Edinburgh, on 26 August 1764. Witnesses : Mr and Mrs Ker. [DUAS.BrMsDC3/12]

HEWET GEORGE, the younger, and his wife Marion Scrimgeour, parents of Alexander was born 6 December and baptised 7 December 1723 in St Andrews; Anne born 25 March and baptised 26 March 1725 in St Andrews, Fife; and Christopher born and baptised 21 March 1727 in St Andrews, Fife. [SER]

HILL, JAMES, minister at Blairgowrie and Mill-hill, Perthshire, 1740; father of Elizabeth baptised 31 January 1741. [TBD#40/45]

HILL, JANE, daughter of Alexander Hill jr. a tailor in Aberdeen, was baptised 21 October 1720. Witnesses : Patrick Ross a merchant and Patrick Gray a wright. [SPAER]

HILL, JEAN, daughter of Alexander Hill a cordiner in the Murroes, was baptised in Dundee on 23 September 1726. [BNDBR]

HILL, JOHN, a merchant in Dundee, 1727. [ECD#24]

HILL, JOHN, possibly son of Reverend John Hill, was confirmed at Whiteloch, Blairgowrie, on 2 September 1750. [TBD#155]

HILL, JOHN, a corporal of the 53rd Regiment, married Sarah Kelvin from Ayr, there, 19 February 1793. [NAS.CH12.26.1]

HILL, JOSEPH, born 1750, a gardener, died 1818. [Montrose Episcopal MI]

HILL, ROBERT, in Dundee, 1727. [ECD#26]

HODGE, HENRY, married Jane Laughland, in Ayr, 25 February 1770. [NAS.CH12.26.1]

HOME, ALEXANDER, a Lieutenant in the Royal Navy, married Elizabeth Stuart from Ladykirk, Berwickshire, in Haddington, East Lothian, on 18 April 1785. Witnesses : Mary Maitland and Eliza Buchanan. [NAS.CH12.2.2.18][HEC]

HOME, JOHN, of Coldingham, Berwickshire, married Margaret Home, of the same parish, in Haddington, East Lothian, on 23 January 1787. Witnesses : James Nisbet and George Swinton.[NAS.CH12.2.2.18][HEC]

HOME, WILLIAM, of Basenrig, married Mrs Margaret Home, daughter of Alexander Home a landwaiter, at Sheriffbrae of Leith on 28 April 1747. Witnesses : the said Alexander Home, Charles Home, Mrs Helen Home, Mrs Ann Home, and Margaret Thomson. [LER][NNQ.8.125]

HONEYMAN, JAMES, son of James Honeyman, minister at Kinneff, Kincardineshire, and his wife Margaret Leask, a cleric who emigrated to New York in 1703, a missionary in Newport, later in Jamaica, Long Island, and in 1708 he settled as a minister in Newport, Rhode Island, died July 1750. [SCHR.14.149][EMA#34][F.5.473] [FPA#122][LIS.5.87/128] [SPAWI.1727.638/817]

HOOD, JOHN, and his wife Jean Adam, in Copegate, Arbroath, Angus, 1752. [SRS.13.76]

HOOPER, WILLIAM, emigrated to New England in 1747, died 14 April 1767. [EMA#34][FPA#75][possibly the William Hopper, a native of Berwickshire, minister in Montrose from 1731 to 1733 when he was deposed. (F.5.414)]

HORN, GEORGE, son of James Horn a baker, was baptised in Aberdeen on 20 September 1720. Witnesses : George Burnet senior and George Robertson a goldsmith. [SPAER]

HORN, PATRICK, in Bauchie, was baptised at Blairgowrie, Perthshire, and also confirmed on 20 March 1742. [TBD#41]

HORN, ROBERT, a farmer in the North Mains of Restalrig, and Jean Mitchell, daughter to William Mitchell a merchant in Edinburgh, resident at the saw-mill, : married in Edinburgh on 7 February 1743 by Alexander McKenzie. [SLIM#619]

HORNE, JOHN, of Stirkoke, Caithness, born 1753, died 1823. [St John's, Edinburgh, MI]

HORNER, JOHN, born 1751, a merchant, died 1829, husband of Joanna Baillie, born 1755, died 1827. [St John's, Edinburgh, MI]

HORSMAN, WILLIAM, born 1758, died 1845, his 1st wife Jane ...., born 1770, died 1833, his 2nd wife Mary Turner, died 1841. [St John's, Edinburgh, MI]

HOSACK, WILLIAM, husband of Margaret Edward died 1799. [Montrose Episcopal MI]

HOUSTOUN, JAMES, a minister who emigrated to Maryland in 1747, schoolmaster at Chester, Pennsylvania. [EMA#34][LIS.5.87]

HOWE, JOHN, an Episcopal preacher, 1694. [NAS.CH1.2.2.1/33]

HOWIE, ALEXANDER, son of Reverend John Howie in Birse, Aberdeenshire, educated at Marischal College, Aberdeen, around 1719, emigrated to Pennsylvania as a minister in 1730, missionary in Whitemarsh and Perkiomen, 1731, in Oxford, Pa., by 1739, moved to Jamaica in 1743. [EMA#34][FPA#104/108/111][LIS.5.69/128]

HUDSON, GEORGE, born 1695, sergeant major of the 36th Regiment of Foot, died 1758, wife Margaret, born 1697, died 1761. [Montrose Episcopal MI]

HUE, Mr, of the Perth Episcopalian Congregation, 1742. [TV.77.21][JWI]

HUNTER, ALEXANDER, an Episcopalian in Leith, 1735. [NAS.CH12.23.156]

HUSBAND, WILLIAM, and his daughter Elizabeth Husband, : confirmed at Whiteloch, Blairgowrie, 30 October 1753. [TBD#155]

HUTCHESON, JOHN, a land surveyor, died 176- aged 40, testament, 1770, Comm. Brechin. [NAS][Montrose Episcopal MI]

HUTTON, JOHN, brushmaker, and his wife Anne Ruddiman, parents of Janet baptised at the Meal Mercat, Edinburgh, on 2 November 1752. Witnesses : Walter Ruddiman and his wife, Mrs Fenton and Mrs Fleming midwife. [DUAS.BrMsDC3/12]

IDELL, WILLIAM, born in Moray, graduated MA from King's College, Aberdeen, 1664, schoolmaster at Chapel of Garioch from 1669, minister at Coull, Aberdeenshire, from 1686 to 1716 when he was deposed as a Jacobite. [F.6.90]

INGLIS, CHARLES, a minister, to Pennsylvania, 1758. [FPA#328]

INGLIS, FRANCES, died 9 January 1791. [Kingston parish MI, Jamaica]

INGLIS, JAMES, born 1660, son of Archibald Inglis minister of St Mungo's in Glasgow, minister in Muthill, Perthshire, from 1689 until his death on 24 October 1732. Husband of Marion Davidson. [F.4.285]

INGLIS, JAMES, a shipmaster, and his wife Martha Spink, in Arbroath, Angus, 1752. [SRS.13.80]

INGLIS, MUNGO, a Episcopalian minister, schoolmaster at the College of William and Mary, 1695. [SCHR.14.138]

INNES, ALEXANDER, a chaplain sent to the Leeward Islands in 1694. [CTB.X.1.514]

INNES, BEROALD, minister of Alves, Morayshire, removed 1689. [EM#153]

INNES, GEORGE, deacon in 1741, minister at Dunning and later Balgowan, Perthshire, 1743. [TBD#38]

INNES, GEORGE, a minister in Aberdeen, Bishop of Brechin from 1778 until his death on 18 May 1781. [Keith#545]

INNES, JAMES, son of John Innes in Mortlach, educated at Marischal College, Aberdeen, 1769-1773, graduated MA, minister at Meiklefolla. [MCA#340]

Scots Episcopalians at Home and Abroad, 1689-1800

INNES, ROBERT, a minister in Caroline County, Virginia, 1752

IRONSIDE, RALPH ANTHONY, of Houghton le Spring, County Durham, married Judith Dunn of Tannochside, at Cockney, Old Kilpatrick, Dunbartonshire, on 16 November 1796. Witnesses : John Hamilton of Barns, James Jackson postmaster in Glasgow, and John Boyes junior of Wellholl. [SA.X.23]

IRVINE, CHARLES, minister of St Philip's, Barbados, from 1692, took the Association Oath of the Clergy in Barbados in 1696. [NA]; Reverend Charles Irvine in St Michael's, Barbados, 1715. [Parish Register][FPA#227]

IRVINE, GEORGE, a minister on the Western Shore of Maryland, 1718. [FPA#29]

JACK, JAMES, a tailor in Dundee, 1727. [ECD#24]

JACKSON, GRISHILD, daughter of Andrew Jackson a writer in Edinburgh and his wife Agnes Law, was born 23 July and baptised 26 July 1727 in St Andrews, Fife. [SER]

JACKSON, Mrs, of the Perth Episcopalian Congregation, 1742. [TV.77.21][JWI]

JAFFREY, ANDREW, probably son of Alexander Jaffrey minister of Kinedward, educated at Marischal College, Aberdeen, minister of Alford until 1716 when he was deposed as a Jacobite. Husband of Marjorie Davidson, parents of William, Robert, Alexander, and Arthur. [F.6.118]

JAFFREY, JOHN, a minister in Lonmay, a beneficiary under the will of Alexander Deuchar in Barbados, 1738 [NAS.CC8.8.100];

JAFFREY, JOHN, a wheelwright in Strichen, Aberdeenshire, and Ann Presley in Fraserburgh, Aberdeenshire, : married on 3 August 1793. [NAS.CH12.32.2]

JAMESON, ..., a child of ...... Jameson, was baptised in Brechin, Angus, on 25 December 1798. [NNQ.14.100]

JAMIESON, WILLIAM, a surgeon in Fraserburgh, Fraserburgh, and Isobel Gordon, : married there on 29 January 1804. [NAS.CH12.32.2]

JAMISON, JOHN, a sailor in Leith, and Mary Seaman a baker there, : married in Edinburgh by Alexander McKenzie on 4 November 1743. [SLIM618]

Scots Episcopalians at Home and Abroad, 1689-1800

JOHNSTON, ALEXANDER, was confirmed in Arpafilie, Ross-shire, in 1770.
[EV#327]

JOHNSTON, ANDREW, a cleric and schoolmaster, who emigrated to emigrated
to Jamaica in 1706. [EMA#37]

JOHNSTON, DAVID, a merchant and guilds-brother of Montrose, Angus,
testament, 1781, Comm. Brechin. [NAS][Montrose Episcopal MI]

JOHNSTON, DONALD, was confirmed in Arpafilie, Ross-shire, in 1770. [EV#327]

JOHNSTON, FRANCIS, a minister who emigrated to North Carolina in 1768.
[EMA#37][FPA#327]

JOHNSTON, GIDEON, a cleric who emigrated to Carolina with his wife and six
children in 1708, in Charleston, SC, 1715, drowned in 1716.
[EMA#37][FPA#131]

JOHNSTON, JANET, was confirmed in Arpafilie, Ross-shire, in 1770. [EV#327]

JOHNSTON, JEAN, daughter of Patrick Johnston a tenant in the Murroes,
Angus, was baptised in Dundee on 25 June 1726. [BNDBR]

JOHNSTON, JAMES, of Clepington, in Dundee, 1727. [ECD#24]

JOHNSTON, JOHN, son of James Johnston a writer in Dundee, was baptised in
James Johnston's house there on 13 August 1723. [BNDBR]

JOHNSTON, THOMAS, a minister who emigrated to Maryland in 1751.
[EMA#37][FPA#301/325]

JOHNSTONE, WILLIAM, a minister who emigrated to Jamaica in 1704, settled
in Vere parish and later in St Andrew's parish, died 1739. [GL#ms10326/40;
FPA#232/249]

JOHNSTON, WILLIAM, son of Peter Johnston in Murraygate, Dundee, was
baptised on 20 June 1724. [BNDBR]

JOLLY, ALEXANDER, Bishop of Moray, 1796, minister at Fraserburgh,
Aberdeenshire. [Keith#543]

JOLLY, ISAAC, a writer and deputy town clerk of Arbroath, Angus, residing in Copegate, Arbroath, 1752. [SRS.13.75]

JOLLIE, THOMAS, in Glen Effock, was father of Margaret Jollie, baptised at Lochlee, Angus, on 16 March 1728. Witnesses : William Archibald and David Archibald both there. Also of Jean Jollie baptised at Lochlee on 15 February 1731. Witnesses : David and William Archibald there. [DUAS.BrMsDC3/174]

JUNOR, MARGARET, was conformed in Fortrose, Easter Ross, 1770. [EV#327]

KEIR, JAMES, of Kilmont, married Margaret, daughter of Alexander Orme of Balvaird, in Edinburgh, 28 April 1750. [DUAS: BrMS3/Dc/12]

KEITH, ALEXANDER, of Ravelston, a trustee of the Carruber's Close congregation, Edinburgh, 1741. [JSC#83]

KEITH, ALEXANDER, a minister in Cruden, Aberdeenshire, a beneficiary under the will of Alexander Deuchar in Barbados, 1738 [NAS.CC8.8.100];

KEITH, ALEXANDER, junior, an under-clerk of Session, a trustee of the Carruber's Close congregation, Edinburgh, 1741. [JSC#83]

KEITH, ALEXANDER, a minister who emigrated to South Carolina in 1745, in St Stephen's parish, S.C., 1766. [EMA#39][FPA#155]

KEITH, BASIL, Governor of Jamaica from 1774 to 1777, son of Robert Keith, died 15 June 1777. [Spanish Town Cathedral MI, Jamaica]

KEITH, GEORGE, born 1638, from Peterhead, Aberdeenshire, educated at Aberdeen University in 1654, initially a Presbyterian, then a Quaker in England and East New Jersey from 1684, a convert to Anglicanism in 1700 he returned to America as a missionary of the Society for the Propagation of the Gospel, he died in 1716. [SCHR.14.146][EMA#39]

KEITH, JAMES, born 1696 in Peterhead, Aberdeenshire, son of Robert Keith, educated at Marischal College, Aberdeen, emigrated to America in 1720, minister in Henrico County, and Hamilton parish, Fauquier County, Virginia, died in Hamilton, 1758. [VMHB.31.327][CCVC#29][OC#216][EMA#38]

KEITH, JOHN, a ship carpenter in Fraserburgh, Aberdeenshire, married Susan Rannie, in Fraserburgh on 15 November 1788. [NAS.CH12.32.2]

KEITH, MARISCHAL, born 4 April 1761, son of James Keith and his wife Anne Barclay in Kinnellar, educated at King's College, Aberdeen, a minister who emigrated to Bermuda in 1792, settled in Warwick and Paget Counties, died 1796. [EMA#39][FPA#246/247/315]

KEITH, ROBERT, born 7 February 1682 at Uras in the Mearns, son of Alexander Keith [died 1683] and his wife ...... Arbuthnot [1638-1707], educated at Marischal College, Aberdeen, tutor to Lord Keith 1703 to 1710, ordained as a deacon 1710, domestic chaplain to Charles, 12th Earl of Errol, minister in Edinburgh 1713, Bishop of Orkney and Caithness, 1727, husband of Isabel Cameron, died January 1757. [TBD#28][Keith#549]

KELLY, JOHN, minister of the Protestant Episcopal Church in Ayr, 1776-1779. [NAS.CH12.26.1]

KELLY, JOHN, and Margaret Barber, both from Maybole, Ayrshire, : married in Ayr, 27 November 1795. [NAS.CH12.26.1]

KELLY, Lady, of the Perth Episcopalian Congregation, 1742. [TV.77.21][JWI]

KEMP, HUGH, MA, a minister who emigrated to Jamaica in 1730. [EMA#39]

KENCARUKIE, of the Perth Episcopalian Congregation, 1742. [TV.77.21][JWI]

KENNER, ..., educated at Glasgow University, a minister who emigrated to Virginia in 1729. [FPA#181]

KENNEDY, JOHN, born in Kingussie, Inverness-shire, 1 June 1748, educated at King's and Marischal Colleges, Aberdeen, assistant minister of St Mark's, East Florida, 1777. [EMA#39][FPA#300]

KERR, DAVID, born 1745, a surgeon who emigrated via London to Jamaica on the <u>Dawes</u> in December 1775. [NA.T47.9/11]; possibly in Trelawney, Jamaica, 1783. [NLS.Melville ms3591/115-130]; born 1745, late of Jamaica, died 1829. [Montrose Episcopal MI]

KER, JAMES, in Dundee, 1727. [ECD#26]

KER, JOHN, a baker in Dundee, 1727. [ECD#24]

KERR, Mrs LEONORA, in Ayr, relict of Robert Kerr of Newfield, was buried in Ayr on 12 September 1795. [NAS.CH12.26.1]

KERR, MARK, Captain of the 9th Regiment of Dragoons on the Irish Establishment, was buried at Irvine on 23 September 1791. [NAS.CH12.26.1]

KEY, JOHN, a tailor in Arbroath, Angus, husband of Helen Tod, 1752. [SRS.13.78][Arbroath MI]

KID, CLEMENTINA DUGALLA, daughter of George Kid, eldest son of the laird of Craigie, was baptised at Woodhill, Angus, by Robert Norie, 21 June 1722. Godfather was her grandfather the laird of Craigie and godmothers : her two grandmothers Madam Maitland and the lady Craigie. [BNDBR]

KID, GEORGE, the younger of Craigie, in Dundee, 1727. [ECD#23]

KID, JAMES, of Craigie, in Dundee, 1727. [ECD#23/24]

KID, THOMAS, a merchant in Dundee, 1727. [ECD#24]

KILGOUR, ROBERT, born at Waulkmill, Cruden, Aberdeenshire, in 1714, graduated from Aberdeen University in 1733, ordained 1737, minister of St Peter's, Peterhead, Bishop of Aberdeen in 1768, Bishop of Edinburgh and Primus of the Scots Episcopal Church in 1782, consecrated Bishop Seabury, died 22 March 1790, husband of Margaret Arbuthnott. [TBD#223][Peterhead MI] [Keith#534]

KILPATRICK, ROBERT, a missionary of the Society for the Propagation of the Gospel at Trinity Bay, Newfoundland, 1730-1731, at New Windsor, New York, 1731-1733, returned to Newfoundland, died there August 1741. [EMA#39][FPA#5][LIS.5.87][SPAWI.1731.422]

KINCAID, THOMAS, a weaver in Restalrig, and Ann Holmes, relict of Thomas Ainskie there, : married by James Wingate, minister, in Edinburgh on 27 March 1731. Witnesses : John Bennet and John Kinkead. [SLIM#358]

KINLOCH, CICIL, daughter to Dr Kinloch, MD in Dundee, was baptised in Dundee on 20 June 1722. Godfather was Dr John Fotheringham, brother german to the late George Fotheringham, laird of Bandeen, and the godmothers : his wife and Mrs Bell Hay, daughter to the late Sir John Hay of Moorie. [BNDBR]

KINLOCH, Sir JAMES, of that Ilk, in Dundee, 1727. [ECD#23]

KINLOCH, JAMES, the younger of that Ilk, in Dundee, 1727. [ECD#24]

KINLOCH, JAMES, son of John Kinloch MD in Dundee, was baptised in his house in Dundee on 1 January 1726. Godfathers : the laird of Kilrie and David Fotheringham MD in Dundee, with Dr Fotheringham's wife as godmother. [BNDBR]

KINLOCH, Dr JOHN, in Dundee, 1727. [ECD#21/23]

KINLOCH, JOHN, son of John Kinloch MD in Dundee, was baptised in Kinloch's house in Dundee on 24 June 1724. Godfathers : Patrick Crichton of Crunan, and John Fotheringham, brother german to the deceased George Fotheringham of Bandene, while the wife of David Fotheringham MD was godmother. [BNDBR]

KINLOCH, JOHN, son of the laird of Kilrie, was baptised in the house of Dr John Kinloch, brother german to the laird of Kilrie, in Dundee on 15 August 1724. Dr John Kinloch and Dr David Fotheringham : godfathers while the wife of Dr John Kinloch was godmother. [BNDBR]

KINNEAR, JOHN, father of a daughter baptised at Lochlee, Angus, on 6 July 1735. Witnesses : Thomas Kinnear in Milntown and David Archibald in Glen Effock. [DUAS.BrMsDC3/174]

KINNEAR, THOMAS, in Milntown, was father of David Kinnear baptised at Lochlee, Angus, on 14 October 1729. Witnesses : John Edward there and David Archibald in Glen Effock. Also of Thomas Kinnear baptised at Lochlee on 13 May 1732. Witnesses : Thomas Jollie in Glen Effock and James Anerdale. [DUAS.BrMsDC3/174]

KINNEAR, WILLIAM, in Inchgrundle, was father of Margaret Kinnear baptised at Lochlee, Angus, on 13 October 1729. Witnesses : David Archibald and Thomas Jollie in Glen Effock. [DUAS.BrMsDC3/174]

KIRKPATRICK, HENRY ERSKINE, a minister who emigrated to the Leeward Islands in 1768. [EMA#39]

KIRKWOOD, THOMAS, schoolmaster at Cranston, and Margaret Alexander, daughter of the late John Alexander minister at Kildrummy, an antenuptial marriage contract, 24 May 1719; schoolmaster in Leith, 1723. [NAS.CH12.23.11/18]

KNOX, JAMES, born in Edinburgh during 1690s, son of Reverend Henry Knox once in Bowden, a cleric who emigrated to St Kitts in 1715, minister in St Kitts, son and heir of Henry Knox minister at Bowden, 1719; a minister at St Mary's, Antigua, 1726, probate 1740 PCC. [NAS.S/H.1719][EMA#39][FPA#276]

KNOX, JAMES, son of James Knox and Mary his wife, was born on 15 December 1797 and baptised in St John the Evangelist, Edinburgh, on 17 December 1797. [NAS.CH12.3.26/2]

KNOX, WILLIAM, son of John Knox and Mary his wife, was born 2 November 1799 and baptised in St John the Evangelist, Edinburgh, on 2 November 1799. [NAS.CH12.3.26/7]

KYD, JAMES, born 1687, a glover in Arbroath, Angus, died 8 December 1761, husband of Euphan Reid, parents of John and Henry. [SRS.13.63][Arbroath MI]

LAING, ELEANOR, died 29 September 1747. [Kingston parish MI, Jamaica]

LAING, JAMES, in Drumcairn, Lethnot, Angus, father of a daughter baptised 15 December 1725. Witnesses : John Gib in Newbigging and Thomas Will. [DUAS.BrMS.DC3/174]

LAING, JAMES, born 1765, died 15 December 1827. [Spanish Town Cathedral MI, Jamaica]

LAING, JOHN, son of James Laing and his wife ..... Chalmers in Tillery, Foveran, was baptised on 24 November 1763. [CBER]

LAING, MALCOLM, born 1718, died 1 August 1781. [Kingston parish MI, Jamaica], probate 1788 PCC. [NLS.ms5028/40]

LAING, PATRICK, a minister in Alford, a beneficiary under the will of Alexander Deuchar in Barbados, 1738 [NAS.CC8.8.100];

LAIRD, ANDREW, a merchant in Dundee, 1727. [ECD#24]

LAIRD, JAMES, a merchant in Dundee, 1727. [ECD#24]

LAIRD, SAMUEL, son of James Laird in the parish of Desartmartin, County Londonderry, graduated MA from Glasgow University 1751, a minister who emigrated to North Carolina in 1755. [EMA#40][FPA#304/327][MAGU#319]

LAMB, JOHN, in Pitblae, and Jean Massie, daughter of William Massie at Berry Mill, Rathen, : married in Fraserburgh, Aberdeenshire, on 29 October 1796. [NAS.CH12.32.2]

LANG, JOHN, a minister who emigrated to Virginia in 1725, minister of Lyins Creek parish, then in St Peter's, New Kent County, Virginia, later by 1731 in St James parish, Anne Arundel County, Maryland. [NAS.GD248/5648][EMA#40][FPA#42/44/178]

LARCHEN, WILLIAM, son of Humphrey Larchen and his wife Margaret Buller, was born 9 July and baptised 17 July 1768 in Haddington, East Lothian. Witnesses : John Blaikie and George Kemp. [NAS.CH12.2.13]

LASON, JAMES, and his wife Margaret Bryce, in Middle, Drumnawhance, Muthill, Perthshire, : parents of James born 13 February and baptised 16 February 1698. [MRB]

LAUDER, FRANCIS, born 22 October 1729 in Auldearn, Nairn, educated at Marischal College, Aberdeen, 1751, a schoolmaster and minister, emigrated to Maryland in 1761. [FPA#301/326]

LAURIE, JOHN, a shipmaster in North Leith, married Ann Drysdale, widow of Gilbert Shirreff late shipmaster in Leith, in Haddington on 20 September 1784. Witnesses : James Mitchell and Mary Humphrey. [NAS.CH12.2.2.18][HEC]

LAW, ALEXANDER, a minister in Kondall, a beneficiary under the will of Alexander Deuchar in Barbados, 1738 [NAS.CC8.8.100];

LAW, GEORGE, a minister in Ellon, Aberdeenshire, a beneficiary under the will of Alexander Deuchar in Barbados, 1738 [NAS.CC8.8.100]; a non-jurant minister in Aberdeen, a Jacobite soldier in 1745. [LPR#12]

LAW, GEORGE, and his wife Janet Denis, parents of Michael born in ... April and baptised in St Andrews, Fife, on 25 April 1723; John born and baptised in St Andrews on 7 February 1726; and Henry born 13 May and baptised on 14 May 1728 in St Andrews, Fife. [SER]

LAW, GEORGE, and Janet Morton, : married in St Andrews, Fife, on 21 July 1760. [SER]

LAW, JAMES, in Dundee, 1727. [ECD#26]

LAW, WILLIAM, a minister residing in South Leith, 1746. [JSC#63]

LAWSON, JOHN, and his wife Ann Drummond in Middle Drumnawhance, Perthshire, : parents of Mary born 18 February and baptised 22 February 1775. [MRB]

LAWSON, WILLIAM, and his wife Mary Murray, in Balloch, : parents of Patrick born 8 May and baptised 12 May 1775. [MRB]

LAWTHER, Mrs, and her sister, of the Perth Episcopalian Congregation, 1742. [TV.77.21][JWI]

LEALL, JONATHAN, and Janet Bowie, : married in Ayr, 30 March 1798. [NAS.CH12.26.1]

LEEL, JAMES, of the Aberdeenshire Militia, and Christian Pirie, daughter of John Pirie in Pitsligo, Aberdeenshire, : married in Fraserburgh on 22 May 1803. [NAS.CH12.32.2]

LEICH, WILLIAM, was confirmed in Fortrose, Easter Ross, 1770. [EV#327]

LEITH, MARY ELIZABETH ANNE, daughter of Colonel James Leith and Augusta his wife, was born 17 November 1798 and baptised in St John the Evangelist, Edinburgh, on 21 December 1798. [NAS.CH12.3.26/5]

LEITH, PATRICK, graduated MA from King's College, Aberdeen, 1676, minister of Lumphanan from 168- until 1716 when he was deposed as a Jacobite. Father of William born 1680, a soldier, died in Aberdeen 26 November 1777. [F.6.106]

LEKLAND, THOMAS, son of Thomas Lekland in the Glass-work, was baptised at North Leith on 26 August 1746. Thomas Sommer and Jeremiah Stamford : godfathers and Mrs Sommer was godmother. [LER][SA.X.10]

LENDRUM, THOMAS, a minister who emigrated to Virginia in 1765, minister in Hanover, Virginia, minister of Annapolis, Maryland, a Loyalist in 1776, moved via the West Indies to England. [EMA#40][NA.AO13.40.151][FPA#308/330]

LESLIE, ALEXANDER, born 1637, son of James Leslie of Warthill and Beatrix Abercrombie, graduated MA from King's College, Aberdeen, in 1657, minister of Crail, Fife, from 1684 until he was deposed in 1689, Episcopal minister there until he died in 1703. [F.5.193]

LESLIE, ALEXANDER, son of Andrew Leslie a periwig-maker in Aberdeen, was baptised 23 December 1720. Witnesses : Alexander Cooper master of the music school of Aberdeen and Alexander Hill a tailor. [SPAER]

LESLIE, ANDREW, a minister who emigrated to South Carolina in 1729, in St Paul's 1731, returned home in 1740. [EMA#40][FPA#142/149][LIS.5.129]

LESLIE, WILLIAM, rector of St John's, Barbados, from 1653, grandson of the laird of Kincraigie, and great grandson of John Leslie the 8th baron of Balquhain, probate 1674, Barbados.

LESLIE, WILLIAM, a minister who emigrated to Antigua in 1718. [EMA#40][Rawlinson ms.C393/94]

LESLIE, WILLIAM, a minister in Holla, a beneficiary under the will of Alexander Deuchar in Barbados, 1738 [NAS.CC8.8.100];

LEVISTON, JOHN, was confirmed in Ballachulish, Argyll, in 1770. [EV#344]

LEWIS, ..., wife of Sergeant Lewis of the 35th Regiment of Foot, was buried in Ayr on 6 February 1791. [NAS.CH12.26.1]

LEWIS, WILLIAM, a sergeant of the 35th Regiment, and Elizabeth James a servant to Mr Buchan in Ayr, : married in Ayr, 23 January 1792. [NAS.CH12.26.1]

LIDDERDALE, ALEXANDER, a gardener, father of Helen baptised at Abbeyhill, Edinburgh, 27 May 1752. Witnesses: Mrs Jean Rose and John Dunbar. Alexdrina, youngest daughter of Harry Allan a writer, was confirmed in Leith on 13 August 1747.

LINDSAY, ALEXANDER, of the Perth Episcopalian Congregation, 1742. [TV.77.21][JWI]

LINDSAY, ANDREW, in Achin, father of James Lindsay baptised at Lochlee, Angus, on 13 May 1732. Witnesses : James Gordon in Glen Catt and David Gold in Achin. [DUAS.BrMsDC3/174]

LINDSAY, DAVID, born 2 January 1603, son of Sir Jeremy Lindsay and his wife Jane Ramsay in Leith, a minister in Wicomico parish, Northumberland County, Virginia, died 3 April 1677. [CCVC#32][Northumberland MI]

LINDSAY, JAMES, in Achin, was father of James Lindsay, baptised at Lochlee, Angus, on 31 March 1727. Witnesses : David Gib and Andrew Lindsay the younger in the Achin. [DUAS.BrMsDC3/174]

LINDSAY, JAMES, of the Perth Episcopalian Congregation, 1742. [TV.77.21][JWI]

LINDSAY, JAMES, an Excise officer in Haddington, East Lothian, married Janet Herriot, a milliner there, in Haddington on 6 December 1788. Witnesses : John Main and William Johnstone. [NAS.CH12.2.2.18][HEC]

LINDSAY, JOHN, in Tilliebearn, Lethnott, Angus, father of Jean baptised 2 September 1724. Witnesses : Andrew Smart in Achurie and John Smart. [DUAS.BrMS.DC3/174]

LINDSAY, JOHN, son of Reverend Henry Lindsay and his wife Mary Simson, rector of St Thomas, Jamaica, graduated Doctor of Divinity at Glasgow University on 12 January 1773. [GUL][F.4.231]

LINDSAY, MARTIN, a writer in Edinburgh and a trustee of the Carruber's Close congregation, 1741. [JSC#84]

LINDSAY, WILLIAM, graduated MA from Glasgow University, to America 1733, ordained in 1735, missionary of the Society for the Propagation of the Gospel in Bristol, Virginia; New England, and Trenton, New Jersey, from 1735 until 1745. [SCHR.14.149][FPA#109][LIS.5.88/129]

LINDSAY, WILLIAM, of the Perth Episcopalian Congregation, 1742. [TV.77.21][JWI]

LINDSAY, WILLIAM, of Feddinch and Elisabeth Balfour, sister of ..... Balfour of Fernie, : married at Dunbog, Fife, 15 August 1762. [SER]

LITSTER, ADAM, married Emma Francis, both from Perth, there on 1 May 1780. Witnesses : John Pierie and William Litster. [NAS.CH12.2.2.18][HEC]

LISTON, ROBERT, of Damhead, His Majesty's Ambassador to the Porte, married Henrietta Merchant, daughter of Nathaniel Merchant from Antigua, on 27 February 1796 at St Andrew's Episcopal Church in Glasgow. Witnesses : Mr and Mrs Jackson, and Miss Thebau. [SA.X.23]

LIVINGSTON, ALEXANDER, son of Reverend Andrew Livingston, an Episcopal minister in Dunfermline, 17.... [F.6.128]

LIVINGSTON, ANDREW, graduated MA from Marischal College, Aberdeen, in 1670, chaplain to the Earl of Kintore, minister of Keig, Aberdeenshire, from 1683 until 1716 when deposed as a Jacobite. Father of William, Andrew, Alexander, Margaret, and James. [F.6.128]

LIVINGSTON, GEORGE, an inn-keeper, father of John baptised in Advocate's Close, Edinburgh, on 6 October 1752. Witness Allan Stewart a surgeon; Mary baptised in Old Bank Close, Edinburgh, on 16 November 1755. Witness was Mr Bell. [DUAS.BrMsDC3/12]

LIVINGSTON, WILLIAM, in Antigua, 1716. [FPA#270]

LIVINGSTON, WILLIAM, son of Reverend Andrew Livingston, an Episcopal minister in Old Deer, dead by 1757. [F.6.128]; a beneficiary under the will of Alexander Deuchar in Barbados, 1738 [NAS.CC8.8.100];

LIVISTON, ANGUS, was confirmed in Ballachulish, Argyll, in 1770. [EV#344]

LIVISTON, DONALD, was confirmed in Ballachulish, Argyll, in 1770. [EV#344]

LIVISTON, DONALD, was confirmed in Ballachulish, Argyll, in 1770. [EV#344]

LONG, ANNE, daughter of Nicolas Long, a mariner and mason in Ayr, and his wife Anne..., was baptised in Ayr on 19 November 1799. [NAS.CH12.26.1]

LONGMUIR, WILLIAM, born 1692 in Grange, schoolmaster at Rothiemay 1716, minister at Rathven 1714, then at Wick 1730-1734, non-jurant minister at Auchinhove, 1761. [EM#323]

LOVE, DAVID, educated at Edinburgh University, a minister in Maryland 1764. [FPA#301]

LOVET, Lady, of the Perth Episcopalian Congregation, 1742. [TV.77.21][JWI]

LOW, CHRISTIAN, daughter of Abraham Low a mason in Hilltown, Dundee, on 6 June 1723. [BNDBR]

LOW, DAVID, late of the Mains of Barras, husband of Isabel Wyse, born 1713, died 1803. [Montrose Episcopal MI]

LOW, DAVID, possibly from Forfar, Angus, a minister who emigrated to Maryland in 1764. [EMA.41][NAS.RS35.20.79]

LOW, Dr DAVID, son of David Low in Brechin, Angus, educated at Marischal College, Aberdeen, 1783-1787, minister at Pittenweem, Fife, later Bishop of Ross. [MCA#360][Keith#551]

LOW, EUPHEMIA, at Dungarthill, was confirmed at Whiteloch, Blairgowrie, Perthshire, on 2 September 1750. [TBD#155]

LOW, GEORGE, a slater, and Mary Milne, both in Fraserburgh, Aberdeenshire, : married there on 4 August 1799. [NAS.CH12.32.2]

LOW, JAMES, in Ardoch, was father of Janet Low, baptised at Lochlee, Angus, on 3 September 1727. Witnesses : David and Charles Campbell. [DUAS.BrMsDC3/174]

LOW, JOHN, in Achlochie, was father of David Low baptised at Lochlee, Angus, on 14 July 1728. Witnesses : David Edward in Milltown and David Jollie in Miln Achin. [DUAS.BrMsDC3/174]

LOW, JOHN, in Glack, father of Elizabeth Low baptised at Lochlee, Angus, on 5 March 1733. Witnesses : John Crofts and Thomas Kinnear in Milntown. [DUAS.BrMsDC3/174]

LOW, THOMAS, in Ardsallerie, was father of David Low baptised at Lochlee, Angus, on 3 March 1728. Witnesses : David Rose, David Edward in Milntown, and David Kinnear in Auchlochie, [DUAS.BrMsDC3/174]

LOWSON, JOHN, in Boguetown, Lethnott, Angus, was father of David baptised 1 August 1724. Witnesses : David Tosh in Old Town and David Smart. [DUAS.BrMS.DC3/174]

LUMSDEN, ANDREW, formerly minister of Duddingston, Bishop of Edinburgh from 1727, died in July 1733. [Keith#527]

LUMSDEN, WILLIAM, a writer in Edinburgh and a trustee of the Carruber's Close congregation, 1741. [JSC#84]

LUNAN, ALEXANDER, born around 1647, son of Reverend William Lunan, graduated MA from King's College, Aberdeen, in 1664, minister of Daviot, Aberdeenshire, from 1672 until 1716 when he was deposed as a Jacobite, Episcopal minister at Meikle Wartle. Husband of Janet Elphinstone, parents of James, Patrick, Robert, Margaret, Elizabeth, Cecilia, and Anna. [F.6.156]

LUNAN, ALEXANDER, a minister in Blair, a beneficiary under the will of Alexander Deuchar in Barbados, 1738 [NAS.CC8.8.100];

LUNAN, ALEXANDER, a minister in Virginia, 1769. [FPA#309/330]

LUNAN, PATRICK, son of Reverend Alexander Lunan and his wife Janet Elphinstone in Daviot, Fyvie, Aberdeenshire, minister at Meikle Wartle who emigrated to Virginia in 1760, settled in Upper Parish, Nansemond County. [EMA#41][NAS.CH12.24.17][FPA#215/330][F.6.156]; a beneficiary under the will of Alexander Deuchar in Barbados, 1738 [NAS.CC8.8.100];

LUNDIE, JAMES or THOMAS, from Buchan, Aberdeenshire, educated at King's College, Aberdeen, 1741, a minister who emigrated to Virginia in 1767. [EMA.41][FPA#309/330]

LYALL, ANDREW, born 1765, a currier in Montrose, Angus, died 1810, husband of Elspet Phase. [Montrose Episcopal MI]

LYALL, ROBERT, in Migvie, was father of Jean Lyall baptised at Lochlee, Angus, in February 1730. Witnesses : John Crokat and James Webster both there. [DUAS.BrMsDC3/174]

LYALL, ROBERT, in Milntown, father of John Lyall baptised at Lochlee, Angus, on 16 April 1732. Witnesses : John Brown in Tillybirnie and Alexander Brown in Milntown. [DUAS.BrMsDC3/174]

LYALL, WILLIAM, son of William Lyall a tailor, was baptised in Aberdeen on 11 September 1720. Witnesses : William Kelly a maltman and William Spence a hook-maker.[SPAER]

LYES, MARGARET, daughter of Alexander Lyes in Seatown of Cowie, was baptised in Stonehaven, Kincardineshire, on 2 April 1761. [ST.ER]

LYNDSAY, JOHN, and his wife Barbara Murray, parents of John born in October and baptised on 6 October 1723 in St Andrews; James born and baptised 22 November 1724 in St Andrews; Janet born 4 December and baptised 5 December 1725 in St Andrews; and Robert born and baptised on 24 April 1727 in St Andrews, Fife. [SER]

LYON, JAMES, a merchant in Dundee, 1727. [ECD#24]; father of Susanna baptised is his house in the Nethergate of Dundee on 7 February 1726. Godfather was Provost Douglas of Forfar, while godmothers : Provost Douglas's wife and Mrs Malcolm. [BNDBR]

LYON, PATRICK, master of Dundee Grammar School 1702 to 1716 when deposed as a Jacobite, 'an elder of a schismatical meeting house', a burgess of Dundee 1713. [REBD#209]

LYON, ROBERT, born 1710, a minister from Perth, a Jacobite chaplain in 1745, executed at Penrith 28 October 1746. [LPR#46][JP#29]

MCALISTER, JAMES, son of Daniel McAlister, a collier in Newton, and his wife Jane ....., was baptised in Ayr on 8 December 1798. [NAS.CH12.26.1]

MCANDREW, PATRICK, and his wife Margaret Dow in Benie, Muthill, : parents of Agnes born 7 February and baptised 12 February 1698. [MRB]

MCAREW, JOHN, and his wife Helen McInis, in Allans, Muthill, Perthshire, : parents of Janet born 10 February and baptised 12 February 1698. [MRB]

MCARTHUR, ANDREW, married Elizabeth Boyd from Monkton, in Ayr, 5 April 1790. [NAS.CH12.26.1]

MCARTNEY, JAMES, a minister who emigrated to North Carolina in 1768. [EMA#42]

MCAULAY, JOHN, a minister who emigrated to Jamaica in 1754. [FPA][EMA#42]

MACBEAN, AENEAS, a Writer to the Signet, born 1776, died 1857. [St John's, Edinburgh, MI]

MCCALLUM, NEIL, a minister who emigrated to Virginia, 1735. [EMA#42][WMQ.2.20/126]

MCCALMAN, NICOL, born before 1674, a cleric who emigrated to America in 1710, minister of St Elizabeth's, St David's, and St Thomas in the East, Jamaica from 1712. [EMA#42][FPA#252]

MCCLEAN, JOHN, a minister, to Virginia, 1773. [FPA#330]

MCCLEISH, DAVID, and his wife Mary Anderson in Mill of Ardoch, : parents of Lilias born 18 April and baptised in Muthill, Perthshire, 19 April 1775. [MRB]

MCCOLL, ANGUS, was confirmed in Ballachulish, Argyll, in 1770. [EV#344]

MCCOLL, MARGARET, was confirmed in Ballachulish, Argyll, in 1770. [EV#344]

MCCOLL, SARAH, was confirmed in Ballachulish, Argyll, in 1770. [EV#344]

MCCONACHIE, WILLIAM, a minister who emigrated to Maryland in 1710, settled on the Western Shore by 1718, in Portobacco and in Durham, died 1742, testament, 1743, Comm. Edinburgh. [EMA#43][FPA#29/35][NAS]

MCCONN, JOHN, son of Ezekial McConn, a sailor in Irvine, and his wife Jane ..., was baptised in Ayr in November 1799. [NAS.CH12.26.1]

MCCORMICK, ROBERT, a minister who emigrated to Maryland in 1775, assistant at St James', Ann Arundel County, Maryland. [EMA#42][FPA#302/326]

MCCULLIE, THOMAS, and his wife Catherine McLaren in Pet, Muthill, Perthshire, parents of Thomas, born and baptised 29 November 1697. [MRB]

MCCULLOCH, JAMES, and his wife Mary Tainsh in Allans, Perthshire, : parents of Helen born 11 July and baptised in Muthill 17 July 1775. [MRB]

MACCULLOCH, RODERICK, from Ardwell, Wigtownshire, a minister who emigrated to Virginia in 1730, settled in Westmoreland County, died 1745. [EMA#42][CAG.I.185/983]

MCCULLOCH, WILLIAM, son of Roderick McCulloch a glover in Aberdeen, was baptised 23 August 1720. Witnesses : William Spence and William Walker hookmakers. [SPAER]

MCDONALD, ALEXANDER, son of Alexander McDonald in Aberdeen, was baptised 20 September 1720. Witnesses : Alexander Allan a saddler and Alexander Leckpost. [SPAER]

MCDONALD, ALEXANDER, in Dundee, 1727. [ECD#26]

MACDONALD, Sir ALEXANDER, of Sleat, Inverness-shire, married Lady Margaret Montgomery, sister of the Earl of Eglinton, in the Countess of Eglinton's lodging, Canongate, 24 April 1739. [DUAS: BrMS3/Dc/12]

MACDONALD, ALEXANDER, was confirmed in Glencoe, Argyll, 1770. [EV#345]

MCDONALD, ALEXANDER, a Lieutenant HEICS, married J. McDowal in Ayr, 1788. [NAS.CH12.26.1]

MCDONALD, ANN, was confirmed in Glencoe, Argyll, in 1770. [EV#345]

MCDONALD, DANIEL, a minister who emigrated to Virginia in 1731. [EMA#42]

MCDONALD, JAMES, son of Arthur McDonald and his wife Janet Wilson in the Mains of Dudwick, was baptised on 25 December 1763. [CBER]

MCDONALD, JAMES, was confirmed in Arpafilie, Ross-shire, in 1770. [EV#327]

MCDONALD, JEAN, was confirmed in Glencoe, Argyll, in 1770. [EV#345]

MCDONALD, JOHN, son of Ronald McDonald, was baptised in South Leith on 18 September 1741. Witnesses : Alexander McDonald, Duncan Campbell, and Mrs Anne McDonald. [LER][SA.X.9]

MACDONALD, JOHN, was confirmed in Glencoe, Argyll, in 1770. [EV#345]

MCDONALD, JOHN, a minister who emigrated to Jamaica, 1792, settled in the parish of St Thomas in the Vale. [EMA#42][FPA]

MCDONALD, MARGARET, daughter of Roger McDonald and his wife Ann McNeill, was baptised in Ayr, 31 October 1776. [NAS.CH12.26.1]

MACDONALD, MARY, was confirmed in Glencoe, Argyll, in 1770. [EV#345]

MACDONELL, BRUCE COTTON LYON, daughter of Archibald MacDonell of Barisdale, was baptised on Castle Hill, Edinburgh, on 17 February 1757. Witnesses : Mr Forbes, Mr Hay, Mrs Isabella MacDonell, and Mrs Bettie MacDonal. [LER][SA.X.11]

MACDONELL, FORBES ALEXANDRA, daughter of Archibald MacDonell of Barisdale (a prisoner in Edinburgh Castle under sentence of execution) and his wife ..... McLeod, daughter of McLeod of Drynagh, was baptised in Edinburgh on 31 March 1754. Witnesses : Charles Leslie, Mrs Leslie, and Mrs MacLauchlen. [LER][SA.X.11]

MACDONELL, KATHARINE, daughter of Archibald MacDonell of Barisdale, was baptised in Edinburgh Castle on 17 July 1760. Witnesses : William McDonald a writer, Messrs MacDonald and Grant belonging to the Castle, and Mrs MacDonald. [LER][SA.X.11]

MCDOUGAL, ALEXANDER, and his wife Ann Ross in Mill of Balloch, : parents of Jean born 10 September and baptised in Muthill, Perthshire, on 19 September 1775. [MRB]

MCDOWELL, JOHN, a minister who emigrated to North Carolina, 1753. [EMA#42]

MCDUFFIE, DUGALD, a merchant in Jamaica, married Janet Campbell from Argyll, at Old Cambus, Berwickshire, on 13 April 1765.[NAS.CH12.2.18][HEC] [Argyll Sheriff Court Book.XVI., 20.3.1765]

MCDUGALL, JOHN, was confirmed in Glencoe, Argyll, in 1770. [EV#345]

MCEWAN, PATRICK, and his wife Janet McLaren, in Blainror, Muthill, : parents of Daniel born 16 January and baptised 20 January 1698. [MRB]

MCFAIR, JOHN, a minister who emigrated to St Vincent, 1798. [EMA#42]

MACFARLANE, ANDREW, minister at Inverness. Bishop of Moray, 1787-1796, Bishop of Ross and Argyll, died 1819. [Keith#543/551]

MACFARLANE, PATRICK, son of John MacFarlane and his wife Jane Robertson, was born 30 April and baptised in St Andrews, Fife, on 1 May 1727. [SER]

MCFARLANE, WALTER, of McFarlane, married Lady Betty, daughter of Alexander Erskine, Earl of Kelly, in Canongate, 23 April 1760. [DUAS: BrMS3/Dc/12]

MCFARQUHAR, COLIN, a printer in Edinburgh, married Jean Scruton, daughter of James Scruton a writing master in Glasgow, on 28 December 1767, in St Andrew's Episcopal Church, Glasgow. [SA.X.21]

MCFARQUHAR, GEORGE, born 1741, a physician "22 years in Jamaica", died 25 December 1786. [St James Church MI, Montego Bay, Jamaica]

MCGAW, SAMUEL, a minister who emigrated to Pennsylvania, 1767. [FPA#328] [EMA#43]

MCGHIE, RICHARD, was confirmed at Thurso, Caithness, on 8 August 1762. [DC#277]

MCGILCHRIST, WILLIAM, son of James McGilchrist of Inchinnan, Renfrewshire, a minister who emigrated to South Carolina in 1741, arrived in Charleston by January 1742. [EMA#42][FPA#151]

MCGILL, Baillie, and his wife Elizabeth Barclay, parents of George baptised "in the Back Stairs" on 13 December 1756. Witnesses : Charles Butler, John Goodwillie, and Agnes Barclay; Agnes baptised "in the back stairs Pt.Ch.", Edinburgh, on 7 August 1758. Witnesses : Elizabeth Barclay, Mr and Mrs Goodwillie; Jean baptised "in the backstairs over the Meal Mercat", Edinburgh, on 25 April 1760. Witnesses : Mrs R. Barclay, Charles Butler and his wife. [DUAS.BrMsDC3/12]

MCGILL, JAMES, born 1701, educated at St Andrews University, emigrated to America 1727, tutor to the family of Colonel John Taylor in Virginia, a minister who returned from London to Maryland in 1728, settled in Queen Caroline parish, died 26 December 1779. [EMA#42][CAG.I.381][FPA#45/169/179]

MAKGILL, ROBERT, Viscount Oxenfurd, married Janet, daughter of Alexander Christie a writer in Edinburgh, in Mrs McGill's House, Fowlis's Close, Edinburgh, 16 June 1748. [DUAS: BrMS3/Dc/12]

MCGOWAN, WALTER, a minister who emigrated to Virginia, 1768. [EMA#43][FPA#309]

MCGRIGGOR, ALEXANDER, son of John McGriggor, a sailor in Ayr, and his wife Mary McCauley, was baptised in Ayr on 25 November 1799. [NAS.CH12.26.1]

MCGRIGOR, JOHN, was confirmed in Arpafilie, Ross-shire, in 1770. [EV#327]

MCGRIGGOR, JOHN, a soldier of Lord Breadalbane's Fencibles, and Mary Webb from Ayr, : married there, 6 April 1795. [NAS.CH12.26.1]

MCGRUTHER, ALEXANDER, born 1669, from Dalchruinn, Muthill, Perthshire, a Jacobite officer, captured at Carlisle on 30 December 1745, died before trial. [P.3.131][TBD#131]

MCHAEN, ROBERT, a minister who emigrated to New Jersey, 1757. [EMA#42]

MCILHONNEL, JOHN, and his wife Helen Morison, in Blainror, Muthill, : parents of James born 24 February and baptised 26 February 1698. [MRB]

MCINNES, ALEXANDER, born 1771, settled in Jamaica 1792, died 9 September 1836. [Spanish Town Cathedral MI, Jamaica]

MCINNES, ANN, was confirmed in Ballachulish, Argyll, in 1770. [EV#344]

MCINNES, DONALD, was confirmed in Ballachulish, Argyll, in 1770. [EV#344]

MCINNES, KATHERINE, was confirmed in Ballachulish, Argyll, in 1770. [EV#344]

MCINNES, MARGARET, was confirmed in Ballachulish, Argyll, in 1770. [EV#344]

MCINTIRE, DAVID, in Glen Effock, was father of William baptised at Lochlee, Angus, on 9 July 1727. Witnesses : William and Thomas Jollie both there. Also of James McIntyre baptised at Lochlee on 4 February 1732. Witnesses : James Campbell in Dalbreak and Thomas Jollie in Glen Effock. [DUAS.BrMsDC3/174]

MCINTIRE, WILLIAM, in Ardfullery, was father of John McIntire baptised at Lochlee, Angus, on 31 August 1729. Witnesses : John Edward and Thomas Kinnear, both in Milntown of Glenesk. [DUAS.BrMsDC3/174]

MCINTOSH, ALEXANDER, a writer in Edinburgh and a trustee of the Carruber's Close congregation, 1741. [JSC#84]

MCINTOSH, ALEXANDER, was confirmed in Inverness by Bishop Forbes of the Episcopal Church, on 29 August 1762. [SA.IX.12]

MCINTOSH, ANDREW, was confirmed in Arpafilie, Ross-shire, in 1770. [EV#327]

MCINTOSH, ANNE, an adult, daughter of Robert McIntosh of Termit, was baptised in Inverness by Bishop Forbes of the Episcopal Church, on 29 August 1762. [SA.IX.12]

MCINTOSH, CHRISTIAN, an adult, daughter of Robert McIntosh of Termit, was baptised in Inverness by Bishop Forbes of the Episcopal Church, on 29 August 1762. [SA.IX.12]

MCINTOSH, JAMES, an adult, son of Robert McIntosh of Termit, was baptised in Inverness by Bishop Forbes of the Episcopal Church, on 29 August 1762. [SA.IX.12]

MCINTOSH, JAMES, a minister who emigrated to Dominica, 1771. [EMA#42]

MCINTOSH, ROBERT, of Termit, and his wife, : confirmed in Inverness by Bishop Forbes of the Episcopal Church, on 29 August 1762. [SA.IX.12]

MCIVER, ALEXANDER, was confirmed in Arpafilie, Ross-shire, in 1770. [EV#327]

MCIVER, ARCHIBALD, son of Robert McIver and his wife Catherine Rice, was baptised in Ayr, 6 November 1776. [NAS.CH12.26.1]

MCIVER ELSPIT, was confirmed in Arpafilie, Ross-shire, in 1770. [EV#327]

MCKAY, ANNA, was confirmed in Arpafilie, Ross-shire, in 1770. [EV#327]

MCKAY, ELSPET, was confirmed in Arpafilie, Ross-shire, in 1770. [EV#327]

MCKAY, FRANCIS, and Eliza Garioch in Abbeyhill, : married by Alexander McKenzie on 5 August 1731. Witnesses : James Goollen a burgess in Edinburgh and John McKay a vintner in Abbeyhill. [SLIM#375]

MCKAY, ISABEL, was confirmed in Arpafilie, Ross-shire, in 1770. [EV#327]

MCKAY, JOHN, and Sarah Godfrey, : married by Alexander McKenzie in Edinburgh on 11 November 1731. Witnesses : William Tibbets a smith in Abbeyhill and John Ewar a writer there. [SLIM#31]

MACKAY, JOHN, a minister who emigrated to the Leeward Islands in 1739. [EMA#42]

MCKAY, MARGARET, was confirmed in Arpafilie, Ross-shire, in 1770. [EV#327]

MACKAY, THOMAS, son of William Mackay of the Sutherland Fencibles and Catharine his wife was born 3December 1797 and baptised in St John the Evangelist, Edinburgh, on 8 December 1797. [NAS.CH12.3.26/2]

MACKAY, WILLIAM, a minister who emigrated to Virginia, 1736. [EMA#42][FPA#193][WMQ.2.20/126]

MCKAY, WILLIAM, was confirmed in Arpafilie, Ross-shire, in 1770. [EV#327]

MACKAY, WILLIAM, a writer in Tolbooth Kirk parish, married Sarah Cleghorne, a spinster in Corstorphine, in Haddington on 3 August 1789. Witnesses : John Taylor and Alexander Thom. [NAS.CH12.2.2.18][HEC]

MCKEAN, DAVID, was confirmed in Fortrose, Easter Ross, 1770. [EV#327]

MCKEAN, ELIZABETH, was confirmed in Fortrose, Easter Ross, 1770. [EV#327]

MCKENLY, WILLIAM, a minister who emigrated to Nevis in 1773. [EMA#42]

MCKENZIE, AENEAS, born 1675, educated in Aberdeen and Edinburgh, a missionary of the Society for the Propagation of the Gospel, to Staten Island or New Jersey in 1705, settled in Virginia. [EMA#43][SCHR.14.149][LIS.5.337/339]

MCKENZIE, ALEXANDER, son of Reverend Hector McKenzie in Inverness, an Episcopal minister in Edinburgh, died 1764. [F.6.457]; residing in Forglen's Back Land, Edinburgh, 1746. [JSC#62]

MCKENZIE, ALEXANDER, born 1739, died 1806, husband of Isabella ......, born 1739, died 1794. [St John's, Edinburgh, MI]

MCKENZIE, ANNA, was confirmed in Fortrose, Easter Ross, 1770. [EV#327]

MCKENZIE, ANNA, was confirmed in Arpafilie, Ross-shire, in 1770. [EV#327]

MCKENZIE, ANNABEL, was confirmed in Arpafilie, Ross-shire, in 1770. [EV#327]

MCKENZIE, DAVID, burgess of Dundee in 1712, a gunsmith in Dundee, 1727. [ECD#24][DBR]

MACKENZIE, DONALD, father of Daniel baptised in Edinburgh on 18 September 1761. [DUAS.BrMsDC3/12]

MCKENZIE, DONALD, was confirmed in Arpafilie, Ross-shire, in 1770. [EV#327]

MCKENZIE, EUPHAM, in Bankhead, was confirmed in Forfar in 1770. [EF#26]

MCKENZIE, EVAN, a soldier of the City Guard, married Mary McDonnell, in Edinburgh, 6 December 1743. [DUAS: BrMS3/Dc/12]

MCKENZIE, HECTOR, born in Sutherland 1645, graduated MA from King's College, Aberdeen in 1665, minister at Kingussie in 1670 and in Inverness from 1688 until his death on 14 June 1719. Father of James, Alexander, and William. [F.6.457]

MCKENZIE, JAMES, an Episcopalian minister in Edinburgh, son of Hector McKenzie a minister in Inverness, a memorial, 1740. [NAS.GD23.4.145]; residing on the West Side of Niddry's Wynd, Edinburgh, 1746. [JSC#63]

MCKENZIE, JOHN, a Writer to the Signet, a trustee of the Carruber's Close congregation, 1741. [JSC#83]

MCKENZIE, JOHN, a minister residing in Gray's Close, Edinburgh, 1746. [JSC#63]

MCKENZIE, JOHN, was confirmed in Fortrose, Easter Ross, 1770. [EV#327]

MCKENZIE, JOHN, from Ross-shire, graduated from King's College, Aberdeen, 1797, later Bishop of Toronto. [KCA#265]

MACKENZIE, JOHN, born 1755, a Lieutenant General, died 1833, eldest son of William Mackenzie of Belmaduthie, Ross-shire. [St John's, Edinburgh, MI]

MCKENZIE, KENNETH, a cleric who emigrated to Virginia in 1711 aboard the Severn, settled in St James parish, Lawn Creek, Virginia. [EMA#43][NAS.NRAS.0040]

MACKENZIE, MURDOCH, a minister in Ross-shire, Inverness, and Elgin, Bishop of Moray 1662 to 1677, Bishop of Orkney 1677 to his death in February 1688. [Keith#228]

MCKENZIE, WILLIAM, a minister who emigrated to Virginia in 1773, settled in Granville, North Carolina, a Loyalist who returned to Scotland in 1779. [EMA#42][NA.AO.12.36.110. etc][FPA#310/330]

MACKERSON, BARBARA, was confirmed at Whiteloch, Blairgowrie, Perthshire, on 2 September 1750. [TBD#155]

MACKIE, FRANCIS, son of John Mackie in Leadside of Stonehaven, Kincardineshire, was baptised in Stonehaven on 13 July 1761. [ST.ER]

MACKIE, JAMES, and Rachel Muirison, late servants in Tirrenhill, Fraserburgh, Aberdeenshire, : married on 27 December 1806. [NAS.CH12.32.2]

MCKINNON, DONALD alias DANIEL, born 9 September 1743 in Sleat, Inverness-shire, educated at King's College, Aberdeen, 1764, a minister who emigrated to Maryland in 1769, assistant at St John's, Maryland, 1768, settled in Westwood, Prince William County, Virginia. [FPA.25.105/108/302/309/326][EMA#42]

MCKINNON, WILLIAM, born 1699, son of Daniel second son of Lachlan McKinnon of McKinnon, late of Antigua, died 8 October 1769. [Bath Abbey MI, England]

MACKNO, ROBERT, a cleric who emigrated to Maryland in 1709. [EMA#43]

MCLACHLAN, DONALD, of that Ilk, married Susanna Campbell, daughter of Colin Campbell of Park, at Park, near Fushinnan, Renfrewshire, on 1 July 1788. Witnesses : George Murdoch in Glasgow formerly a merchant and Provost there, Major James Campbell, Captain of the 42nd [Black Watch] Regiment, the bride's father, mother, sister, and other ladies. [SA.X.22]

MACLAMBURGH, SAMUEL, possibly educated at Glasgow University in the 1690s, a cleric who emigrated to Maryland in 1711. [EMA#43]

MCLANE, HENRY, a minister who emigrated to Dominica in 1764. [EMA#43]

MCLAREN, DONALD, gardener to Lady Bruce, married Elizabeth Milne, in North Leith on 10 September 1740. Witnesses : Robert Stewart, James McKay, John Chalmers, Janet Stewart, and Margaret May. [LER][NNQ.8.125]

MCLAREN, PATRICK, and his wife Janet McCara, in Struthill, Muthill, : parents of Margaret born 11 February and baptised 15 February 1698. [MRB]

MCLAURINE, ROBERT, born 1717, a minister to Virginia, 1750, settled in St James, Southam parish, Va., died July 1773. [FPA#199/307/329][EMA#43][CCVC#54]

MACLEAN, ..., minister in Morvern, Dunoon, and Eastwood, Bishop of Argyll 1680 until his death in 1687. [Keith#292]

MCLEAN, JOHN, a minister who emigrated to Virginia, 1773. [EMA#42]

MCLENNAN, ANNA, was confirmed in Fortrose, Easter Ross, 1770. [EV#327]

MCLENNAN, WILLIAM, was confirmed in Fortrose, Easter Ross, 1770. [EV#327]

MACLEOD, MARGARET, daughter of MacLeod of Cadboll, was confirmed in Leith on 24 February 1772. [SA.IX.14][LER]

MCMILLAN, JOHN, son of John McMillan, a travelling chapman, and his wife Janet...., was baptised in Ayr on 22 July 1799. [NAS.CH12.26.1]

MCMORLAND, HUGH, son of James McMorland, a laborer in Maybole, and his wife Elizabeth ...., was baptised in Ayr on 30 November 1798. [NAS.CH12.26.1]

MCMORRAN, JAMES, a cleric who emigrated to Maryland in 1710. [EMA#43]

MCMURDO, ELEANOR, daughter of Douglas McMurdo and Mary Clementina his wife, was born 15 March 1798 and baptised in St John the Evangelist, Edinburgh, on 16 April 1798. [NAS.CH12.3.26/3]

MCNAB, WILLIAM, deceased, and his wife Margaret Moir in Drumbuie, Muthill, : parents of Helen born 17 July and baptised 20 July 1774. [MRB]

MCNAUGHTON, DUNCAN, from Perthshire, a minister in Wicomico parish, Northumberland County, Virginia, 1799-1805, and in St Stephen's parish, Northumberland County, Va., 1805-1809, died 16 May 1809. [WMQ.2.19.4] [Northumberland MI]

MCNEILL, GEORGE, son of Archibald McNeill and Georgina Anne his wife, was born 6 July 1798 and baptised in St John the Evangelist, Edinburgh, on 20 July 1798. [NAS.CH12.3.26/5]

MCNISH, JOHN KILLEAN, a surgeon, married Christian Kerr, both of Barony parish, Glasgow, on 1 February 1796 at Lancefield. Witnesses : John McNish his father, Mr Dick of Glasgow, Hatton Bowman there, and Mr Johnston at Anderton. [SA.X.23]

MCNIVEN, JAMES, and his wife Margaret Ogilbie in Blainror, Muthill, Perthshire, : parents of Archibald, born 12 November and baptised 15 November 1697. [MRB]

MACNOE, ROBERT, educated at Glasgow University, a missionary in Virginia for the Society for the Propagation of the Gospels from 1709. [SCHR.14.147]

MCPHAIL, DONALD, was confirmed in Ballachulish, Argyll, on 7 July 1770. [EV#311/344]

MCPHERSON, JOHN, born 1725, a minister who emigrated to Maryland in 1751, settled in St Anne's parish, Annapolis, and in William and Mary parish, Charles County, died 1785. [FPA#301/325][EMA#43][CCMC#54]

MACQUEEN, ALEXANDER, and his wife Mary Duncan, parents of Elizabeth born on 29 October and baptised in St Andrews on 30 October 1722; Jane born 15 January and baptised 17 January 1724 in St Andrews; Margaret born 3 February and baptised 5 February 1727 in St Andrews; and John born in April and baptised 24 April 1729 in St Andrews. [SER]

MACQUEEN, GEORGE, a cleric who emigrated to Maryland in 1702. [EMA#43] [SCHR.14.149]

MCRAE, CHRISTOPHER, born 1733, son of Christopher McRae in Urquhart, Inverness-shire, educated at Marischal College, Aberdeen, 1753, assistant at St Paul's, Hanover County, Virginia, 1765, returned to Virginia from London in 1766, minister in Surrey County, Virginia, and at Littleton parish, Cumberland County, Virginia, 1773 to 1785, died in Powhattan County on 22 December 1808. [EMA#43][OC#2/35][FPA#308/330]

MCRAH, DONALD, was confirmed in Arpafilie, Ross-shire, in 1770. [EV#327]

MCRAH, ISABEL, was confirmed in Arpafilie, Ross-shire, in 1770. [EV#327]

MCRAH, MARTHA, was confirmed in Arpafilie, Ross-shire, in 1770. [EV#327]

MACROBERT, ARCHIBALD, a minister who emigrated to Virginia in 1761, settled in the parishes of Dale and of St Patrick. [EMA#43][FPA#330]

MACSPARRAN, JAMES, educated at Glasgow University, graduated MA, 1720, emigrated to New England as a missionary of the Society for the Propagation of the Gospel in 1722, in Rhode Island 1725, incumbent of St Paul's in the Pettiquamscot Purchases and in King's County, R.I. 1736; settled at Narragansett, died in December 1757.
[APCCol.1725.85/390][EMA#43][SCHR.14.149]
[FPA#12/122][LIS.5.88][SPAWI.1727.638/817]

MCTAGGART, ANGUS, and Elizabeth Farquhar, : married in Ayr, 18 June 1792. [NAS.CH12.26.1]

MCWHANNEL, MARY, daughter of Duncan McWhannel and his wife Mary McCraw in Craigneich, was baptised in Muthill on 1 December 1734. [TBD#72]

MADISON, THOMAS, son of Robert Madison at the Mill of Mains, was baptised in Dundee on 18 July 1726. [BNDBR]

MAGAN, MARY ANNE, daughter of Michael Magan and his wife Hannah, was born 3 September 1798 and baptised in St John the Evangelist, Edinburgh, on 26 November 1798. [NAS.CH12.3.26/5]

MAICH, DAVID, in Achronie, was father of James baptised at Lochlee, Angus, on 23 November 1729. Witnesses : Thomas Kinnear in Milntown, Walter Innes in Achsallerie, and William McIntire there. [DUAS.BrMsDC3/174]

MAIDEN, JOHN, son of John Maiden a weaver in Cottarton of Craigie, was baptised in Dundee on 7 October 1726. [BNDBR]

MAITLAND, CHARLOTTE, daughter of Lieutenant Colonel Frederick Maitland and his wife Catherine Warsam, was born 30 April 1799 and baptised in St John the Evangelist, Edinburgh, on 12 June 1799. [NAS.CH12.3.26/7]

MAITLAND, DAVID, educated at Marischal College, Aberdeen 1701-1705, minister at Forgue. [MCA.II.281]

MAITLAND, JOHN, a cleric who emigrated to Carolina in 1708. [EMA#43]

MAITLAND, JOHN, from Aberdeenshire, a minister in Forgue, a beneficiary under the will of Alexander Deuchar in Barbados, 1738 [NAS.CC8.8.100]; a non-jurant minister in Careston, Angus, a Jacobite in 1745. [LPR#180] [ECD#69]

MAITLAND, RICHARD, son of Richard Maitland minister of Inverkeithny, educated at Marischal College, Aberdeen, 1665-1668, schoolmaster at Foveran, Aberdeenshire, 1671, minister of Nigg from 1674 to 1716 when deposed as a Jacobite. Husband of (1) Susanna Irvine, (2) Katherine Mylne, (3) Mary Keith, father of Richard, Margaret, Charles, Christian, Catherine, John, Richard, Elspeth, Anna, Alexander, Patrick, William, and Helen. [F.6.69]

MALCOLM, ALEXANDER, a minister who emigrated to Massachusetts in 1740, settled in Marblehead during 1741, later in Annapolis, Maryland. [EMA#43][EUL.Laing ms 2/91] [FPA#75][LIS.5.88/129/301]

MALCOLM, DAVID, the younger, in Blackcraig, father of David Malcolm baptised 22 March 1732 at Lochlee, Angus. Witnesses : Andrew Lindsay in Achin and David Gold there. [DUAS.BrMsDC3/174]

MALCOLM, JAMES, at Mithill, married Bettie, daughter of John Durward a schoolmaster in Kirkcaldy, Fife, in South Leith on 11 April 1738. Witnesses : Archibald Balfour son of Dr Balfour in Kirkcaldy, Richard Seaman a baker in Leith, Katherine Durward sister of the bride, and Elizabeth Seaman sister of the aforesaid Richard Seaman. [LER][NNQ.8.125]

MALTMAN, WILLIAM, and his wife Isobel McNiel in Wester Drumnawhance, : parents of Margaret born 28 August and baptised in Muthill, Perthshire, on 3 September 1775. [MRB]

MANDERSON, WILLIAM, of West Kirk parish, Edinburgh, married Margaret Orr of the same parish, in Haddington, East Lothian, on 30 January 1787. Witnesses : John Clark and James Nisbet. [NAS.CH12.2.2.18][HFC]

MANDERSTON, JAMES, a merchant and dyer in Dundee, 1727. [ECD#24]

MANN, AGNES, at Glamis Castle, was confirmed in Forfar in 1770. [EF#26]

MANN, WILLIAM, and Agnes Kerr, both from St Quivox, : married in Ayr, 13 March 1791. [NAS.CH12.26.1]

MANZIE, CHARLES, husband of Catherine Burness, born 1788, died 1813. [Montrose Episcopal MI]

MANZIE, JAMES, born 1733, died 1811, married in 1762 to Margaret Kinnear, born 1737, died 1820. [Montrose Episcopal MI]

MARJORIBANKS, ANDREW, a trustee of the Carruber's Close congregation, Edinburgh, 1741. [JSC#83]

MARJORIBANKS, or SCOTT, Mrs MARGARET, in North Leith, was baptised in South Leith on 14 December 1751. [LER][SA.X.10]

MARR, CATHARINE, daughter of Alexander Marr and his wife Agnes Conon in Chapelhall, Ellon, Aberdeenshire, was baptised 1 April 1776. [CTER]

MARSHALL, ALEXANDER, married Jane Bruce, in Ayr, 12 March 1770. [NAS.CH12.26.1]

MARSHALL, JAMES, a shoemaker in Dundee, 1743. [ECD#65]

MARSHALL, MUNGO, a minister who emigrated to Virginia in 1744, settled in St Thomas parish, Orange County, died 1758. [EMA#43][WMQ.2.1.154][FPA#199]

MARSHALL, SAMUEL, a minister who emigrated to Maryland in 1698. [EMA#44]

MARSHALL, THOMAS, a minister who emigrated to Maryland in 1698. [EMA#44]

MARSHALL, WILLIAM, a wright in Leith, and Mary Pollock, : married by Alexander McKenzie on 6 December 1728. Witnesses : Thomas Gourlay a wright in Leith, and John Pollack a wright in Edinburgh. [SLIM#317]

MARSHALL, WILLIAM, a minister who emigrated to Barbados in 1800. [EMA#44]

MARTIN, ANDREW, son of James Martin, a private in the 23 Light Dragoons, and his wife Elizabeth ....., was baptised in Ayr on 8 December 1798. [NAS.CH12.26.1]

MARTIN, JEAN, daughter of William Martin in Logie, by Dundee, was baptised on 3 July 1723. [BNDBR]

MARTIN, JOHN, a brewer in Dundee, 1727. [ECD#24]

MARTIN, Mrs, of the Perth Episcopalian Congregation, 1742. [TV.77.21][JWI]

MASON, ANNA, daughter of Alexander Mason in Seatown of Cowie, was baptised in Stonehaven, Kincardineshire, on 2 September 1759. [ST.ER]

MASSIE, WILLIAM, at Berry Mill, and Margaret Cruden, : married in Fraserburgh, Aberdeenshire, on 7 June 1800. [NAS.CH12.32.2]

MASSON, BARBARA, daughter of John Masson the younger of Cowie, was baptised in Stonehaven, Kincardineshire, on 4 October 1761. [ST.ER]

MATHESON, ROBERT, a wright burgess in Dundee in 1727, in Dundee, 1727. [ECD#26][DBR]

MATHEW, DAVID, a dyer in Murraygate, Dundee, 1727. [ECD#24]; father of Patrick, baptised in Dundee on 14 August 1722; and Janet baptised in Dundee on 25 May 1724. [BNDBR]

MATTHEW, THOMAS, a tailor in Fraserburgh, Aberdeenshire, and Marjory Fraser, : married there on 31 December 1791. [NAS.CH12.32.2]

MAULE, ROBERT, a minister who emigrated to North America in 1707, died in South Carolina, 1716. [EMA#44][FPA#132]

MAULE, ..., Countess of Panmure, of the Episcopal meeting house in Arbroath, Angus,1729-1731. [NAS.GD45.13.26]

MAURICE, JEAN, daughter of William Maurice a weaver in Seagate, Dundee, was baptised in Dundee, on 25 February 1723. [BNDBR]

MAWER, JOHN, a dyer in Dundee, 1727. [ECD#24]

MAXTON, JAMES, of the Perth Episcopalian Congregation, 1742. [TV.77.21][JWI]

MAXTON, JAMES, of Cultoquhey and his wife Marjory Graeme, : parents of Patrick born at Cultoquhey, Fowlis, Perthshire, on 24 January and baptised there on 4 February 1775. [MRB]

MAXWELL, JOHN, from Glasgow, educated at Edinburgh University around 1658, to Jamaica in 1662, a physician and cleric in Port Royal, died in Jamaica 1673, probate 1673 Jamaica.

MEAL, ROBERT, in Dundee, 1727. [ECD#26]

MEGGET, ARCHIBALD, of Gifford, East Lothian, married Elizabeth Wells from Darlington, in Haddington, East Lothian, on 6 November 1771. Witnesses T. Innocent and James Fairbairn. [NAS.CH12.2.18][HEC]

MELDRUM, ANDREW, minister of Mertoun, papers, 1690? [NRAS.105.5.39]

MELDRUM, WILLIAM, a minister who emigrated to Virginia in 1756, minister in Winchester parish, and later Frederick parish.
[EMA#45][OC#285/303][FPA#330]

MELVIL, JAMES, a sailor now at Leith, married Agnes Elder, in St Andrews on 16 January 1773. [SER]

MEMESS, JEAN, daughter of Robert Memess minister of St James's, Stonehaven, was born and baptised in Stonehaven, 8 July 1759. [ST.ER]

MEMESS, ROBERT, son of Reverend Robert Memess, was born 28 July, baptised 29 July 1760, and died 28 July 1762 in Stonehaven. [ST.ER]

MENZIES, ADAM, a minister who emigrated to Virginia, 1751.
[EMA#45][FPA#307/329]

MERCER, ROBERT, and **MARGARET,** : confirmed at Pindreich, Blairgowrie, Perthshire, on 4 October 1753. [TBD#155]

MERCER, Lady, from Meiklour, of the Perth Episcopalian Congregation, 1742.
[TV.77.21][JWI]

MESSENGER, JOSEPH, from Dumfries-shire, a minister who emigrated to Virginia in 1772, settled in St John's, Pitscataway, Maryland.
[EMA#45][St John's parish register, fo.415][FPA.309/330]

MICHIE, WILLIAM, and Eupham Taylor both merchants, : married in Fountain Close, Edinburgh, 22 December 1750. [DUAS: BrMS3/Dc/12]

MIDDLETON, JAMES, son of David Middleton in Lumgair, was baptised in Stonehaven, Kincardineshire, on 3 September 1759. [ST.ER]

MIEN, JAMES, married Mary Sutor, in South Leith, on 8 July 1755.
[LER][NNQ.8.127]

MILLAR, ARTHUR, minister of Inveresk before 1689, minister of the Church of Ireland, Bishop of Edinburgh and Primus, died in October 1727. [Keith#526]

MILLER, CHRISTIAN, daughter of William Miller in Whitfield, was baptised in Dundee on 12 January 1723. [BNDBR]

MILLER, DAVID, son of James Miller in Logie, was baptised in Dundee on 18 July 1722. [BNDBR]

MILLER, JAMES, son of James Miller and his wife Katherine Mason was born 3 June and baptised 10 June 1770 in Haddington, East Lothian. Witnesses : George Mason and Bartholemew Bower. [NAS.CH12.2.13]

MILLER, MARGARET, daughter of James Miller in Cottarton of Dudhope, was baptised in Dundee on 27 January 1726. [BNDBR]

MILLER, PATRICK, and his wife Helen Moir in Kincardine, Crieff, Perthshire, : parents of Jean born 16 September and baptised 22 September 1775. [MRB]

MILLAR, ROBERT, born 1778, a merchant, died 1861, husband of Else Bolette Hoyer, born 1781, died 1830. [Montrose Episcopal MI]

MILLER, THOMAS, in Dundee, 1727. [ECD#26]

MILLER, WILLIAM, and Janet Ferguson, in Blainror, Muthill, Perthshire, : parents of William born 18 January and baptised 20 January 1698. [MRB]

MILLER, WILLIAM, in Dundee, 1727. [ECD#26]

MILLS, HENRY, son of John Mills and his wife Harriet Stamper, was baptised in Ayr, 16 October 1776. [NAS.CH12.26.1]

MILN, ALEXANDER, in Glen Mark, was father of James Milne baptised at Lochlee, Angus, on 29 March 1731. Witnesses : Alexander Clark and John High both in Droustie. Also of Anes Miln baptised at Lochlee on 21 July 1735. Witnesses : Harry Lindsay in Kinie and John Watt in Glenmark. [DUAS.BrMsDC3/174]

MILN, ALEXANDER, son of Alexander Milne and his wife Margaret Sangster in Mill of Alatahn, Udny, Aberdeenshire, was baptised in 1775. [CTER]

MILNE, ANNE, was confirmed in Forfar, Angus, in 1770. [EF#26]

MILNE, ELIZABETH, was confirmed in Forfar, Angus, in 1770. [EF#26]

MILNE, FRANCIS, a cleric who emigrated to Maryland in 1707. [EMA#45]

MILNE, JAMES, sometime Episcopal minister in Aberdeen, testament, 20 June 1769, Comm. Aberdeen. [NAS]

MILN, JANET, daughter of ....Miln in Lochill, was born 10 August and baptised 19 August 1768 in Haddington, East Lothian. Witnesses : Thomas Miln and John Skirven. [NAS.CH12.2.13]

MILNE, JANET, was confirmed in Forfar, Angus, in 1770. [EF#26]

MILNE, JEAN, was confirmed in Forfar, Angus, in 1770. [EF#26]

MILN, JOHN, a minister who emigrated to New York in 1727, a missionary of the Society for the Propagation of the Gospel at Albany, NY, 1728-1736, later in Monmouth, New Jersey, from 1737-1745. [EMA#45][LIS.5.88/129]

MILNE, MARGARET, daughter of ......Milne in Reidside, was born 11 April and baptised 18 April 1768 in Haddington, East Lothian. Witnesses : John Shirver and Richard Allan. [NAS.CH12.2.13]

MILNE, MARGARET, was confirmed in Forfar, Angus, in 1770. [EF#26]

MILNE, WILLIAM, and his wife Isobel, married in Arbirlot, Angus, 1732, residing in Arbroath, 1752. [SRS.13.89]

MILNE, WILLIAM, son of John Milne in Craigton, Peterculter, educated at Marischal College, Aberdeen, 1788-1792, minister in Muchalls. [MCA#369]

MINNIMAN, ALEXANDER, and his wife Katherine Steel, parents of James born on ... May and baptised in St Andrews, Fife, on 30 May 1723; and William born on 15 October and baptised on 19 October 1725. [SER]

MINTO, ROBERT, born 1740, died in Trelawney parish, Jamaica, 5 May 1803. [Lottery MI, Jamaica]

MITCHELL, ALEXANDER, son of Alexander Mitchell and his wife Elspet Simpson in Tillicorthie, Udny, Aberdeenshire, was baptised 9 July 1768. [CBER]

MITCHELL, ANDREW, son of Charles Mitchell of Pitedie, was baptised in Leith on 2 October 1756. Witnesses : Reverend William Forbes, Mrs Kathereine Forbes, Mrs Marion Forbes, and Miss Ramsay. [LER][SA.X.11]

MITCHELL, GEORGE, born 30 July 1742 in Fendraught, Aberdeenshire, a minister to Frederickstown, Maryland, in 1769, assistant minister at Stepney, Maryland, 1774, a Loyalist. [FPA#302/326][NAAO12102.173, etc]

MITCHELL, HELEN, daughter of James Mitchell and his wife Margaret ...., was born 31 December 1729, and baptised in St Andrews 1 January 1730.[SER]

MITCHELL, JAMES, born 1730, a merchant in Montrose, Angus, died 1795, his first wife Ann Auchterlony born 1738, died 1778, his second wife Helen Forbes, born 1730, died 1790. [Montrose Episcopal MI]

MITCHELL, JAMES, a maltman, husband of Rachel McKenzie, parents of Maria, in Marketgate, Arbroath, Angus, 1752. [SRS.13.82]

MITCHELL, JEAN, daughter of Charles Mitchell of Pitedie, was baptised in South Leith on 1 November 1757. Witnesses : William Forbes, Mrs Katherine Forbes, and Mrs Marion Forbes. [LER][SA.X.11]

MITCHELL, JEAN, daughter of William Mitchell and his wife Elizabeth Mitchell in Haddo, Foveran, Aberdeenshire, was baptised on 14 January 1764. [CBER]

MITCHELL, JOHN, a merchant in Riga, Latvia, father of James, born 1740, died 1791. [Montrose Episcopal MI]

MITCHELL, MARGARET, daughter of Charles Mitchell of Pitedie, was baptised in South Leith on 7 December 1760. Witnesses : William Forbes, Mrs Katherine Forbes, Marion Forbes, and Miss Lindsay. [LER][SA.X.11]

MITCHELL, MARJORY and JEAN, daughters of William Mitchell a farmer, : baptised in Aberdeen on 17 November 1720. Witnesses : John Lyall a maltman and Thomas Fiddess a farmer. [SPAER]

MITCHELL, ROBERT, a barber and wigmaker journeyman in Leith, married Barbara Fotheringham a shopkeeper in the Canongate, in the house of James Oliphant a wigmaker in the Canongate, on 24 December 1747. Witnesses : James Oliphant, John Armour, and George Yorston. [LER][NNQ.8.125]

MITCHELL, THOMAS, was confirmed at Whiteloch, Blairgowrie, Perthshire, on 2 September 1750. [TBD#155]

MITCHELL, WILLIAM, son of Charles Mitchell of Pitedie, was baptised in South Leith on 20 January 1759. Witnesses : William Forbes, Mrs Katherine Forbes, Marion Forbes, and Miss Lindsay. [LER][SA.X.11]

MITCHELL, ..., a soldier, married ...... Thomson, daughter of George Thomson a mason in Brechin, Angus, on 9 December 1798. [NNQ.14.100]

MOFFAT, WILLIAM, in the Ground of Balgay, father of William baptised in Dundee on 10 March 1724, and of Isobel baptised in Dundee on 21 January 1726. [BNDBR]

MOIR, ANDREW, and his wife Janet Moir, in Crofthead, Blackford, Perthshire, : parents of William born 9 March and baptised 20 March 1775. [MRB]

MOIR, HELEN, daughter of Andrew Moir and his wife Ann Gray in Crofthead of Farmton, was born 18 March and baptised 20 March 1750 in Muthill, Perthshire. [TBD#132]

MOIR, JAMES, a minister who emigrated to North Carolina in 1739, brother of Reverend Henry Moir in Auchtertool, Fife, a Presbyterian who converted to Anglicanism, died in Edgecombe County, North Carolina, on 31 December 1766. [EMA#46][SM.29.278][FPA#149][LIS.5.129] possibly in Edinburgh, 1727. [NAS.CH12.23.63; RD2.204.1]

MOIR, WILLIAM, of Lonmay, and his wife Worthley Stewart, parents of Mary baptised on 19 Marcg 1758 in Byre's Close, Edinburgh. Witnesses : Mrs Stewart grandmother, Dugal Ged with his wife and daughter, Nathaniel Spens, Mrs John Moir, and Mr Johnston a midwife. [DUAS.Br.MS3.DC/12]

MOIR, WILLIAM, of New Grange, the younger, married Cornelia Isabella Aitken a spinster, both of St Vigeans, Angus, in Haddington on 22 August 1795. Witnesses : Sarah Fairbairn and Helen Walker. [NAS.CH12.2.2.18][HEC]

MONCRIEFF, ROBERT, a minister who emigrated to Antigua in 1749. [EMA#46][FPA#283]

MONCRIEFF, Lady, of the Perth Episcopalian Congregation, 1742. [TV.77.21][JWI]

MONCURE, JOHN, born 24 April 1710, son of Robert Moncure and his wife Jean Grant in Kinneff, Kincardineshire, emigrated to America in 1733, minister and teacher in Overwharton parish, Stafford County, and later Old Acquia parish, Virginia, died 10 March 1764, buried at Acquia. [VG#424][CCVC#37][OC#198][AcquiaMI][FPA#190]

MONORGAN, WILLIAM, son of Alexander Monorgan and his wife Helen Ramsay, was born in December and baptised in St Andrews on 5 December 1722. [SER]

MONRO, ALEXANDER, DD, Principal of Edinburgh University, Bishop of Argyll, 1688. [Keith#292]

MONZIE, Lady, of the Perth Episcopalian Congregation, 1742. [TV.77.21][JWI]

MOORE, ALEXANDER, an Episcopal minister, 1710. [NAS.CH12.12.5]

MORE, Reverend GEORGE, born 1744, died 1827, husband of Catherine ...., born 1749, died 1827. [St John's, Edinburgh, MI]

MORE, JOHN, a bookbinder in Edinburgh, married Mary, daughter of John Patullo sometime a shipbuilder in Montrose, Angus, at Leith, 18 November 1742. [DUAS: BrMS3/Dc/12]

MORE, JOHN, was confirmed in Fortrose, Easter Ross, in 1770. [EV#327]

MORGAN, Dr WILLIAM, a minister who emigrated to Jamaica in 1773; former rector of Kingston, Jamaica, later Professor of Philosophy in Marischal College, Aberdeen, testament, 1789, Comm. Aberdeen. [NAS][EMA#46]

MORICE, ROBERT, son of James Morice, minister, and his wife Cecilia White, was born and baptised 22 August 1728 in St Andrews. ("he died a little thereafter")[SER]

MORICE, WILLIAM, in Dundee, 1727. [ECD#26]

MORISON, ANDREW, a merchant in Dundee, 1727. [ECD#24]

MORISON, DAVID, and his wife Janet Drummond, in Lentibbert, Muthill, : parents of James born 11 February and baptised 12 February 1698. [MRB]

MORRISON, JAMES, a minister who emigrated to Virginia in 1776. [EMA#46]

MORRISON, JOHN, a minister who emigrated to Virginia in 1699, later in Nevis. [EMA#46][DP#335]

MORRISON, JOHN, a minister in Birse, Aberdeenshire, a beneficiary under the will of Alexander Deuchar in Barbados, 1738 [NAS.CC8.8.100];

MORRISON, KENNETH, born 1715, a minister who emigrated to Barbados in 1745, minister of St Joseph's from 1747 to 1750, and of St James from 1751 to 1775. [EMA#46][Barbadian parish registers]

MORRISON, LUCINDA, daughter of James Morrison, a weaver in Ayr, and his wife Mary ...., was baptised in Ayr on 19 March 1799.[NAS.CH12.26.1]

MORRISON, ROBERT, a barber, and his wife .... Ramsay, parents of Alexander baptised in Edinburgh on 16 February 1756. Witnesses : Alexander White and John Graeme a plumber. [DUAS.BrMsDC3/12]

MORTON, JAMES, married Margaret Stalker, in Newhaven on 4 April 1738. Witnesses : Thomas Morton father of the bridegroom, and David Stalker father of the bride. [LER][NNQ.8.125]

MOSSCROP, JOHN, a farmer in Edram, Berwickshire, married Agnes Grieve from Eyemouth, Berwickshire, in Haddington on 8 September 1788. Witnesses : John Clarke and James Mitchell. [NAS.CH12.2.2.18][HEC]

MUDIE, DAVID, town clerk of Arbroath, Angus, husband of Katherine Spink, residing in Copegate, Arbroath, 1752. [SRS.13.75]

MUIR, DAVID, a brewer in Abbeyhill, and Charlotte Mitchell, daughter of Walter Mitchell, King's porter in the Abbey, : married by Alexander McKenzie on 9 December 1741. [SLIM#587]

MULLO, ALEXANDER, a tailor, married Christian Robertson, daughter of Mrs Balvaird, in Dundee 22 July 1743. [ECD#63]

MUNN, RICHARD, a minister who emigrated to Jamaica in 1795. [EMA#47]

MUNRO, HARRY, a missionary of the Society for the Propagation of the Gospel who emigrated to New York in 1765, settled in Albany, a Loyalist in 1776, died in Edinburgh during 1797. [EMA#47][FPA#304/327] [NA.AO12.24.36][NAS.RD3.289/717]

MUNRO, JOHN, from Catewell, Ross and Cromarty, emigrated in 1650, a minister at St John's on the Pamunkey River, King and Queen County, Virginia, died 1724. [WMQ.2.13.231]

MURDOCH, GEORGE, born 1678, a minister in Virginia, around 1723, in Prince George's parish, Maryland, 1730. [FPA#38/41/168]

MURISON, PATRICK, a shoemaker burgess of Arbroath, married Nicola Guthrie in 1725, residing in Marketgate, Arbroath, 1752. [SRS.13.89][Arbroath MI]

MURRAY, ALEXANDER, was transported in 1651, a minister in Ware parish, Mockjack Bay, Virginia, 1653-1672, dead by 1703. [CCVC#38][WMQ.2.2.157] [RoyalSociety,MSS1.369]

MURRAY, ALEXANDER, son of William Murray and his wife Magdalene Gellie, Episcopal minister at Banff, 17.... [F.6.161]; a minister in Banff, a beneficiary under the will of Alexander Deuchar in Barbados, 1738 [NAS.CC8.8.100];

MURRAY, ALEXANDER, graduated Master of Arts in 1746, a missionary of the Society for the Propagation of the Gospel who emigrated to Pennsylvania in 1762, and settled in Reading, Pennsylvania, graduated as a Doctor of Divinity from King's College, Aberdeen, on 17 February 1784. [KCA#103][EMA#47][FPA#305/328]

MURRAY, ALEXANDER, Lieutenant of the 22nd Regiment of Foot, married Isobel Wordie, daughter of John Wordie of Cambusbarron, in St Andrew's Episcopal Church, Glasgow, on 28 October 1771. [SA.X.21]

MURRAY, Mrs ANN, of the Perth Episcopalian Congregation, 1742. [TV.77.21][JWI]

MURRAY, ANNE, daughter of Lady Clardon, Sinclair or Murray, was confirmed at Thurso, Caithness, on 8 August 1762. [DC#277]

MURRAY, BARBARA, daughter of Lady Clardon, Sinclair or Murray, was confirmed at Thurso, Caithness, on 8 August 1762. [DC#277]

MURRAY, BETTIE, daughter of Lady Clardon, Sinclair or Murray, was confirmed at Thurso, Caithness, on 8 August 1762. [DC#277]

MURRAY, GEORGE, a bookseller in Montrose, Angus, married Jean Mercer of Brechin, Angus, on 21 January 1798. [NNQ.14.99]

MURRAY, HENRY, son of Gilbert Murray minister of Crieff, Perthshire, graduated MA from St Andrews in 1678, minister at Dunkeld from 1688 until deposed in 1701; an Episcopalian preacher in Perth, 1703 -1715, 1722-1735, died 1735; husband of Ann Young. [NAS.B59.28.83][TBD#47][F.4.155]

MURRAY, JAMES, and his wife Anna Glass, in Alangrow, Muthill, Perthshire, parents of Lilias, born 22 December and baptised 24 December 1697. [MRB]

MURRAY, JAMES, of Abercairnie, married Lady Christian Montgomery, in the Countess of Eglinton's lodging above John Jollie's, Edinburgh, 16 February 1737. [DUAS: BrMS3/Dc/12]

MURRAY, JEAN, daughter of Lady Clardon, Sinclair or Murray, was confirmed at Thurso, Caithness, on 8 August 1762. [DC#277]

MURRAY, JOHN, minister in Deskford, ordained 1698, died 1 March 1719, husband of Jean Ord, parents of James who died 5 May 1717. [F.6.285]

MURRAY, JOHN, son of Henry Murray in Dundee, was baptised on 8 May 1723. Godfather was Andrew Ogilvy of Templehall, and godmother was Lady Westhall. [BNDBR]

MURRAY, JOHN, from St Ninian's Stirlingshire, married Isabella Lindsay, second daughter of the late Hercules Lindsay, Professor of Law at the University of Glasgow, and his wife Cecilia Murray, on 14 January 1789 at St Andrew's Episcopal Church in Glasgow. Witnesses : Sir William Murray of Polmais, William Murray a cordiner in Edinburgh, and Mrs Oswald of Shieldhall. [SA.X.22]

MURRAY, JOHN, son of ...... Murray a bookseller, was baptised in Montrose, Angus, on 5 June 1800. [NNQ.14.154]

Scots Episcopalians at Home and Abroad, 1689-1800

MURRAY, MARGARET, daughter of Peter Murray in Stonehaven, Kincardineshire, was baptised in Stonehaven on 30 December 1760. [ST.ER]

MURRAY, MARGARET, daughter of Lady Clardon, Sinclair or Murray, was confirmed at Thurso, Caithness, on 8 August 1762. [DC#277]

MURRAY, THOMAS, an Episcopal preacher in Baledgarno, Inchture, Perthshire, 1723. [NAS.B59.30.48]

MURRAY, WILLIAM, born in the Garioch, Aberdeenshire, graduated MA from King's College, Aberdeen, in 1667, minister of Inverurie, Aberdeenshire, from 1679 until 1716 when he was deposed as a Jacobite, husband of Magdalen Gellie, parents of William, Katherine, Alexander, Peter, and Sarah. [F.6.161]

MURRAY, WILLIAM, son of Reverend William Murray and his wife Magdalene Gellie, educated at Marischal College, Aberdeen, 1709-1713, an Episcopal minister in Old Aberdeen, baptismal registers, 1730-1752. [NRAS.2698.1.5.9][MCA#290][F.6.161]; a beneficiary under the will of Alexander Deuchar in Barbados, 1738 [NAS.CC8.8.100]

MURRAY, WILLIAM, burgess of Dundee in 1726, a tailor in Dundee, 1727. [ECD#24][DBR]

MURRAY, WILLIAM, of Polmaise, married Elizabeth, daughter of Alexander Gibson of Pentland, at Addieston, Edinburgh, 10 February 1738. [DUAS: BrMS3/Dc/12]

MURRAY, WILLIAM, 'engaged to be pedagogue to Drummond alias McGregor of Balhadie in the town of Stirling', was baptised in South Leith on 19 January 1771. [SA.IX.12][LER]

MURRAY, Mr, a goldsmith, of the Perth Episcopalian Congregation, 1742. [TV.77.21][JWI]

MURRAY, Mrs, of the Perth Episcopalian Congregation, 1742. [TV.77.21][JWI]

MURRAYSHALL, Lady, of the Perth Episcopalian Congregation, 1742. [TV.77.21][JWI]

MYLNE, Miss GRAHAM, daughter of Thomas Mylne of Mylnefield, born 1767, died 1841. [St John's, Edinburgh, MI]

NAIRN, WILLIAM, a minister who emigrated to Bermuda in 1722, moved to Varina parish Virginia, 1727, then to Wiltshire, England, 1728. [EMA#47][FPA#180/242]

NAIRN, ..., of Baldovan, in Dundee, 1727. [ECD#23]

NAPIER, JAMES, born 1707, died 1762. [Montrose Episcopal MI]

NASH, JAMES, born 1756, Captain of the 26th Regiment of Foot, died 1838, his wife Janet Ritchie, born 1769, died 1846. [St John's, Forfar, MI]

NEILL, HUGH, a minister who emigrated to Pennsylvania, 1750, in Queen Anne County, Maryland, 1771. [EMA#47][FPA#46/328]

NEILSON, WILLIAM, a merchant in Edinburgh and trustee of the Carruber's Close congregation, 1741. [JSC#83]

NEISH, ALEXANDER, in Dundee, 1727. [ECD#26]

NEISH, HENRY, and Jean Griffes, : married in St Andrews, Fife, on 30 October 1760. [SER]

NEISH, HENRY, and his wife Margaret Blair, parents of Katherine born 30 January and baptised 31 January 1724 in St Andrews, and John born 9 February and baptised 10 February 1727 in St Andrews, Fife. [SER]

NEUTH, JOHN, married Christian Quayle, in Ayr, 2 June 1777.[NAS.CH12.26.1]

NICHOLSON, ALEXANDER, a plumber, and his wife .....Murray, parents of Jacobina Stewart baptised on Castle Hill, Edinburgh, 11 June 1752. Witnesses: Mr Webster and daughter Christian; Margaret baptised on Castle Hill on 26 August 1753. Witnesses: Mr and Mrs Thomson; Charles baptised on 16 March 1755 on Castle Hill. Witnesses : Robert Murray, Mr and Mrs Thomson, Mrs Ballentine, and Mrs Pringle; Alexander baptised on 2 January 1758 on Castle Hill. Witnesses: Mrs Mabone and Mrs Thomson. [DUAS.Br.MS3.DC/12]

NICOL, JOHN, a wright, father of Francis baptised in Edinburgh on 24 June 1759. Witnesses : Mrs Craigie and Jean Leslie. [DUAS.Br.MS3.DC/12]

Scots Episcopalians at Home and Abroad, 1689-1800

NICOLL, JOHN, in Blackhills, father of David Nicoll baptised at Lochlee, Angus, on 26 November 1727. Witnesses : David Smart in Greenburn, Edzell, and David Rose in Balyordie. [DUAS.BrMsDC3/174]

NICOLSON, GEORGE, and Jane Stephen, from Longside, : married in Fraserburgh, Aberdeenshire, on 1 March 1794. [NAS.CH12.32.2]

NICOLSON, JOHN, son of James Nicolson in Gilmerton was born 5 March 1770 and baptised in Haddington, East Lothian. Witnesses : James Fairburn and James Tait. [NAS.CH12.2.13]

NIDDRIE, GEORGE, and Margaret Rennie, both in Fraserburgh, Aberdeenshire, : married there on 8 January 1789. [NAS.CH12.32.2]

NISBET, ALEXANDER and FRANCIS, twin sons of Alexander Nisbet and Janet Knox, : born 5 December and baptised 9 December 1770 (?) in Haddington, East Lothian. [NAS.CH12.2.13]

NISBET, REDE, a merchant on Nevis pre 1789, saught ordination in the Church of England. [FPA#287]

NISH, DUNCAN, and his wife Elspet McLaren, in Blainror, Muthill, Perthshire, : parents of Duncan and Elspet, twins, born 13 December and baptised 14 December 1697. [MRB]

NIVEN, JOHN, and his wife Jean Gordon, in Borland, Muthill, Perthshire, : parents of James, born 14 November and baptised 17 November 1697. [MRB]

NIVING, Reverend NINIAN, a Jacobite in 1745; letters, 1743/1746, died 1763. [NAS.CH12.12.110; 12.23.359/499] [TBD#203]

NIVISON, JOHN, educated at Glasgow University, to Virginia 1752, an assistant minister at St Anne's, Albemarle County, Virginia, 1751. [FPA#307/329]

NOBLE, DONALD, was confirmed in Arpafilie, Ross-shire, in 1770. [EV#327]

NOBLE, JAMES, was confirmed in Arpafilie, Ross-shire, in 1770. [EV#327]

NOBLE, JEAN, was confirmed in Arpafilie, Ross-shire, in 1770. [EV#327]

NOBLE, MARGARET, was confirmed in Arpafilie, Ross-shire, in 1770. [EV#327]

NORIE, DAVID, and Elisabeth MacIntire from Linton, : married in St Andrews, Fife, on 26 February 1768. [SER]

NORIE, ROBERT, born 1647, son of Reverend Robert Norie, graduated MA from St Andrews in 1667, minister in Dundee from 1686 to 1689, deprived 29 August 1689, deposed 26 December 1716, an Episcopal minister in Dundee , consecrated as a Bishop of Brechin in the non-jurant church in 1724, husband of Isabel Guthrie, died in March 1727. [F.5.320][Keith#545/552][ECD]

NORTON, CATHERINE MONCRIEFF, daughter of Henry Norton and his wife Catharine, was born 23 October 1798 and baptised 10 November 1798. [NAS.CH12.3.26/7]

NOURSE, WALTER, son of John Nourse and his wife Elizabeth, was born 11 August 1797 and baptised in St John the Evangelist, Edinburgh, on 24 September 1797. [NAS.CH12.3.26/2]

OCHTERLONY, JOHN, of Flemington, born 1667 son of Alexander Ochterlony minister of Carmyllie, graduated MA from Marischal College, Aberdeen, 1685, assistant minister in Carmyllie around 1690, then at Aberlemno, an Episcopalian and a Jacobite, deposed, in 1726 he was consecrated a bishop of the non-jurant church and was assigned the diocese of Brechin, of the Seagate Chapel in Dundee, he died in Dundee during May 1742. He married Margaret, elder daughter of John Graham a merchant bailie of Dundee, and their son Alexander, a merchant in Montrose settled in Philadelphia. [F.5.277][EF#108][TBD#10/49]

OGILVIE, DAVID, of Peattie, born 1649, son of David Ogilvie and his wife Margaret Hallyburton, graduated MA from St Andrews in 1669, schoolmaster at Inverkeillor, deacon at Kirriemuir, chaplain to the Bishop of Brechin, 1680, minister of Birse from 1685 until 1697, deposed as a non-jurant, settled in Kirkton of Kettins, died there December 1714. Husband of Beatrix Cabel, parents of David, George, Elizabeth, and Margaret. [F.6.83]

OGILVIE, GEORGE, born 1731, late of Langley Park and of Tayock, near Montrose, and of Langley estate in Jamaica, died at Langley Park in 1791. [Montrose Episcopal MI]

OGILVIE, HARRY, burgess of Dundee in 1727, a merchant in Dundee, 1727. [ECD#24][DBR]

OGILVIE, JAMES, from Banff, a minister who emigrated to Virginia in 1771, settled in Hampshire County, 1771, and in Charles City in 1772, rector of Westover, a Loyalist, in London by 1781. [NA.AO13.32.166, etc] [AOB.2.427][EMA#48][OC#319][FPA#310/330]

OGILVIE, JOHN, Captain of the brig <u>Royal George of Leith</u>, married Louisa, widow of Captain Alexander Ogilvie in London, in Haddington, East Lothian, on 8 September 1789. Witnesses : Thomas Salmon, Margaret Ogilvie, and Anne Ogilvy. [NAS.CH12.2.2.18][HEC]

OGILVIE, THOMAS, minister at Brechin, Angus, 1743. [ECD#69]

OGILVIE, THOMAS, minister at Kinalie, 1744. [Keith#548]

OGILVIE, Mrs, in Copegate, Arbroath, Angus, 1752. [SRS.13.74]

OGILVY, CATHERINE, in Glasclune, was confirmed at Whiteloch, Blairgowrie, Perthshire, on 2 September 1750. [TBD#155]

OGILVY, CHARLES, son of Dr Ogilvy, was confirmed in Forfar in 1770. [EF#26]

OGILVY, JEAN, was confirmed at Craighall, Blairgowrie, Perthshire, on 7 August 1748. [TBD#155]

OGILVY,...... a son of the Earl of Airlie, of the Perth Episcopalian Congregation, 1742. [TV.77.21][JWI]

OGILVY, MARGARET, daughter of .... Ogilvy, deceased, son of Ogilvy of Newhall, was baptised on 9 April 1724 in the house of the Lady Dowager of Monorgan in Dundee. Godfathers : the laird of Monorgan and Thomas Crichton a surgeon apothecary in Dundee, while the godmothers : his wife and Mrs James Pilmor, daughter of the Lady Dowager of Monorgan. [BNDBR]

OGILVY, MARGARET, daughter of Henry Ogilvy of Templehall a merchant in Dundee, was baptised in his house in the Murraygate of Dundee on 25 June 1726. [BNDBR]

OGILVY, MARY, daughter of Dr Ogilvy, was confirmed in Forfar, Angus, in 1770. [EF#26]

OGILVY, THOMAS, son of Henry Ogilvy of Templehall, was baptised at Ogilvy's house in Murraygate, Dundee, on 2 June 1724. [BNDBR]

OLIPHANT, CHARLES, daughter (sic), of James Oliphant a merchant, was born and baptised in Leith on 28 March 1748. Witnesses : Mr Cheyne a surgeon, Mrs Cheape, and Mrs Binning. [SA.IX.13][LER]

OLIPHANT, EBENEZER, a jeweller in Edinburgh and a trustee of the Carruber's Close congregation, 1741. [JSC#84]

OLIPHANT, WILLIAM, and Margaret Murray, : married in Fraserburgh, Aberdeenshire, on 13 August 1791. [NAS.CH12.32.2]

ORME, ALEXANDER, of Balvaird, a writer in Edinburgh and a trustee of the Carruber's Close congregation, 1741. [JSC#84]

ORMONT, ISOBEL, was confirmed in Forfar, Angus, in 1770. [EF#26]

ORR, SAMUEL, a minister who emigrated to the Leeward Islands in 1710, minister of St Philip's, Antigua, 1726. [EMA#48][FPA#276]

ORR, WILLIAM, a minister who emigrated to South Carolina in 1736, an assistant minister in Santee, S.C., 1737, to St Philip's, Charleston, 1740, to St John's parish, Colleton County, S.C., 1750. [EMA#48][FPA#148/150/153]

ORROCK, WALTER, a merchant in Fife, father of Helen baptised in Morrison's Close, Edinburgh, 3 December 1752. Witnesses Mrs White, Mrs Mossman, Mrs Mercer, and Dougal Ged. [DUAS.BrMsDC3/12]

OUCHTERLONIE, JOHN, was consecrated in Edinburgh on 29 November 1726, Bishop of Brechin from 1731 until 1742. [Keith#543]

OUCHTERLONY, ROBERT, born 1737, minister in Montrose, Angus, 1743, died 1816, his wife Anne Renny, born 1724, died 1787. Their children – James born 1768, died 1820, his wife Alithea Bridget Pert died 1826; Robert, born 1776, died 1827, his wife Mary Munde born 1797, died 1853. [Montrose Episcopal MI] [ECD#69]

OUCHTERLONY, ROBERT, born 1776, late of Kingston, Jamaica, died 1827. [Montrose Episcopal MI]

PAGAN, WILLIAM, of Linnburn, born 1751, died 1836, husband of Katherine ..., born 1755, died 1843. [St John's, Edinburgh, MI]

PANTON, GEORGE, a schoolmaster from Jedburgh, Roxburghshire, educated at Marischal College, Aberdeen, a minister who emigrated to America in 1772, settled in Trenton, New Jersey, as a missionary, rector of St Michael's, Trenton, a Loyalist chaplain in New York in 1780, via Halifax, Nova Scotia, to Kelso, Scotland, by 1788. [NA.AO12.15.8, etc][SA1#107]

PARGILLIES, WILLIAM, a resident of South Leith, married Helen Crokatt, a servant to the family of Captain Hugh Clerk, in Mrs Fraser's House, Borthwick Close, Edinburgh, on 9 September 1757. Witnesses : George Donald, George Cuthbertson, Mrs Fraser, and Mr Ogilvie. [LER][NNQ.8.127]

PARK, JAMES, an apothecary, and spouse ....MacLean, parents of Eunice baptised in Dickson's Land, Edinburgh, on 15 May 1760. Witnesses : Hector McLean, a writer, and Mrs McLachland; James Allan baptised in Dickson's Laand, Edinburgh, on 8 April 1763. Witnesses : Major McLean, Hector McLean, ...Campbell, and Mrs McIlmeath. [DUAS.BrMsDC3/12]

PARTINGTON, WILLIAM, son of William Partington was born 17 August and baptised on 21 August 1768 in Haddington. Witnesses : Archibald Smith and James Miller. [NAS.CH12.2.13]

PATERSON, ALEXANDER, a brewer, married Elizabeth Gibson a servant, in Hackerton's Wynd, Edinburgh, 24 September 1748; parents of Alexander baptised on 17 March 1754 at the 'back of the Canongate'. Witnesses : Thomas Mack and his wife Jean Rose, and Euphan Taylor; Andrew baptised in Canongate on 7 May 1756; John baptised in Canongate 23 September 1759. [DUAS: BrMS3/Dc/12]

PATERSON, ISABEL, was confirmed in Arpafilie, Ross-shire, in 1770. [EV#327]

PATERSON, JOHN, born 1632, Bishop of Galloway, Bishop of Edinburgh pre 1687, Bishop of Glasgow from 1687 to 1688 when deposed, died in Edinburgh on 8 December 1708. [Keith#64/270]

PATERSON, MARY, daughter of John Paterson in Boorhills, was baptised 25 October 1763. [CBER]

PATERSON, ROBERT, a journeyman wright, married Janet Jaffrey a servant maid, in the house of Mrs Elmsel in South Leith on 26 June 1753. Witnesses : Lauchlan Farquharson, Mrs Elmsel, Anne Elmsel, and Betty Cheyne. [LER][NNQ.8.125]

PATERSON, ROBERT, son of John Paterson in Cowie, was baptised in Stonehaven, Kincardineshire, on 20 April 1758. [ST.ER]

PATERSON, WILLIAM, son of William Paterson in Aberdeen, educated at Marischal College, Aberdeen, 1777-1781, graduated MA, an Episcopal minister and Dean of Ross. [MCA#352]

PATTERSON, JOHN, a minister who emigrated to Maryland in 1768, assistant at St Mary Ann's. [EMA#49][FPA#302/326]

PATTON, Mrs, of the Perth Episcopalian Congregation, 1742. [TV.77.21][JWI]

PEARSON, ALEXANDER, a shipmaster in Arbroath, Angus, 1752. [SRS.13.79]

PEDDIE, JOHN, a glover in Arbroath, Angus, married Nicola Guthrie in 1734, 1752. [SRS.13.62]

PENDER, GEORGE S, minister of the Protestant Episcopal Church in Ayr, 1780. [NAS.CH12.26.1]

PETRIE, ARTHUR, minister at Mucklefolla, Aberdeen, 1777, Bishop of Ross and Caithness, Bishop of Moray, died 1787.[Keith#542]

PETRIE, ISABEL, widow of George White a tailor, in Rotten Row, Arbroath, Angus, 1752. [SRS.13.56]

PETRY, COLIN, tenant of Auchentender of Clinkstown in Forgue, Aberdeenshire, brother of George Petry of Newton of Prema, now at Miln of Gairth, and Isobel Alexander, daughter of John Alexander, minister at Kildrummy, and his wife Anna Gordon, antenuptial contract of marriage, 3 April 1711. [NAS.CH12.23.5][TBD#1]

PETTIGREW, CHARLES, son of James Pettigrew, a minister who emigrated to North Carolina in 1775, died 1807. [EMA#50][FPA#304]

PEW, MARY, daughter of John Pew a farmer, was baptised at Leith Links on 14 February 1748. Witnesses : Jeremy and William Pew, also Anne and Elizabeth Pew. [LER][SA.X.10]

PHILIPS, ROBERT, of the Prince of Wales Dragoons (?), and Anne Middleton, : married in Ayr, 27 July 1797. [NAS.CH12.26.1]

PIRIE, CHARLES, son of William Pirie and his wife Margaret Young in Boat of Kinharochy, Aberdeenshire, was baptised 30 June 1764. [CBER]

PIRIE, WILLIAM, son of James Pirie and his wife Elspeet Martin in Mill of Tory, Udny, Aberdeenshire, was baptised 14 January 1776. [CTER]

PITEUCHAR, Lady, of the Perth Episcopalian Congregation, 1742. [TV.77.21][JWI]

PITTENDREACH, JAMES, farmer in Kirkton of Tyrie, Pitsligo, Aberdeenshire, and Sophia Ramsay, alias Mrs Lachlan Milne, in Pitsligo, : married in Fraserburgh on 26 September 1795. [NAS.CH12.32.2]

PORTER, MARGERY, daughter of Alexander Porter and his wife Margaret Ruthven, was born and baptised on 18 August 1723 in St Andrews, Fife. [SER]

PORTERFIELD, ANDREW, son of Robert Porterfield and his wife Janet Smith, was born on 5 October and baptised on 10 October 1722 in St Andrews, Fife. [SER]

POWELL, AILSIE, daughter of John Powell, was born 3 April and baptised 10 April 1768 in Haddington, East Lothian,. Witnesses : William Audland and Bartholemew Bower. [NAS.CH12.2.13]

POWELL, THOMAS, son of John Powell, was born 27 July and baptised 31 July 1761 in Perth. Witnesses : Mrs Stewart and Mrs Waldon. [NAS.CH12.2.13]

PRESLEY, CHARLES, a merchant in Fraserburgh, and Margaret Moir from Lonmay, : married in Fraserburgh on 15 July 1798. [NAS.CH12.32.2]

PRESLEY, JAMES, a weaver in Fraserburgh, a widower, and Isobel Cardno, a widow, : married in Fraserburgh on 14 June 1794. [NAS.CH12.32.2]

PRESLEY, JOHN, a shoemaker in Fraserburgh, Aberdeenshire, and Jean Sinclair, : married in Fraserburgh on 13 September 1788. [NAS.CH12.32.2]

PROCTOR, WILLIAM, from Banff or Elgin, educated at college in Aberdeen, 1733, to America 1740, a minister who died in Nottoway parish, Amelia County, Virginia, died in December 1761.
[AJ#741][VMHB.10.298][SM.24.167][GM.32.145][FPA#220/349]

PROVOST, MARGARET, was confirmed in Arpafilie, Ross-shire, in 1770. [EV#327]

PURVIS, Sir ALEXANDER, of Eccles, Berwickshire, married Mary Hume of Coldingham, in Haddington on 21 June 1775. [NAS.CH12.2.2.18][HEC]

RAE, DAVID, a minister residing in Old Assembly Close, Edinburgh, 1746. [JSC#63]

RAIT, DAVID, son to David Rait in Wallace of Craigie, was baptised in Dundee on 4 October 1726. [BNDBR]

RAITT, DAVID, in Dundee, 1727. [ECD#26]

RAITT, Dr GEORGE, in Dundee, 1727. [ECD#23]

RAITT, JAMES, born 9 February 1689, son of William Raitt of Pitforthy, Episcopal minister in Kiriemuir and Dundee from 1727, consecrated Bishop of Brechin in 1742, died 13 January 1777.
[NAS.CH12.12.1530][F.5.365][TBD#33][Keith#545][ECD]

RAIT, JOHN, son to David Rait in Wallace of Craigie, was baptised in Dundee on 3 January 1725. [BNDBR]

RAIT, WILLIAM, of Pitforthy,born 1653 son of Reverend William Rait in Dundee, MA King's College, Aberdeen, 1677, minister at Monikie from 1680 until deposed as a Jacobite in 1716, husband of Isobel Yeaman, parents of George, James, Barbara, and Margaret. [F.6.365]

RAMSAY, ALEXANDER, a butcher in Duns, Berwickshire, married Frances Spears from Berwick on Tweed, in Haddington on 23 November 1795. Witnesses : Alexander Thom and Thomas Temple. [NAS.CH12.2.2.18]

RAMSAY, DANIEL, of Falla, born 1760, a merchant in Edinburgh, died 1824, husband of Catherine Hamilton, born 1762, died 1825. [St John's, Edinburgh, MI]

RAMSAY, GEORGE, burgess of Dundee 1719, a merchant in Dundee, 1727. [DBR][ECD#24]

RAMSAY, GEORGE, junior, in Dundee, 1727. [ECD#21]

RAMSAY, GILBERT, born 1650s, educated at King's College, Aberdeen, 1673, ordained by the Bishop of Galloway in 1686, to Antigua in 1686, minister at St Paul's, Antigua until 1692, moved to Barbados, minister of Christ Church from 1692 until 1727, died in Bath, England, 5 May 1728. Probate 1720 PCC, [Bath Abbey MI][NAS.RD3.143.507][Car.3.268][CA.2.243]

RAMSAY, JAMES, son of Robert Ramsay minister of Dundonald, minister at Kirkintilloch, next at Linlithgow, Dean of Glasgow 1673, Bishop of Dunblane , Bishop of Ross from 1684 to 1688 when he was deposed, died in Edinburgh on 22 October 1696, buried in Canongate. [Keith#204]

RAMSAY, JAMES, a merchant in Dundee, 1727. [ECD#24]

RAMSAY, JAMES, a minister who emigrated to the West Indies in 1761, rector of St John's Capisterre, St Kitts, 1770. [EMA#51][FPA#285]

RAMSAY, JOHN, minister at Stonehaven, Kincardineshire, 1743. [ECD#60]

RAMSAY, JOHN, a minister who emigrated to Virginia in 1751, settled in St Ann's, Albemarle County. [EMA#51][FPA#214/307/329]

RAMSAY, JOHN, of the Isle of May in the parish of Crail, Fife, and Isabel Brunton in St Andrews, : married there 18 December 1752. [SER]

RAMSAY, JOHN, a minister who emigrated to Jamaica in 1759. [FPA]

RAMSAY, KATHERINE, was confirmed in Forfar, Angus, in 1770. [EF#26]

RAMSAY, PETER, a stabler, and his wife .... Mackenzie, parents of James, baptised at Cowgate Port, Edinburgh, on 15 February 1753. Witnesses : John Ramsay collector, and William Sutherland brewer; Peter baptised at Cowgate Port, on 5 April 1754. Witness was John Ramsay a collector; William baptised at Cowgate Port, on 1 April 1758. Witnesses : William Ramsay, William Sutherland and his wife, James Ramsay, and James Ramsay a banker. [DUAS.Br.MS3.DC/12]

RANKEILLOUR, DAVID, and his wife Margaret Skinner, parents of Catherine born and baptised on 19 October 1723 in St Andrews; Christian born 28 June and baptised 29 June 1725 in St Andrews; John was born and baptised 31 May 1727 in St Andrews; and Margaret born and baptised 21 May 1729 in St Andrews, Fife. [SER]

RANKEN, ALEXANDER, born 1647, MA St Andrews, 1667, an Episcopal preacher at Benvie, Angus, 1692 to 1703, died in Dundee 7 April 1729. [NAS.CH1.2.3.2/166-183][F.5.351]

RANKEN, DAVID, born 1663, son of Alexander Ranken of Pottie a merchant bailie of Perth, graduated MA from St Andrews in 1677, minister at Bendochy from 1692 until 1700, then an Episcopal preacher in Skinner's Close, Edinburgh, consecrated Bishop of the non-jurant church in Edinburgh 1727, died 17 November 1728, husband of Euphan Blair who died 1736. [NAS.CH12.26.1][Keith#553]

RANKEN, ROBERT, a wine merchant in Leith, married Janet Williamson, daughter of the late James Williamson a merchant there, at Leith Links on 12 February 1738. Witnesses : George Fenwick grandfather of Janet, John Cheyne a surgeon in Leith, James Angus a writer in Edinburgh and his wife.[LER][NNQ.8.125]

RANKIN, ALEXANDER, from Aberdeen, and Sarah Furiston, late servant at Memsie, : married at Memsie on 23 February 1797. [NAS.CH12.32.2]

RANKIN, CHRISTIAN, was confirmed in Glencoe, Argyll, in 1770. [EV#345]

RATTRAY, CHRISTIAN, was baptised as anadult in South Leith on 17 December 1743, and confirmed on 22 December 1743.[LER][SA.IX.13; X.10]

RATTRAY, JAMES, a brewer in Dundee, 1727. [ECD#21/24]

RATTRAY, JANET, daughter of John Rattray a surgeon in Edinburgh, was confirmed in Leith on 15 March 1755. [SA.IX.13][LER]

RATTRAY, JOHN, son of Rt. Rev. Dr Rattray of Craighall, married Christian, daughter of the late George Main a jeweller in Edinburgh, in the Citadel of Leith on 3 February 1742. Witnesses : Mrs Anne Main, Mrs Rachel Houstoun, and James McKay. [LER][NNQ.8.125]

RATTRAY, MARGARET, daughter of John Rattray a surgeon, was baptised at the Citadel of Leith on 23 June 1746. Dr John Clerk was godfather, Lady Elphinstone junior and Mrs Anne Mayne : godmothers. She was confirmed on 15 March 1755. [LER][SA.IX.13; X.10]

RATTRAY, MARJORY, was confirmed at Craighall, Blairgowrie, Perthshire, on 5 July 1747. [TBD#155]

RATTRAY, RACHEL, and WILLIAM RATTRAY, children of the late Mr Rattray a surgeon in the Canongate, : baptised as adults in South Leith on 29 October 1743. [LER][SA.IX.13; X.10]

RATTRAY, Dr THOMAS, a minister since 1727, Bishop of Dunkeld from 1727 until his death on 12 May 1743, Primus from 1739. [Keith#537]

RATTRAY, THOMAS, was confirmed at Whiteloch, Blairgowrie, Perthshire, on 2 September 1750. [TBD#155]

RAW, JOHN, married Janet McGill, in Ayr, 18 August 1789. [NAS.CH12.26.1]

REAY, JOHN, born 1754, minister of St Peter's for 28 years, died 1808. [Montrose Episcopal MI]

REID, HUGH, was confirmed in Fortrose, Easter Ross, 1770. [EV#327]

REID, JANE, daughter of William Reid and Effie Baron, who married in Edinburgh on 1 February 1728, was born 26 September and baptised in St Andrews on 28 September 1728. [SER]

REID, JOHN, graduated MA from Marischal College, Aberdeen, in 1669, schoolmaster of Banchory-Ternan, minister of Durris, Kincardineshire, from

1675 until 1715 when he was deposed as a Jacobite, dead by April 1728. Husband of (1) Isabel Fraser, (2) Margaret Cruden. [F.6.53]

REID, JOHN, a minister who emigrated to North Carolina in 1745. [EMA#52]

REID, MARY, was confirmed in Fortrose, Easter Ross, 1770. [EV#327]

REID, SARAH, daughter of Robert Reid and his wife Christian Graham in Kirkoswald, Ayrshire, was baptised in Ayr on 14 July 1798. [NAS.CH12.26.1]

REID, WILLIAM, of Auchmillan, and Barbara, daughter of John Alexander minister at Kildrummy, Aberdeenshire, an antenuptial marriage contract, 21 February 1721; later in Crumpstone, marriage tocher discharge, 15 January 1720. [NAS.CH12.23.6/14]

REID, ..., of Affleck, in Dundee, 1727. [ECD#23]

REID, ..., of Torfbeg, in Dundee, 1727. [ECD#23]

RENNIE, CHARLES, a blacksmith, and Margaret Mackie, daughter of Charles Mackie a mason in Fraserburgh, Aberdeenshire, : married there on 15 August 1802. [NAS.CH12.32.2]

RENNIE, JOHN, born in London, 13 November 1748, a minister who emigrated to Georgia in 1773, settled in St Phillip's parish, chaplain at the Zouberbuhler estate, a Loyalist in 1776, moved to England. [EMA#52][FPA#301/325] [NA.AO12.99.184]

RENNY, HENRY, born 1738, died 1836, husband of Mary Henderson, born 1760, died 1838. [Montrose Episcopal MI]

RENNY, ROBERT, educated at Glasgow and Aberdeen universities around 1755, a minister who emigrated to Virginia in 1764, settled in Overwharton parish. [EMA#52][FPA#308/330]

RENNY, THOMAS, born 1765, a shipmaster in Montrose, died 1825. [Montrose Episcopal MI]

REOCH, JAMES, a procurator, father of Isobel baptised in Blackfriars Wynd, Edinburgh, on 11 August 1752. Witnesses : Thomas Sinclair writer, Patrick Edie surgeon, and Mrs Reoch. [DUAS.BrMsDC3/12]

RHIND, JOSEPH, a weaver in Dundee, 1743. [ECD#65]

RHIND, MARGARET, daughter of John Rhind in Stonehaven, was baptised in Stonehaven, Kincardineshire, on 31 July 1760. [ST.ER]

RICHARD, ANDREW, and Helen Alice in Balloch, : parents of Ann born 16 August and baptised in Muthill, Perthshire, on 19 August 1774. [MRB]

RICHART, THOMAS, and his wife Helen Watson, in Middle Drummanawhance, Muthill, Perthshire, : parents of Janet, born 19 December and baptised 22 December 1697. [MRB]

RICHIE, ALEXANDER, and his wife Jane Petie, parents of Laurence born and baptised in St Andrews on 14 December 1727, and Jane born on 10 July and baptised in St Andrews, Fife, on 12 July 1729. [SER]

RICHIE, PETER, son of George Richie in Pitcarrow, was baptised in Dundee on 23 March 1726. [BNDBR]

RIND, GRISEL, daughter of David Rind in the Ground of Balgay, was baptised in Dundee on 1 February 1726. [BNDBR]

RITCHIE, ANDREW, son of William Ritchie in Peterculter, Aberdeenshire, educated at Marischal College, Aberdeen, 1781-1785, graduated MA, minister in Cuminestown and in Forgue. [MCA#357]

RITCHIE, DAVID, born 1753 in Perth, a minister who emigrated to Dominica in 1801, settled in St George, Grenada, and in Dominica. [EMA#52][FPA#293/319] [GM.72.181]

RITCHIE, DAVID, 'one of the managers of the chapel', died in Brechin, Angus, on 23 March 1798. [NNQ.14.99]

RITCHIE, JOHN, quartermaster aboard the ship of war Amazon, married Mary Lawtie, in South Leith on 12 September 1760. Witnesses : Mrs Crockat, the mother of the bride, Janet and Jean Chapman, and Anne Bennet. [LER][NNQ.8.127]

RITCHIE, ..., daughter of Mr Ritchie a writer in Brechin, Angus, was baptised on 25 August 1798. [NNQ.14.100]

RIDDOCH, CHRISTIAN, daughter of James Riddoch minister of St Paul's Chapel, Aberdeen, testament, 7 January 1779, Comm. Aberdeen. [NAS]

ROBB, ALEXANDER, and Isabel Davie, both in Fraserburgh, Aberdeenshire, : married there on 23 April 1789. [NAS.CH12.32.2]

ROBB, WILLIAM, in Crimond, and Rebecca Catto in Rathen, : married in Fraserburgh, Aberdeenshire, on 31 July 1794. [NAS.CH12.32.2]

ROBE, MARGARET, was confirmed in Forfar, Angus, in 1770. [EF#26]

ROBERT, DAVID, at Lochhead, was confirmed in Forfar, Angus, in 1770. [EF#26]

ROBERT, ISOBEL, at Lochhead, was confirmed in Forfar, Angus, in 1770. [EF#26]

ROBERTSON, AGNES, daughter of James Robertson in Hilltown, Dundee, was baptised in Dundee on 1 November 1725. [BNDBR]

ROBERTSON, ALEXANDER, a merchant in Dundee, 1727. [ECD#24]

ROBERTSON, ALEXANDER, a merchant in Leith, married Elizabeth Anderson, relict of John Ranken, in South Leith on 3 February 1761. Witnesses : Convenor Simpson, Thomas Clark, David Clark, Mrs Simpson, Mrs Clark, and Mrs Rearson. [LER][NNQ.8.127]

ROBERTSON, ALEXANDER, a minister residing at the foot of Carrubber's Close, Edinburgh, 1746. [JSC#63]

ROBERTSON, ALEXANDER, a minister who emigrated to Jamaica in 1775, settled in Clarendon, Jamaica, 1775. [EMA#52][FPA]

ROBERTSON, CHARLES, of the Perth Episcopalian Congregation, 1742. [TV.77.21][JWI]

ROBERTSON, DAVID, of Bleaton, was baptised at Whiteloch, Blairgowrie, Perthshire, on 30 October 1753. [TBD#155]

ROBERTSON, DONALD, and his wife Ann Comrie in West Mains of Drummond, Perthshire, : parents of a daughter born 18 August and baptised 20 August 1774. [MRB]

ROBERTSON, ELIZABETH, was baptised at Whiteloch, Blairgowrie, Perthshire, on 30 October 1753. [TBD#155]

ROBERTSON, ELSPET, daughter of John Robertson and his wife Jane Low, was born ...January and baptised 22 January 1724 in St Andrews, Fife. [SER]

ROBERTSON, GEORGE, born in Struan, Perthshire, 1668, educated at St Andrews University, chaplain on board a man-of-war in 1692, a schoolmaster and minister who emigrated in 1693, settled in Bristol parish, Virginia, from 1693 until his death in 1739. [SCHR.14.142][FPA#177/190]

ROBERTSON, GEORGE, minister at Ardrie-dynat near Aberfeldy, Perthshire, 1744, imprisoned in Perth Tolbooth after the '45. [TBD#38/119]

ROBERTSON, HARRY, servant to Lord Minto, and his wife Margaret Napier, parents of Elliot baptised 30 May 1752 in Bell's Wynd, Edinburgh, on 30 May 1753. baptised 16 March 1776.

ROBERTSON, JAMES, a minister who emigrated to Virginia in 1718, settled in Westover parish, Va., later in Coventry parish, Maryland, by 1723. [EMA#52][FPA#36]

ROBERTSON, JAMES, in Dundee, 1727. [ECD#26]

ROBERTSON, JAMES, a packman, married Margaret Scott a servant, in Edinburgh, 30 April 1754; parents of Catharine baptised 22 April 1755. Witness Patrick Scott. [DUAS: BrMS3/Dc/12]

ROBERTSON, JAMES, a vintner, father of James baptised in Caltoun, Edinburgh, on 22 July 1764. [DUAS.BrMsDC3/12]

ROBERTSON, JAMES, son of John Robertson in Stonehaven, Kincardineshire, was baptised there on 16 March 1758. [ST.ER]

ROBERTSON, JAMES, of Dunork, and Mrs Jean Seaton, relict of Mr Corstorphin of Nydie, : married in St Andrews on 21 October 1766. [SER]

ROBERTSON, JAMES, son of James Robertson of the Princess of Wales' Fencibles and his wife Janet....., was baptised in Ayr on 8 March 1799. [NAS.CH12.26.1]

ROBERTSON, JOHN, educated at Marischal College, Aberdeen, 1671-1675, minister of Strathdon from 1681 until 1717 when deposed as a Jacobite, died at Whitehouse of Cromar in 1772. Father of Joseph, Charles, William, John, George, James, Janet, Margaret, Isobel, Isobel Elizabeth, Sophia, and Rebecca. [F.6.138]

ROBERTSON, JOHN, a minister in St Vincent, probate 1776, PCC.

ROBERTSON, JOSEPH, a non-jurant minister in Haddington, East Lothian, a Jacobite in 1745. [LPR#138]

ROBERTSON, ROBERT, minister in St Paul's, Nevis, 1726, 1727. [FPA#275] [SPAWI.1727.771xi]

ROBERTSON, ROBERT FORBES, son of James Robertson a mirror manufacturer, was baptised in Cowgate, Edinburgh, on 26 March 1771. Witnesses : Alexander Robertson, Malcolm McDermit, and John Coupland. [SA.IX.12][LER]

ROBERTSON, THOMAS, a shipmaster in Flushing, The Netherlands, married Helen Wood, daughter of the late Alexander Wood, in St Andrews, Fife, on 1 March 1778. [SER]

ROBERTSON, THOMAS, a minister who emigrated to Hudson Island, North America, in 1786. [EMA#52]

ROBERTSON, WILLIAM, a minister in Lochside, a beneficiary under the will of Alexander Deuchar in Barbados, 1738 [NAS.CC8.8.100];

ROBERTSON, WILLIAM, in Longley, minister at Peterhead, Aberdeenshire, 1742. [EV#357]

ROBERTSON, WILLIAM, a minister in Dundee, 1743. [ECD#65]

ROBERTSON, Mrs, of the Perth Episcopalian Congregation, 1742. [TV.77.21][JWI]

RODGER, PHILLIP, and Margaret McLean, both from St Quivox, : married in Ayr, 10 April 1797. [NAS.CH12.26.1]

ROLLAND, PATRICK MIDDLETON, daughter (sic) of Mr Rolland a shipmaster, was born on 30 October 1752 and baptised in Leith on 2 November 1752. Mr

Grant was surety, while George Anderson, the two grandmothers, and Mrs Grant, : witnesses. [SA.IX.13][LER]

RONALD, ALEXANDER, a minister who emigrated to Virginia in 1760. [EMA#52][FPA#308/330]

ROSE, ALEXANDER, son of the Prior of Monymusk, married Euphame Threipland at Kilspindie, Perthshire, on 27 April 1676, parents of Patrick born 31 December in Perth, Alexander born 2 January 1679 in Perth, Arthur born 22 September in Perth – died 8 April 1700, Euphame born 4 December 1683 in Glasgow, Barbara born February 1685 in Glasgow, John born 30 April 1687 in Glasgow, Anna born 9 May 1689 in Edinburgh, James born 29 February 1692 in the Citadel of Leith, David born 2 March 1694 in Canongate, Alexander born 19 April 1696 in Canongate, and Charles born 4 October 1698 in Canongate. He graduated MA from King's College, Aberdeen, a divinity student in Glasgow, minister in Perth, Bishop of Moray, 1686-1687, Bishop of Edinburgh 1687 to 1688 when deposed, Primus in 1704, a minister in Edinburgh 1713, died 20 March 1720 in White Horse Close, Canongate, buried at Restalrig. [JSC][Keith#64/155]

ROSE, ALEXANDER, born 1653 son of David Rose of Earlsmill, Nairn, graduated MA from King's College, Aberdeen, 1673, schoolmaster at Inverness 1673-1680, minister of Cairney, Drumdelgie and Ruthven, 1680 -1716, deposed as a Jacobite in 1716, died in 1720, husband of Anna Gordon, parents of Alexander and David Episcopal minister at Lethnot. [F.6.303][TBD#2]

ROSE, ALEXANDER, 'who is to be pedagogue to Mr Stevenson's children near Dunfermline – he has two brothers, priests in America', letter, 1742. [NAS.CH12.23.302]

ROSE, CHARLES, son of John Rose and his wife Mary Grant in Wester Alves, Moray, emigrated to Barbados in 1732, in St Peter's, Parham, Antigua, 1732, later in Virginia by 1736, minister of Copley parish, Virginia, died 1761. [SA1#31][EMA#53][WMQ.2.22.532][FPA#279]

ROSE, CHARLES, [nephew of Reverend Patrick Rose in Barbados], a schoolmaster in Christ Church, Barbados, from 1728 to 1731, rector of St Peter's, Antigua, from 1732, Depute Judge of the Admiralty Court there, graduated Doctor of Law at King's College, Aberdeen, 28 January 1748; in Antigua 1753. [F.Ab#447][NAS.CS96/644][FPA#192/234/283]

ROSE, CHARLES, Bishop of Dunblane and Dunkeld, from 1774 until his death in April 1791. [TBD#9][Keith#540/548]

ROSE, DAVID, MA, son of the minister of Cairney, was ordained in Aberdeen in 1723, later minister at Woodside of Dunlappie, was father of George Rose born 17 January and baptised 18 January 1744, also of Stewart Rose born 22 October and baptised 23 October 1747, and of Margaret born 1741 who died in Montrose during 1831. Reverend David Rose died in 1758 and was buried in Lethnot Church, Angus. [DUAS.BrMsDC3/174]

ROSE, GEORGE, born 17 January 1744, married Theodora, daughter of John Dues of Antigua, he died in January 1818. [DUAS.BrMsDC3/174]

ROSE, JAMES, a minister in Fife, Bishop of Glasgow from 1726 until his death in March 1733. [Keith#552]

ROSE, JAMES, a minister in Old Aberdeen, a beneficiary under the will of Alexander Deuchar in Barbados, 1738 [NAS.CC8.8.100];

ROSE, JOHN, a merchant, married Catherine, daughter of Dr Chalmers in St Paul's, Aberdeen, on 27 September 1772. [SPAER]

ROSE, PATRICK, a minister who emigrated to Barbados in 1727, minister of St Andrew's in 1730, minister of St James's there from 1740 to 1741. [EMA#53][St James's parish register][FPA#231]

ROSE, PATRICK, in Inchbrakie, near Crieff, Perthshire, was ordained a deacon, 1768. [TBD#225]

ROSE, ROBERT, born 1704, son of John Rose and his wife Mary Grant, in Wester Alves, Moray, emigrated to Virginia in 1725, minister of St Anne's parish, Essex County, 1725 to 1746, of St Anne's parish, Albemarle County, 1747 to 1751, died 30 June 1751, buried Richmond, Virginia. [VMHB.87.361][OC#2/48]

ROSS, AENEAS, possibly son of Reverend George Ross in Delaware, a Society for the Propagation of the Gospel missionary to Pennsylvania in 1741, minister in Oxford and Whitemarsh by 1743. [EMA#53][FPA#18/110/111][LIS.5.129]

ROSS, ALEXANDER, was confirmed in Arpafilie, Ross-shire, in 1770. [EV#327]

ROSS, ARTHUR, son of Alexander Ross minister of Birse, educated at St Andrews, minister in Aberdeenshire, in Glasgow 1665 to 1676, Bishop of Argyll , Bishop of Glasgow 1679, Bishop of St Andrews 1684 to 1689 when deposed, died 13 June 1704. [Keith#43]

ROSS, DANIEL, a tailor, married Elizabeth Clerk a servant maid, in Edinburgh, 10 June 1757. [DUAS: BrMS3/Dc/12]

ROSS, GEORGE, born around 1680 in Ross-shire, educated at Edinburgh University, emigrated to New Jersey in 1705, minister of New Castle parish, Delaware, from 1705 until 1708, prisoner in France 1711, later in Chester, Pennsylvania, 1713-1754, died 1754. [SCHR.14.147][EMA#53][FPA#17/109][LIS.5.69/89]

ROSS, HUGH, and Jean Campbell, both of Catrine, Sorn parish, Ayrshire, : married in Ayr, 15 August 1796. [NAS.CH12.26.1]

ROSS, ISABEL, daughter of John Ross a flesher, was baptised in Aberdeen on 11 September 1720. Witnesses : Alexander Charles an advocate and Robert Weir a periwig-maker. [SPAER]

ROSS, JEAN, daughter of Patrick Ross a merchant in Aberdeen, was baptised in Aberdeen on 24 October 1720. Witnesses : James Robertson late a bailie, and Hugh Ross a pewterer. [SPAER]

ROSS, JOHN, educated at Aberdeen University, a minister who emigrated to Maryland in 1754, settled in All Hallows parish, Worcester County, Maryland, died 1780 at Snowhill on the Eastern Shore of Maryland. [EMA#53][NAS.CS16.1.179][FPA#301]

ROSS, JOHN, son of the laird of Ardnage, Aberdeenshire, an Indian trader at Fort Pitt, then a planter and merchant in East Florida, manager of William Elliot's estate in East Florida before 1775, elected a Member of the East Florida

Assembly in 1781, land grant in Indiantown Creek there, a Loyalist who settled in Dominica in 1785. [NAS.GD180]

ROSS, MARGARET and **SOPHIA,** daughters of John Ross in East Florida by a negro slave, : baptised in Ardnadge, Ellon, Aberdeenshire, on 16 September 1782. [CTER]

ROSS, ROBERT, born 1774, from Dornoch, Easter Ross, a grocer in Edinburgh, died 1861. [St John's, Edinburgh, MI]

ROSS, WILLIAM, a barber and wigmaker in Arbroath, Angus, 1752. [SRS.13.79]

ROWE, BENJAMIN, a collier from the parish of St Quivox, and Jean Samson of the Newton, : married in Ayr, 7 June 1800. [NAS.CH12.26.1]

ROW, ROBERT, son of John Row, a collier in Newton, and his wife Janet ....., was baptised in Ayr on 29 November 1799. [NAS.CH12.26.1]

RUDDIMAN, ROBERT, son of Walter Ruddiman junior, a printer, was baptised in Edinburgh on 3 July 1759. Witnesses : Robert and William Auld, Mrs Auld, and Mrs Hay. [LER][SA.X.11]

RUDDIMAN, THOMAS, Keeper of the Advocate's Library and a trustee of the Carruber's Close congregation, Edinburgh, 1741. [JSC#84]

RUSSELL, ANDREW, from the parish of Cupar, Fife, married Sophia Pirie, in St Andrews on 14 November 1771. [SER]

RUSSELL, JOHN, a writer, and spouse Margaret Fraser, parents of Margaret baptised in Milne's Square, Edinburgh, 8 March 1761. [DUAS.BrMsDC3/12]

RUTHERFORD, JOHN, of the Perth Episcopalian Congregation, 1742. [TV.77.21][JWI]

RYAN, THOMAS, married Elizabeth Russel, in Ayr, 27 January 1779. [NAS.CH12.26.1]

SAMPSON, JEAN, in Little Milne, was confirmed in Forfar in 1770. [EF#26]

SANDERS, ROBERT, of the Perth Episcopalian Congregation, 1742. [TV.77.21][JWI]

SANDERSON, PATRICK, born 1759, a banker, died 1830, husband of Helen Christie, born 1772, died 1849. [St John's, Edinburgh, MI]

SANDFORD, DANIEL KEYR, son of Reverend Daniel Sandford and his wife Helen Frances, was born on 3 February 1798 and baptised in St John the Evangelist, Edinburgh, on 26 February 1798. [NAS.CH12.3.26/3]

SANDISON, JANET, daughter of Thomas Sandison a mason in Aberdeen, was baptised 25 September 1720. Witnesses : Robert Smith a blacksmith and Alexander Frazer a glover. [SPAER]

SANGSTER, JAMES, a Writer to the Signet, a trustee of the Carruber's Close congregation, Edinburgh, 1741. [JSC#83]

SCHOLICK, JOSEPH, a soldier of the Princess of Wales Light Dragoons, and Janet Orr, from Kirkoswald, Ayrshire, : married in Ayr, 16 April 1798. [NAS.CH12.26.1]

SCOTT, ALEXANDER, born 20 July 1686, son of John Scott and his wife Marjory Stuart in Dipple, Morayshire, a minister who emigrated to Virginia in 1710, settled in Overwharton parish, Stafford County, died 1 April 1738, buried at Dipple, Stafford County, testament 1739, Comm. Edinburgh. [NAS.CC8.8.101][EMA#53][OC#197][SNQ.2.24][F.4.402][Aquia MI][FPA#177]

SCOTT, CHARLOTTE SOPHIA, daughter of Walter Scott, an advocate, and his wife Margaret Charlotte, was born 24 October 1799, and baptised in St John the Evangelist, Edinburgh, on 15 November 1799. [NAS.CH12.3.26/7]

SCOTT, DAVID, born 1758, a mason in Montrose, Angus, died 1827, his wife Jane Aitken, born 1756, died 1839. [Montrose Episcopal MI]

SCOTT, HERCULES, of Brotherton, husband of Helen Ramsay born 1681, died 1767.[Montrose Episcopal MI]

SCOTT, JAMES, born 1699 in Dipple, Morayshire, son of Reverend John Scott and his wife Helen Grant, emigrated to America before 1719, minister of Dettingen parish, Prince William County, Virginia, and later Westwood parish there, died 1782. [VG#593][NAS.RS29.5.228/7; 216/8; 172][OC#198]

SCOTT, JAMES, son of James Scott a Writer to the Signet, was baptised in North Leith on 2 May 1751. James Scott of Hawden was godfather, Mrs Girzel and Rachel Marjoribanks (aunts of the child) : godmothers. [LER][SA.X.10]

SCOTT, JOHN, minister of Dipple, Morayshire, died 1725.[EM#153]

SCOTT, JOHN, a cleric who emigrated to Jamaica in 1716, minister of St Catherine's, Spanish Town, from 1716. [EMA#54][FPA#253/255]

SCOTT, JAMES, a mariner in Dundee, 1727. [ECD#24]

SCOTT, JOHN, of Lees, a letter, 1738. [NAS.GD1.1052]

SCOTT, JOHN, born in Virginia February 1745, educated at King's College, Aberdeen, a minister who emigrated to Maryland in 1769, settled in Dettingen parish, Prince William County, Virginia, husband of Elizabeth Innes, probate 1785 Fauquier County. [EMA#54][FPA#302/326]

SCOTT, JOHN, was confirmed in Forfar, Angus, in 1770. [EF#26]

SCOTT, JOHN, from Old Deer, Aberdeenshire, and Ann Massie, daughter of the late William Massie, : married at Berry Mill, Aberdeenshire, on 19 January 1799. [NAS.CH12.32.2]

SCOTT, JOHN, of Criggie, late merchant in Gothenburg, Sweden, died 1778, testament, Comm. Brechin. [NAS]; husband of Agnes Aitken, died 1807. [Montrose Episcopal MI]

SCOTT, ROBERT, a cleric who emigrated to Maryland in 1708, minister of All Faith's parish, Maryland. [EMA#54][FPA#37]

SCOTT, THOMAS, born 1771, a merchant, died 1834, his wife Jean Ranken, born 17724, died 1826. [St John's, Edinburgh, MI]

SCOTT, WILLIAM, of Hightown, a merchant in Edinburgh, married Elizabeth, daughter of Robert Graeme, in Kinloch's Close, Edinburgh, 24 June 1762. [DUAS: BrMS3/Dc/12]

SCOTT, WILLIAM, a minister who emigrated to the West Indies in 1764, a minister on Nevis, 1770. [EMA#54][FPA#286]

Scots Episcopalians at Home and Abroad, 1689-1800

**SCOTT, ..., **a child of George Scott a mason, was buried in Brechin, Angus, on 15 May 1800. [NNQ.14.154]

SCOUGAL, PATRICK, born 1610,son of Sir John Scougal of that Ilk, a minister in East Lothian, Bishop of Aberdeen from 1664 to his death on 16 February 1682. [Keith#133]

SCRIMGEOUR, JOHN, a minister at Nomine, Westmoreland County, Virginia, probate, 1693 PCC.

SCROGIE, JOHN, son of James Scrogie and his wife Margaret Muir, in Nether Ulaw, Aberdeenshire, was baptised on 9 October 1763. [CBER]

SETON, WILLIAM, a Writer to the Signet, a trustee of the Carruber's Close congregation, Edinburgh, 1741. [JSC#83]

SEATON, Reverend WILLIAM, born 1679, Dean of Dunkeld, died in Forfar, Angus, on 13 February 1754. [TBD#161]

SEMPILL, GEORGE, a minister in Perth, 1743. [ECD#72]

SEMPLE, JAMES, born 18 May 1730, son of Reverend James Semple and his wife Margaret Glennie in Dreghorn, Ayrshire, a minister, to Virginia, 1760, settled in St Peter's, New Kent County, died 1787. [FPA#330][WMQ.1.26.176]

SEMPLE, JOHN, born 17 October 1727, son of Reverend James Semple and his wife Margaret Glennie in Dreghorn, emigrated in 1752, settled in Rosemount, King and Queen County, Virginia, died 1773, probate 6 May 1783, Prince William County, Va. [WMQ.1.9.175; 2.22.345][CAG.1.900]AGB.1.243] [VMHB.92.282][NAS.B10.15.7082; CS230.19.21]

SEMPLE, THOMAS, a butcher in Berwick on Tweed, married Jane Robertson, of the same parish, in Haddington, East Lothian, on 19 January 1792. Witnesses : William White and James Nisbet. [NAS.CH12.2.2.18][HEC]

SETON, JANET, daughter of the late George Seton an Episcopalian minister at Burghton and then at Fyvie, Aberdeenshire, widow of Lachlan Seton a sergeant of the Regiment of Foot Guards, 1714. [NAS.GD18.2701]

SETON, JAMES, on St Vincent, 1792. [FPA#291]

SETON, WILLIAM, Dean of Dunkeld, a non-jurant minister in Forfar, Angus, from 1727, 1743, later in Dundee, a Jacobite in 1745, a letter of 1751. [LPR#234][TBD#5/21/42][NAS.CH12.23.764]

SEYMOUR, JAMES, educated at King's College, Aberdeen, a minister who emigrated to Georgia, 1771, settled in St Paul's parish, a Loyalist army chaplain in St Augustine, Florida, died at sea. [FPA#300/325][NA.AO12.102.101]

SHANKS, JOHN, in Glencatt, was father of David Shanks baptised at Lochlee, Angus, on 9 July 1727. Witnesses : David Edward and John Edward in Miln. [DUAS.BrMsDC3/174]

SHANKS, JOHN, and his wife Sarah Gillespie or Glasford, a weaver in Arbroath, Angus,1752. [SRS.13.80]

SHARP, JAMES, and his wife Margaret, in Strageth, Muthill, Perthshire, parents of Jean born 30 December 1697 and baptised 2 January 1698. [MRB]

SHARP, JOHN, educated at King's College, Aberdeen, a minister who emigrated to Virginia in 1699, settled in Virginia and New York, and in the Leeward Islands in 1701. [EMA#54][F.Ab.442][KCA#99]

SHARP, WILLIAM, and his wife Margaret Hamilton, parents of William born on 27 June and baptised on 28 June 1723 in St Andrews; Margaret born 27 October and baptised 6 November 1724 in St Andrews; William born on 15 May and baptised on 21 May 1726, in St Andrews; Penelope born 23 April and baptised 27 April 1727, in St Andrews; William born on 28 January and baptised on 29 January 1729. [SER]

SHARP, WILLIAM, son of William Sharp and his wife Anne More, was born on 24 August and baptised 27 August 1728 at Leuchars Castle. [SER]

SHAW, JOHN, a writer, married Christian, daughter of the late Robert Murray a merchant tin Edinburgh, in Mr Shand's house, 29 April 1738. [DUAS: BrMS3/Dc/12]

SHIELS, HECTOR, a wright, married Anne, daughter of the late William Garrioch in Leith, in South Leith on 28 June 1743. Witnesses : Dr Garrioch, William Frazer, Alexander Tod, and John Young. [LER][NNQ.8.125]

SIBBALD, CHARLES, son of James Sibbald of Kinkell and his wife Margaret Strachan, was born and baptised on 17 August 1723 in St Andrews, Fife. [SER]

SIBBALD, CHARLES, and Anne Irons, : married on 6 August 1786 in St Andrews. [SER]

SIME, JOHN, a Writer to the Signet, and his wife .....Ravenscroft, parents of John baptised at powderhall, Edinburgh, on 5 October 1755. Witnesses : William Gordon, Mrs Scott, and Mrs Alexander of Alloa; James baptised at Cotes near the Colt-bridge, on 2 August 1758. Witnesses : Mrs Andrew Alves and Miss Maxwell. [DUAS.Br.MS3.DC/12]

SINCLAIR, ANNE, at Thurdystaff, was confirmed at Thurso, Caithness, on 8 August 1762. [DC#277]

SINCLAIR, JEAN, Lady Barrack, daughter of Sinclair of Freswick, was baptised and confirmed in Leith on 2 August 1769. Witnessed by Mrs Forbes. [SA.IX.12/14][LER]

SINCLAIR, ROBERT, born 1685, a missionary of the Society for the Propagation of the Gospels at Newcastle, Delaware, from 1709 to 1711. [SCHR.14.147]

SINCLAIR, ..., Lady Scotscaddell, was confirmed at Thurso, Caithness, on 8 August 1762. [DC#277]

SIVEWRIGHT, KATHERINE, daughter of John Sivewright in Brechin was batised on 30 May 1798. [NNQ.14.99]

SIVEWRIGHT, NORMAN, son of Alexander Sivewright, educated at Marischal College, Aberdeen, 1744-1748, minister in Brechin, 1769. [NAS.CH12.13.43] [MCA#317][TBD#227]

SIVEWRIGHT, ..., daughter of Alexander Sivewright in Upper Tenements, Brechin, Angus, was baptised on 13 May 1798. [NNQ.14.99]

SKENE, ELIZABETH, relict of James Milne sometime Episcopal minister in Aberdeen, testament, 29 December 1762, Comm. Aberdeen. [NAS]

SKENE, GEORGE, born 1727, baptised 9 October 1749 in Blairgowrie, Perthshire. [TBD#151]

SKENE, GEORGE, a minister, to South Carolina, 1761,rector of Prince Frederick parish, South Carolina, 1762, dead by 1766. [FPA#154/155/329]

SKENE, GEORGE, of Careston, son of James Skene in Aberdeen, educated at Marischal College, Aberdeen, ordained Deacon to serve at Blacklunans 1750, ordained 1752, minister at Forfar from 1754 to 1797, died in Forfar, Angus, on 19 April 1797. [EF#25/31] [MCA#357]

SKENE, JOHN, youngest son of Reverend Skene, was confirmed in Forfar, Angus, in 1770. [EF#26]

SKINNER, JOHN, baptised in 1662, son of Laurence Skinner minister of Brechin, minister of Brechin 1687 to 1697, intruded there but deposed, prosecuted and imprisoned, banished from the Presbytery of Brechin in 1710, died in Edinburgh around 1725. Husband of (1) Margaret Little, (2) Jean Guild, father of Margaret. [F.5.380][NAS.CH1.2.42.1]

SKINNER, JOHN, was baptised, as an adult, in Leith on 8 June 1740, and confirmed 9 June 1740. 'Engaged to be tutor to the laird of Salloway's son in Shetland'. [LER][SA.X.9]

SKINNER, JOHN, minister at Keithock, 1743. [ECD#69]

SKINNER, JOHN, born 1721, son of John Skinner schoolmaster in Echt, educated at Marischal College, Aberdeen, 1735-1739, an Episcopal minister in Longside, Aberdeen, ca.1751, died 1807, father of Bishop John Skinner. [NAS.NRAS.2784][MCA#311]

SKINNER, JOHN, son of Reverend Skinner in Aberdeenshire, minister in Aberdeen from 1775, Bishop of Aberdeen from 1786 until his death on 13 July 1816. [Keith#536]

SKINNER, JOHN, born 1769, son of Reverend John Skinner in Aberdeen, educated at Marischal College, Aberdeen, 1783-1787, minister in Banff, Dean of Dunkeld and pastor of St John's, Forfar, for 44 years, died 1841. [MCA#361] [St John's, Forfar, MI]

SKINNER, JOHN, a Lieutenant of Marines, Chatham Division, his wife Maria Susannah Ogilvy, born 1766, died 1788. Montrose Episcopal MI]

SKINNER, WILLIAM, born about 1687, a schoolmaster who emigrated to Philadelphia in 1718, later, from 1722, a missionary of the Society for the Propagation of the Gospels in Amboy, New Jersey, from 1722 until his death in 1758. [SCHR.14.149][EMA.55][LIS.5.89/130][JCTP.1737.37]

SMAILES, AGNES, daughter of Henry Smailes, a collier in Newton, and his wife Barbara ..., was baptised in Ayr on 4 November 1798. [NAS.CH12.26.1]

SMEATON, WALTER, a coachman in the Canongate, Edinburgh, married Jean Shirreff of Haddington, at Captainhead on 8 January 1783. Witnesses : James Shirreff, Richard Shirreff, and J. Henderson. [NAS.CH12.2.2.18][HEC]

SMALL, ROBERT, MA, ordained 1738, missionary of the Society for the Propagation of the Gospel at Christ Church, South Carolina, died September 1739. [LIS.5.89/130]

SMART, ANDREW, in Witton, Lethnott, Angus, father of Andrew baptised 6 September 1725. Witnesses : David Smart there and James Duncan in Meigie. [DUAS.BrMS.DC3/174]

SMART, DAVID, in Witton, Lethnott, Angus, was father of a daughter baptised 21 April 1724. Witnesses : David Tosh in Oldtown and John Lowson in Boguetown. [DUAS.BrMS.DC3/174]

SMART, JOHN, in Wharleston, Lethnott, father of John baptised 17 May 1725. Witnesses : John Lindsay in Tilliebearn and John Duthy in Glen.... [DUAS.BrMS.DC3/174]

SMIETON, JOHN, and his wife Helen Niel, in Tombain, Muthill, Perthshire, : parents of William, born 25 November and baptised 27 November 1697. [MRB]

SMITH, ALEXANDER, a barber and wig-maker in Arbroath, a Jacobite in 1745, residing on Shorehead, Arbroath, Angus, in 1752. [SRS.13.76]

SMITH, ALEXANDER, a journeyman blacksmith, married Helen Greig, in South Leith, on 11 June 1762. Witnesses : David Fife, James Lawson, David Fyfe's wife, etc. [LER][NNQ.8.127]

SMITH, ALEXANDER, born 1756, late shoremaster in Montrose, Angus, died in Stonehaven in 1840, his wife Isobel Renny, born 1766, died in Montrose in 1845. [Montrose Episcopal MI]

SMITH, ELIZABETH, in Little Miln, was confirmed in Forfar, Angus, in 1770. [EF#26]

SMITH, HENRY, a merchant in Dundee, 1727. [ECD#24]

SMITH, HUGH, of Boulogne, France, married Elizabeth Seton of Touch, in Linlithgow, 21 September 1745. [DUAS: BrMS3/Dc/12]

SMITH, JAMES, a merchant in Dundee, 1727. [ECD#24]

SMITH, JAMES, jr., a writer in Edinburgh, married Mrs Katherine, daughter of the late William Ferguson a farmer in Dirleton, at the house of Mrs Kirkwood in South Leith on 14 November 1747. Witnesses : Harry Maule, Hugh Rose, James Smith sr., writers, and Mrs Mary Kirkwood and Mrs Isabel Kirkwood. [LER][NNQ.8.125]

SMITH, JAMES, and Meade Struthers, both of Ayr, : married there, 6 March 1793. [NAS.CH12.26.1]

SMITH, JOHN, a merchant in Dundee, 1727. [ECD#23]

SMITH, WILLIAM, born near Aberdeen in 1727, educated in Aberdeen around 1747, emigrated to New York as a tutor in 1751, returned from London to Pennsylvania in 1753, settled in Chester parish, Kent County, Maryland, first Provost of the College of Philadelphia 1754, Archbishop of Maryland, died at the Falls of Schulkill on 14 May 1803, buried in Philadelphia. [AP#323][EMA#56][SA1#111][FPA#114/328][LIS.5.69][DAB.17.353]

SMITH, WILLIAM, nephew of Reverend Alexander Lunan, was confirmed on 17 November 1769. [SA.IX.14][LER]

SMITH, WILLIAM, an Episcopal minister in Aberdeen from 1734, husband of Mary Turner testament, 23 May 1775, Comm. Aberdeen. [NAS.CH12.12.19]

SMITH, WILLIAM, born 1754 in Aberdeen, son of Dr William Smith. A minister who died in New York on 6 April 1821. [WA]

Scots Episcopalians at Home and Abroad, 1689-1800

SMITH, Mr, of the Perth Episcopalian Congregation, 1742. [TV.77.21][JWI]

SMITH, ..., daughter of Provost Smith, married John Geikie, a cattledealer and farmer at Keithock on 17 December 1797. [NNQ.14.99]

SMITH, ..., two sons of James Smith jr. : baptised in Brechin, Angus, on 30 March 1798, and a daughter on 25 March 1800. [NNQ.14.99/154]

SNELLS, Mrs, of the Perth Episcopalian Congregation, 1742. [TV.77.21][JWI]

SOMERVILLE, JEAN, daughter of Robert Somerville and Katherine Instend his wife, was born 1 January 1775 and baptised in Haddington on 9 January 1775. Witnesses : John Buchanan and Bartholemew Bower. [NAS.CH12.2.13]

SOUTAR, FRANCIS, a wright in Arbroath, Angus, husband of Katherine Gray, 1752. [SRS.13.64]

SOUTAR, JAMES, born 1712, a merchant and brewer in Applegate, Arbroath, Angus, spouse of Margaret Wilson, parents of Robert born 1752. [SRS.13.59]

SOUTER, ROBERT, son of Robert Souter a tailor in Dundee, was baptised in Dundee on 27 July 1725. [BNDBR]

SPARK, ROBERT, son of John Spark in Montrose, Angus, educated at Marischal College, Aberdeen, 1776-1780, minister in Drumlithie and Laurencekirk, Kincardineshire. [MCA#351]

SPEAR, JOSEPH, Captain in the Royal Navy, born 1754, died 1826. [St John's, Edinburgh, MI]

SPEED, THOMAS, son of James Speed a merchant in Dundee, was baptised in Mrs White's house in Dundee, on 20 October 1722. [BNDBR]

SPENCE, ALEXANDER, died in Brechin, Angus, 24 June 1800. [NNQ.14.154]

SPENCE, JAMES, son of George Spence and his wife Christian Thorn in Inch, Aberdeenshire, to Jamaica in 1698, a schoolmaster and minister in St Mary's, Jamaica, died 1737. [APB.3.57][EBR.102/6294]

SPENS, NATHANIEL, born 1694, an Episcopal clergyman, died in Pittenweem, Fife, in 1772. [DUAS.Br.MS3.DC/12]

SPENS, NATHANIEL, a surgeon, and his wife Mary, daughter of James Mulliken of that Ilk, parents of Jean baptised 5 November 1757 in Old Assembly Close, Edinburgh. Witnesses : Mrs Mulliken, Lathallan and his lady, Miss Douglas, Mrs Houston; Janet, baptised in the Old Assembly Close, on 15 June 1759. Witnesses : Lady Lathallan, William Ingles, Mrs McDowell, and Mrs Douglas; of James baptised in Nydie's Wynd, on 9 November 1761. Witnesses : Robert and Mrs Douglas; Thomas baptised in Martin's Wynd, on 8 August 1763. Witnesses : John McPherson and Mrs Douglas; Alexander baptised in Nydrie's Wynd, on 17 August 1764. Witnesses : Sir Robert Douglas and John McPherson. [DUAS.BrMsDC3/12]

SPENS, THOMAS, of Lathallan, married Janet, daughter of Sir Robert Douglas of Glenbervie, in 1721, parents of Thomas, Robert, William, Nathaniel, Alexander, and three daughters. [DUAS.Br.MS3.DC/12]

SPOONER, JOSEPH, born 1728, minister of St Peter's chapel for 22 years, died 1779, wife Christian Dickson, born 1745, died 1782. [Montrose Episcopal MI]

STEPHEN, ANDREW, a brewer in Broughton, married Marjory Murray, daughter of the late John Sutherland portioner of Keam, in Fountain Close, Edinburgh, 22 April 1740. [DUAS: BrMS3/Dc/12]

STEPHEN, JOHN, born 1740 in Gaitly, a minister who emigrated to Tobago in 1764 and later in Maryland, died there 1784. [EMA#57][FPA#318]

STEPHEN, WILLIAM, married Katherine Dorward in 1748, parents of Jean, residing in Millgate, Arbroath, Angus, 1752. [SRS.13.88]

STEPHEN, WILLIAM, from New Machar, Aberdeenshire, graduated from King's College, Aberdeen, 1764, a minister in Jamaica. [KCA#244]

STEPHEN, WILLIAM, from the parish of Craig, Angus, and Isabel Stuart in Fraserburgh, Aberdeenshire, married there on 3 June 1804. [NAS.CH12.32.2]

STEUART, JOHN, a minister who emigrated to New York in 1770. [EMA#57]

STEVEN, ALEXANDER, a merchant in Montrose, Angus, husband of Mary Davidson, parents of James died 1794, David born 1789, died 1796, Thomas, born 1805, died 1807, Alexander, born 1790, died 1807, and Robert, born 1796, died 1807. [Montrose Episcopal MI]

STEVENSON, JOHN, a merchant in Arbroath, Angus, married Margaret Spark in 1731, parents of John later a surgeon in Arbroath, 1752. [SRS.13.74]

STEVENSON, JOHN, master of the sloop Otter of London, married Helen Booth from Peterhead, in Haddington, East Lothian, on 9 October 1791. Witnesses : Adam Stevenson and Thomas Hay. [NAS.CH12.2.2.18][HEC]

STEWART, ALEXANDER, a cleric who emigrated to New York in 1703. [EMA#57]

STEWART, ALEXANDER, a minister who emigrated to North Carolina in 1753. [EMA#57][FPA#304/327]

STEWART, ALEXANDER, confirmed in Ballachulish, Argyll, in 1770. [EV#344]

STEWART, ANDREW, was baptised at Glasclune, near Blairgowrie, Perthshire, on 20 March 1742. [TBD#41]

STEWART, ANN, was confirmed in Ballachulish, Argyll, in 1770. [EV#344]

STEWART, ARCHIBALD, a merchant in Edinburgh and trustee of the Carruber's Close congregation, 1741; and his wife Charlotte Baillie, : parents of John baptised in Smith's Land, Edinburgh, on 15 November 1754. Witnesses : John Hamilton, John McFarlane, and James Guild – all writers, also Alexander Stewart and Nellie Murray. [JSC#83] [DUAS: BrMS3/Dc/12]

STEWART, CECILIA, daughter of Alexander Stewart and his wife Margaret Fairfoul, was born 7 November and baptised on 7 November 1727 in Leuchars, Fife. [SER]

STEWART, CHARLES, a shoemaker, married Elizabeth Threipland a mantua maker, in Canongate 11 April 1758; parents of James baptised in Canongate on 4 February 1759. Witnesses : Mrs James Smyth, Mrs Joseph Robertson, and John Graham a writer. [DUAS: BrMS3/Dc/12]

STEWART, DANIEL, of the 2nd Battalion of Argyllshire Fencibles, and Elizabeth Davies from St Quivox, : married in Ayr on 30 August 1795. [NAS.CH12.26.1]

STEWART, DONALD, a chairman, father of Aneas baptised in Edinburgh on 11 July 1752. Witnesses : James Stewart, Aneas and Margaret Campbell. [DUAS.BrMsDC3/12]

STEWART, DUNCAN, born 1660, son of Donald Stewart of Invernahyle, graduated MA from Glasgow University 1675, minister at Dunoon 1689, deprived in 1690, an Episcopalian preacher who intruded at Blair Atholl, Perthshire, from 1709 to 1718, dead by 1730. [F.4.144]

STEWART, GILBERT, a merchant, married Margaret Gardens relict of ..... Hunter a merchant, at Bonnyhaugh, Edinburgh, 13 October 1742. [DUAS: BrMS3/Dc/12]

STEWART, HUGH, a chairmaster, father of Katherine baptised in Kennedy's Close, Edinburgh, on 4 December 1762. [DUAS.BrMsDC3/12]

STEWART, JAMES, a writer, married Alison Ruddiman, at Thomas Ruddiman's house, Parliament Close, Edinburgh, 4 September 1747; parents of Thomas Ruddiman baptised in Writer's Court, on 17 September 1754. Witnesses : William Inglis, Isabel Bailie, and Lady Mackenzie; Cecilia baptised at Moultrie's Hill, on 3 August 1758. Witnesses : Messrs Paton, Gray, W. Ruddiman, and Hutton; Charles baptised at Moulter's Hill, on 18 September 1760; William baptised at Moulter's Hill, on 10 June 1763. Witnesses : William Inglis, John Hutton, ...Munro, and ....Gardener; Frances baptised 5 October 1764. Witnesses : Mrs Stewart of Loudon, W. Ruddiman, Robert Gray, and Mrs Threipland. [DUAS: BrMS3/Dc/12]

STEWART, JAMES, of Allanbank, an advocate, father of Margaret baptised on 22 October 1752 in Smith's Land, Edinburgh. Witnesses : Mrs Smith, Mrs Barbara Smith, Barbara Walkinshaw and William Sellar. [DUAS.BrMsDC3/12]

STEWART, JOHN, born 1716, a glover, of the Perth Episcopalian Congregation, 1742, died 27 February 1782. [TV.77.21][JWI][Greyfriars MI]

STEWART, JOHN, son of John Stewart a writer in Edinburgh, and his wife Christian Graham, was baptised by Alexander Howie an Episcopal minister, on 30 April 1750. [NAS.GD38.1.907]

STEWART, JOHN, the younger of Allanbank, married Agnes, daughter of Charles Smith of Boulogne, France, at Murray's Hall near Stirling, 9 October 1750. [DUAS: BrMS3/Dc/12]

STEWART, JOHN, a minister at Tain, Easter Ross, 1761. [EV#360]

STEWART, JOHN, was confirmed in Arpafilie, Ross-shire, in 1770. [EV#327]

STEWART, JOHN, was confirmed in Ballachulish, Argyll, in 1770. [EV#344]

STEWART, JOHN, and his wife Janet Richard in Crieff, Perthshire, : parents of Henry born 16 April and baptised 18 April 1775. [MRB]

STEWART, JOHN, a minister, from London to Georgia, 1781. [FPA#325]

STEWART, JOHN, eldest son and second child of Charles Stewart and his wife Amelia Oliphant, was born at Ardblair on 7 August 1799 and baptised on 25 August 1799, by Hugh Duncan an Episcopal minister at Over Lethanty, Perthshire. [NAS.GD38.1.1160]

STEWART, LILY, was confirmed in Ballachulish, Argyll, in 1770. [EV#344]

STEWART, THOMAS, born 1766, son of James Stewart of Rothesay, Bute, a minister who emigrated to Jamaica in 1792, died in Westmoreland parish, Jamaica, 19 May 1820. [FPA][Savanna la Mar MI][EMA#57]

STEWART, WALTER, ordained 1711, assistant minister in Perth and Auchterarder, minister at Doune 1722 -1728, to Kilmaveonaig, Blair Atholl, Perthshire, in 1728. [TBD#38]

STEWART, WILLIAM, a chairman, married Mary Fairgrieve, near the Netherbow, Edinburgh, 23 December 1747; parents of William baptised in Bell's Wynd, Edinburgh, 23 January 1753. Witness James Stewart a chairmaster. [DUAS: BrMS3/Dc/12]

STEWART, Mrs, was confirmed in Ballachulish, Argyll, in 1770. [EV#344]

STIRLING, ELIZABETH, born 1759, died 1827, wife of William Hamilton, Professor of Anatomy at Glasgow University. [St John's, Edinburgh, MI]

STIRLING, JAMES, a minister who emigrated to Maryland in 1737, later in Massachusetts. [EMA#57][FPA#81]

STIRLING, JOHN, only son of Sir Alexander Stirling of Glorat, married Gloryanah Fulsome, daughter of Samuel Fulsome of Stratford, Connecticut, in St Andrew's Episcopal Church, Glasgow, on 28 January 1774, witnesses Jean Graham vintner at the Saracen's Head, and her father John Leckie aged 64, in the presence of Sir Alexander Stirling of Glorat and his Lady. [SA.X.21]

STIRLING, MARY, daughter of Sir Harry Stirling of Ardoch, was confirmed on 2 November 1743 in Leith. [SA.IX.13][LER]

STIRLING, ROBERT, born 1772, son of William Stirling of Keir, died in Hampton, St James parish, Jamaica, 28 September 1808. [Kingston Cathedral MI, Jamaica]

STIRLING, Mr, of the Perth Episcopalian Congregation, 1742. [TV.77.21][JWI]

STORMOND, Lady, of the Perth Episcopalian Congregation, 1742. [TV.77.21][JWI]

STRACHAN, ADAM, a schoolmaster who emigrated to the Leeward Islands in 1700. [EMA#57]

STRACHAN, DAVID, a cleric who emigrated to Virginia in 1715. [EMA#57]

STRACHAN, JAMES, a cleric who emigrated to Jamaica in 1713. [EMA#57]

STRACHAN, JAMES, from Auchendoir, Aberdeenshire, a chairman, and wife Jean Touch, parents of Jean baptised in Edinburgh on 13 February 1761. Witnesses : Mrs Jean Rutherford, Adam Hay, and Peter Urquhart. [DUAS.BrMsDC3/12]

STRACHAN, JAMES, married..... Beverley, in Brechin, Angus, on 29 March 1800. [NNQ.14.154]

STRACHAN, JOHN, Bishop of Brechin from 1788 until his death on 28 January 1810. [Keith#546]

STRACHAN, JOHN, born 1777, died near the Cape of Good Hope in 1795. [Montrose, Episcopal MI]

STRACHAN, JOHN, born 1770, a merchant in Montrose, Angus, died 1823. (father of James Ford Strachan a member of the Legislative Council of Victoria, Australia) Wife Helen Howie, born 1774, died 1799. [Montrose Episcopal MI]

STRACHAN, JOHN, born in Aberdeen on 12 April 1778, educated at King's College, Aberdeen, settled in Cornwall, Lower Canada, in 1799, Bishop of Toronto, graduated as a Doctor of Divinity from King's College in 1811, died there on 1 November 1867. [GM.NS3/5.105][ANQ][KCA]

STRACHAN, PATRICK, an Episcopal preacher in Mains parish, 1707. [NAS.CH1.2.27.3/242]

STRACHAN, ROBERT, born 1753, a butcher in Montrose, Angus, died 1802, his wife Jean Wilkie, born 1753, died 1802. [Montrose Episcopal MI]

STRACHAN, ..., daughter of James Strachan a wright in Brechin, Angus, was buried 28 October 1799. [NNQ.14.153]

STRAITON, DAVID, born 1759, a shoemaker, died 1842, husband of Isobel Strachan, born 1757, died 1837. [Montrose Episcopal MI]

STRANGE, BETTY, was confirmed in Forfar, Angus, in 1770. [CF#26]

STRANGE, JAMES, born 1753, died 1840, husband of Anne ...., born 1767, daughter of Viscount Melville, died 1852. [St John's, Edinburgh, MI]

STRATON, ALEXANDER, born 1763, late Envoy to the Court of Sweden, died Bromley, 1832. [Montrose Episcopal MI]

STRATON, GEORGE, an Episcopal minister in Brechin, Angus, journal, 1776-1819. [NRAS.2701.3.5.15]; born 1744, minister in Brechin for 25 years, died 1820, married (1) Margaret Graham, daughter of Captain John Graham of Duchray in Perthshire, she died 10 August 1781, (2) Euphemia Cleric of Hillhead, Caputh, 2 November 1808. [Brechin Cathedral MI][NNQ.14.96]

STROBACH, ANTHONY, a glass engraver, married Sarah Davidson a resident of Glasgow on 25 August 1788 at St Andrew's Episcopal Church in Glasgow. Witnesses : George Younger a merchant, Robert Miller a coppersmith, and Simon Sorge or Soreg a clockmaker. [SA.X.22]

STUART, ALEXANDER, son of Alexander Stuart and his wife Margaret Fairful, was born on 15 May 1723, baptised in Leuchars, Fife, on 19 May 1723. [SER]

STUART, ARCHIBALD, son of Archibald Stuart, a weaver in Muirkirk, Ayrshire, and his wife Janet ...., was baptised in Ayr on 17 August 1798. [NAS.CH12.26.1]

STUART, DAVID, emigrated to America, 1715, minister of St Paul's parish, King George County, Virginia, 1722 to 1749, died 1749. [OC#187][CCVC#49]

STUART, ELIZA, was confirmed in Forfar, Angus, in 1770. [EF#26]

STUART, FRANCIS, Captain of the 26th Infantry Regiment, married Mary Nicholson, a spinster from London, in Haddington, East Lothian, on 6 August 1772. [NAS.CH12.2.2.18][HEC]

STUART, GEORGE, married Jane Bright, in Ayr, 30 January 1779. [NAS.CH12.26.1]

STUART, JAMES, a minister who emigrated to Virginia in 1766. [EMA#57][FPA#309/330]

STUART, JAMES, of Haddington, married Mary, widow of the Francis Stuart a Major of the 26th Infantry Regiment in Edinburgh on 21 March 1780. Witnesses : Mary Boyd, Alexander Wood, and David Boyd. [NAS.CH12.2.2.18][HEC]

STUART, JEAN, was confirmed in Forfar, Angus, in 1770. [EF#26]

STUART, JOHN, a minister who emigrated to New York, 1770. [FPA#327]

STUART, MARGARET, was confirmed in Forfar, Angus, in 1770. [EF#26]

STUART, WILLIAM, a minister who emigrated to Virginia in 1746. [EMA#57]

STURROCK, ANNIE, in Pitreuchy, was confirmed in Forfar in 1770. [EF#26]

STURROCK, JEAN, in Pitreuchy, was confirmed in Forfar in 1770. [EF#26]

SUTHERLAND, ELIZABETH, daughter of Lieutenant Duffus and his wife Lady Sinclair of Olrich, was confirmed in Leith on 29 August 1767. [SA.IX.14][LER]

SUTHERLAND, ISABELLA, grand-daughter of Sutherland of Wester, was confirmed at Wester, Caithness, on 12 August 1762. [DC#277]

SUTHERLAND, ..., of Woodend, father of Euphame baptised in the house of William Sutherland a brewer on 2 April 1756. Witnesses : Mrs Budge, Peter Ramsay, and ...Richardson. [DUAS.BrMsDC3/12]

SUTHERLAND, WILLIAM, grand-son of Sutherland of Wester, was confirmed at Wester, Caithness, on 12 August 1762. [DC#277]

SUTTER, JAMES, a farmer on the Links of Montrose, Angus, husband of Margaret Ferrier, born 1738, died 1791. [Montrose Episcopal MI]

SWAN, WILLIAM, born 1658, son of Reverend Alexander Swan and Jean Leslie, educated at King's College, Aberdeen, minister at Pitsligo, Aberdeenshire, from 1689 until he was deposed in 1716 as a Jacobite, an Episcopal minister in Fraserburgh and later at Cairns of Pittulie, died 1742, husband of Grizel Robertson, parents of Alexander and William. [F.6.234]

SWANSON, JANET, and her son, : confirmed at Thurso, Caithness, on 8 August 1762. [DC#277]

SYME, THOMAS, a non jurant preacher in Ardgask, Errol, Perthshire, a Jacobite soldier in 1745. [LPR#236]

TASKER, JAMES, son of William Tasker a smith in Cottarton of Craigie, was baptised in Dundee on 4 September 1725. [BNDBR]

TASKER, WILLIAM, in Dundee, 1727. [ECD#26]

TAYLOR, GEORGE, a sailor in Leith, and Penelope Ramsay : married on 1 September 1738 by Alexander McKenzie in 1 September 1738. Witnesses : Robert Broun and Alexander Arbuthnott, both in Edinburgh. [SLIM#520]

TAYLOR, JAMES, a minister at Thurso, Caithness, a beneficiary under the will of Alexander Deuchar in Barbados, 1738 [NAS.CC8.8.100]; 1761. [EV#361]

TAYLOR, JOSEPH, of the Perth Episcopalian Congregation, 1742. [TV.77.21][JWI]

TAYLOR, ..., an Episcopalian minister who emigrated to America in 1785. [NAS.CH12.224.595]

TEMPLE, ROBERT, and his wife Margaret Turnbull, in Cloysterseat, Udny, Aberdeenshire, parents of Charles baptised 14 March 1764. [CBER]

TEMPLE, ROBERT, and his wife Margaret Simpson in Crawhill, Aberdeenshire, parents of Elizabeth and Margaret baptised 9 October 1777. [CTER]

TENNANT, WILLIAM, a heel-maker, married Margaret Turnbull, in Edinburgh, 30 July 1750. [DUAS: BrMS3/Dc/12]

THOMSON, ALEXANDER, in Dundee, 1727. [ECD#26]

THOMSON, ALEXANDER, was confirmed at Thurso, Caithness, on 8 August 1762. [DC#277]

THOMPSON, ANDREW, born 1673, educated at Marischal College, Aberdeen, 1691, resident of Stonehaven, Kincardineshire, a cleric who emigrated to Virginia in 1712, settled Elizabeth City, Hampton County, died 1 September 1719, testament confirmed, 3 May 1727, Commissariat of Edinburgh. [NAS][EMA#58]

THOMSON, CHARLES FRIER, son of John Deas Thomson and his wife Rebecca, was born on 9 December 1797 and baptised in St John the Evangelist, Edinburgh, on 19 January 1798. [NAS.CH12.3.26/3]

THOMPSON, GAVIN, a surgeon in the Royal Navy, married Isabella Nairn from Edinburgh, in Haddington, East Lothian, on 15 October 1775. [NAS.CH12.2.2.18][HEC]

THOMSON, JAMES, and his wife Margaret Duncan, parents of Margaret born 24 June and baptised 27 June in St Andrews, Fife; Andrew born 29 August and baptised 30 August 1724; Elizabeth born and baptised in St Andrews on 5 January 1727; and Christian born on 25 December and baptised on 26 December 1728 in St Andrews. [SER]

THOMSON, JAMES, in Whigington was father of David Thomson, baptised at Lochlee, Angus, on 16 October 1727. Witnesses : David Rose minister in Lethnott and Lochlee and John Nicoll in Shenlie. Also of Anna Thomson baptised at Lochlee on 15 February 1731. Witnesses : John Thomson there and Donald Nicoll in Shealie. [DUAS.BrMsDC3/174]

THOMSON, JAMES, son of James Thomson in Aberdeen, educated at Marischal College, 1745 to 1748, to America in 1767, a tutor then minister in Leeds parish, Fauquier County, Virginia, from 1769, died 1812. [EMA#59][OC#219]

THOMSON, JAMES, a wheelwright, married (1) Florence Dunbar, in South Leith on 27 June 1754. Witnesses : John Barrass, Walter Scott, Mrs Crokatt and her daughter, also Isabell Hood; (2) Janet Grant, in South Leith, on 16 July 1761. Witnesses : Thomas Dow, Donald Cameron, Marjory Grant, and Mrs Murray. [LER][NNQ.8.127]

THOMSON, JOHN, educated at Marischal College, Aberdeen, 1715, and at Edinburgh University, emigrated 1739, minister at St Mark's parish, Culpepper County, Virginia, 1740- to 1772, died 1772. [EMA#58][OC#2/77, 78]

THOMSON, JOHN, in Whigingtown, was father of David Thomson baptised at Lochlee, Angus, on 5 July 1730. Witnesses : David Rose minister at Tullybirnie, David Archibald in Glen Effock, and David Campbell in Ardoch. [DUAS.BrMsDC3/174]

THOMSON, JOHN, born 1738, died 1812, his wife Jean Guise, born 1758, died 1839. [Montrose Eplscopal MI]

THOMSON, JOHN DEAS, son of John Deas Thomson and his wife Rebecca, was baptised in St John the Evangelist, Edinburgh, on 6 June 1799. [NAS.CH12.3.26/7]

THOMSON, ROBERT, son of George Thomson a merchant in Aberdeen, educated at Marischal College, Aberdeen, chaplain to the laird of Edzell, minister of Lethnot and Navar, Angus, from 1685 to 1716, deposed as a Jacobite. [F.5.399]

THOMSON, THOMAS, a schoolmaster in Edinburgh, married Dorothea Moor, at Leith Bowling Green on 3 October 1738. Witnesses : Captain McLeod, William Seton a Writer to the Signet, Mrs Renny, and Mrs Margaret Forbes. [LER][NNQ.8.125]

THOMPSON, THOMAS, son of William Thompson, a weaver in Newton on Ayr, and his wife Marion ..., was baptised in Ayr on 23 June 1799. [NAS.CH12.26.1]

THOMSON, WILLIAM, and Anne McKenzie, relict of David Fisher, late staymaker in Edinburgh, married in Edinburgh on 21 July 1742. [SLIM#617]

THOMPSON, WILLIAM, son of John Thompson and his wife Ann Argo in Pitmeddan, Udny, Aberdeenshire, was baptised 1776. [CTER]

THORNTON, CHARLES, born 1757, died 1833, wife Jane Wood, born 1762, died 1836. [St John's, Forfar, MI]

THORNTON, SUSANNA, was confirmed in Forfar, Angus, in 1770. [EF#26]

THOW, ANDREW, in Arksallerie, was father of Agnes Thow baptised at Lochlee, Angus, on 26 March 1730.Witnesses : James Innes and William McIntire. [DUAS.BrMsDC3/174]

THOW, ROBERT, in Turnabrain, father of Jean Thow baptised at Lochlee, Angus, on 31 August 1735. Witnesses : William Nicoll in Boddam and Andrew Tow in Achsallarie. [DUAS.BrMsDC3/174]

THREIPLAND, Sir STUART, a physician in Edinburgh, married (1) Mrs Janet Sinclair, at Scotstoun, Renfrewshire, 5 March 1753; parents of David baptised in Fountains Close, Edinburgh, on 3 December 1753. Witnesses : Mrs Harper, Mr Budge, and Sir Stuart Threipland; Janet baptised in Fountains Close, on 24 January 1755. Witnesses : Mrs Ferguson, Mrs Harper, and Mrs Sinclair; (2) Janet Murray of Pennyland, in Anchor Close,on 24 July 1761; parents of Patrick baptised in Kinloch's Close, on 9 November 1762; Richard baptised 7 December 1763 in Kinloch's Close. Witnesses : William Budge, Mrs Budge, and Donald Robertson. [DUAS: BrMS3/Dc/12] a member of the Carruber's Close congregation in Edinburgh, 1786. [JSC#82]

TINDAL, MATTHEW, was confirmed in Forfar, Angus, in 1770. [EF#26]

TOD, ANDREW, a merchant in Dundee, 1727. [ECD#24]

TOSH, DAVID, in Finacht, Lethnott, Angus, was father of Elizabeth baptised 27 April 1724. Witnesses : Andrew Smart in Achurie and John Lowson. [DUAS.BrMS.DC3/174]

TOSH, ..., a schoolmaster who emigrated to Jamaica in 1700. [EMA#60]

TOSHOCH, JANET, daughter of John Toshoch and his wife Janet Brown, was born 14 February and baptised 15 February 1728 in St Andrews, Fife. [SER]

TOWER, CHRISTIAN, daughter of Robert Tower a merchant in Aberdeen, was baptised 27 August 1720. Witnesses : William Smith, blacksmith, and William Clerk, gardener. [SPAER]

TOWER, ISABEL, an adult, was baptised in Leith on 14 September 1755. [LER][SA.X.11]

TOWSON, JOHN, son of John Towson a gauger in Dundee, was baptised in Dundee on 23 August 1726. [BNDBR]

TRAIL, AGNES, daughter of William Trail and his wife Isabel Patrick, was born and baptised on 28 March 1724 in St Andrews, Fife. [SER]

TRAIL, MARGARET, daughter of Thomas Trail and his wife Jane Shield, was born on 10 April and baptised on 12 April 1728 in St Andrews, Fife. [SER]

TROTTER, GEORGE, a minister who emigrated to Maryland in 1698. [EMA#60]

TROUP, Captain WILLIAM, and Ann Leslie, : married in Fraserburgh, Aberdeenshire, on 5 March 1791. [NAS.CH12.32.2]

TUFFIE, WILLIAM, of the 44th Regiment, married Grizell Campbell of Ayr, there, 4 April 1790. [NAS.CH12.26.1]

TURING, INGLIS, born 1743, son of Reverend Alexander Turing and his wife Anna Brown in Foveran, Aberdeenshire, emigrated to Jamaica in 1772, rector of St Thomas in the Vale, Jamaica, died in November 1791. [GC#57][GM.61.1235] [EMA#60]

TYTLER, WILLIAM, a Writer to the Signet, father of Patrick baptised in the Cowgate, Edinburgh, on 17 April 1759. Witnesses : Messrs Guthrie and Lindsay. [DUAS.Br.MS3.DC/12]

URE, MARGARET, daughter of Provost Ure, was confirmed in Forfar in 1770. [EF#26]

URQUHART, JAMES, a minister, 1761. [EV#360]

URQUHART, JOHN, a minister in Virginia before 1725, served in William and Mary, then in All Faiths parish, later in Maryland in 1733. [FPA#38] [EMA#61]

URQUHART, JOHN, a shoemaker in Memsie, and Elizabeth Milne, : married in Fraserburgh, Aberdeenshire, on 5 June 1803. [NAS.CH12.32.2]

URQUHART, WILLIAM, a cleric who emigrated to New York in 1704, rector of Jamaica parish, Queen's County, Long Island, died 1709, probate 1710, N.Y. [EMA#61]

VALLANCE, WILLIAM, son of William Vallance and Elizabeth his wife, was born 27 March 1798 and baptised in St John the Evangelist, Edinburgh, on 5 April 1798. [NAS.CH12.3.26/2]

VARE, ALEXANDER, a barber in Rosehearty, and Sophia Hepburn near the Kirk of Pitsligo, : married in Fraserburgh on 11 July 1793. [NAS.CH12.32.2]

VINT, HUGH, son of John Vint and his wife Mary Gibson, was baptised in Ayr on 31 October 1776. [NAS.CH12.26.1]

WAITTE, JAMES, son of William Waitte a painter in Ayr, and his wife Mary ...., was baptized in Ayr on 22 November 1799. [NAS.CH12.26.1]

WAITE, JEAN, daughter of James Waite, a painter, and his wife Mary ...., was buried in Ayr on 3 March 1791. [NAS.CH12.26.1]

WAITTE, WILLIAM, and Mary McKee, both of Ayr, : married there 15 October 1794. [NAS.CH12.26.1]

WALKER, ALEXANDER, minister at Luthermuir, at Perth by 1789. [TBD#121]

WALKER, ARTHUR, son of George Walker in Fyvie, educated at Marischal College, Aberdeen, 1756-1760, minister in Old Meldrum. [SPAER]

WALKER, GEORGE, a minister in Fintry, a beneficiary under the will of Alexander Deuchar in Barbados, 1738 [NAS.CC8.8.100];

WALKER, JAMES, born 1757, died 1843, his wife Mary Ouchterlony, born 1763, died 1854. [Montrose Episcopal MI]

WALKER, JAMES, son of William Walker in Buckie's Miln, educated at Marischal College, Aberdeen, 1775-1779, minister in Huntly. [MCA#349]

WALKER, JAMES, son of Alexander Walker in Fraserburgh, Aberdeenshire, educated at Marischal College, Aberdeen, 1785-1789, graduated MA, later Bishop of Edinburgh. [MCA#364]

WALKER, WILLIAM, a minister in Slains, Aberdeenshire, a beneficiary under the will of Alexander Deuchar in Barbados, 1738 [NAS.CC8.8.100];

WALLACE, DAVID, and his wife Margaret Watson, parents of Marjory and Charles, a merchant in Arbroath, Angus, 1752. [SRS.13.85]

WALLACE, JAMES, born 1677, from Errol, Perthshire, a minister who settled in Elizabeth County, Virginia, died 1712. [WMQ.3.168][FPA]

WALLACE, JOHN, Provost and manufacturer in Arbroath, Angus, 1752, married Elizabeth Mudie, 1729, parents of Marion born 1731. [SRS.13.64]

WALLACE, JOHN, a watchmaker, and Mary Hay, : married in Fraserburgh, Aberdeenshire, on 31 August 1800. [NAS.CH12.32.2]

WALLACE, PATRICK, Provost of Arbroath, Angus, 1752, husband of Agnes ...., parents of Thomas, and Patrick. [SRS.13.64]

WALTON, HELEN, daughter of James Walton and his wife Margaret Ross, was born in Leuchars on 12 August and baptised in St Andrews, Fife, on 17 August 1723. [SER]

WARDEN, JAMES or JOHN, minister of James City, Waynoa, and Martins Brandon, Virginia, from 1711; in Va., 1724. [SCHR.14.142][EMA#177][FPA#170]

WARDEN, SAMUEL, a cleric who emigrated to Virginia in 1712. [EMA#64]

WATERSTON, ELSPET, in Lochhead, was confirmed in Forfar in 1770. [EF#26]

WATERSTON, MAY, in Lochhead was confirmed in Forfar in 1770. [EF#26]

WATTERS or FINLAYSON, CHRISTIAN, and daughters Janet and Christian, : confirmed at Thurso, Caithness, on 8 August 1762. [DC#277]

WATSON, DAVID, a vintner and merchant, married Mrs Frances, daughter of the late John Norris a landwaiter, in the house of Morris on the Shore of Leith on 5 March 1753. Witnesses : Thomas Fotheringham, ... MacKenzie, Betty and Susan Norris. [LER][NNQ.8.125]

WATSON, HELEN, was confirmed in Forfar, Angus, in 1770. [EF#26]

WATSON, JAMES, and Mary Norie, : married in St Andrews, Fife, on 20 September 1765. [SER]

WATSON, JANET, was confirmed in Fortrose, Easter Ross, 1770. [EV#327]

WATSON, JONATHAN, a minister in Banff and in Laurencekirk, Bishop of Dunkeld from 1792 to 1808. [Keith#540]

WATSON, JOHN, a soldier of the Loyal Durham Fencibles, married Catherine Hendry, in Ayr, 23 August 1797. [NAS.CH12.26.1]

WATSON, ROBERT, son to William Watson a maltman in Dundee, was baptised in Dundee on 23 November 1722. [BNDBR]

WATT, CHARLES, an adult, was baptised in Leith on 14 September 1755. [LER][SA.X.11]

WATT, DAVID, son of David Watt in Glen Einnick, was the father of Jean, baptised at Lochlee, Angus, on 30 January 1728. Witnesses : Thomas and John Jollie in Glen Effock. [DUAS.BrMsDC3/174]

WATT, DAVID, in Westbank, father of Alexander Watt baptised at Lochlee, Angus, on 22 March 1732. Witnesses : David Kinnear in Achlochie and Thomas Kinnear in Milntown. [DUAS.BrMsDC3/174]

WATT, JOHN, in Achrallerie, Angus, baptised in April 1735. Witnesses : Alexander Miln in Glen Mark and James Campbell in Dalbreak. [DUAS.BrMsDC3/174]

WEBSTER, ANDREW, son of James Webster and his wife Isabel Laas in New Parish, Aberdeenshire, was baptised 20 April 1776. [CTER]

WEBSTER, Dr CHARLES, minister of Old St Paul's, Edinburgh, husband of ... Graham of Balgowan, a chaplain to the troops in the West Indies, died in St Vincent's during 1795. [JSC#89]

WEBSTER, DAVID, was confirmed in Forfar, Angus, in 1770. [EF#26]

WEBSTER, HERCULES, son of James Webster was buried in Brechin, Angus, on 20 May 1799. [NNQ.14.152]

WEBSTER, JOHN, in Migvie, father of Jean Webster baptised 17 October 1735 at Lochlee, Angus. Witnesses : James Campbell in Dalbreak and John Christison in Cairncross. [DUAS.BrMsDC3/174]

WEBSTER, bailie JOHN, father of James and Janet confirmed in Forfar, Angus, 1770. [EF#26]

WEBSTER, WILLIAM, of the Perthshire Militia, married Jean Logan from Ayr, there, 15 September 1799. [NAS.CH12.26.1]

WEBSTER, ..., wife of Alexander Webster, was confirmed in Forfar, Angus, in 1770. [EF#26]

WEBSTER, ..., child of James Webster in the Tenements, Brechin, Angus, was baptised 12 August 1798 and another on 5 March 1800. [NNQ.14.100/154]

WEDDERBURN, Dr JOHN, in Dundee, 1727. [ECD#21/23]

WEDDERBURN, JOHN, the younger of Blackness, in Dundee, 1727. [ECD#24]

WEDDERBURN, MARGARET, daughter of John Wedderburn eldest son of the laird of Blackness, baptised at Blackness on 30 August 1725. Godfather was Dr John Wedderburn in Dundee, and godmothers : Lady Fullarton and Lady Blackness. [BNDBR]

WEMYSS, WALTER, of Lathocar, married Janet Law, daughter of Captain Law of Pittilloch, at Kemback, Fife, on 30 September 1776. [SER]

WEST, JOHN, born 1756 in Logie, Fife, son of Rev. West and his wife Margaret Mein, educated at St Andrews University in 1776, a minister who emigrated to Jamaica in 1785, died there on 17 October 1817. [EMA#62][FPA#21/316]

**WESTERMAN, ..., daughter of ..... Westerman the quartermaster of the 35th Regiment, was buried at Ayr on 16 November 1790. [NAS.CH12.26.1]

WHITE, ALEXANDER, a minister in St David's, King William County, Virginia, from 1754 to 1775. [VMHB.82.101][FPA#205]

WHITE, CHARLES, a merchant in Dundee, 1727. [ECD#21/23]

WHITE, GEORGE, graduated MA from Marischal College, Aberdeen, in 1657, minister in Ayr 1664-1679, minister of Maryculter from 1679 to 1716 ,deposed as a Jacobite, died in 1724. Husband of Marion Cockburn, parents of George, James, Alexander, Agnes, and Catherine. [NAS.CH1.2.26.4/349-354] [F.6.61]

WHITE, JAMES, son of George White minister at Maryculter, a minister who settled in Jamaica by 1692, minister in Vere from 1714. [APB.2.188][FPA#255]

WHITE, ROBERT, son of Charles White a merchant in Dundee, minister at Eassie, Angus, around 1730. [TBD#30]; minister in Cupar, Fife, Bishop of Dunblane, 1735 until 1761, Primus in 1761, died August 1761. [Keith#548]

WHITESIDE, ANTHONY, from Ayr, and Catherine Agnew, from Newton St Quivox, : married in Ayr, 15 September 1794. [NAS.CH12.26.1]

WIGHTMAN, WILLIAM, a surgeon in Eyemouth, Berwickshire, married Ann De Lisle from Dunbar, in Haddington on 1 August 1782. [NAS.CH12.2.2.18][HEC]

WILD, JOHN, in Lochhead, was confirmed in Forfar, Angus, in 1770. [EF#26]

WILD, JOHN BEAUMONT, son of Robert Wild and his wife Elizabeth ...., was buried at Ayr on 17 August 1790. [NAS.CH12.26.1]

WILL, DAVID, in Kinnie, was father of a daughter baptised at Lochlee, Angus, on 11 April 1728. Witnesses : John Nicoll and John Lindsay; Jean Will baptised 12 February 1730 at Lochlee. Witnesses : John Nicoll there and John Nicoll in Shealie; Thomas Will, baptised at Lochlee on 27 February 1732. Witnesses : John Nicoll in Kinnie and John Christison in Cairncross, and Thomas Stuart in Achurie, Lethnott. [DUAS.BrMsDC3/174]

WILLIAMSON, ALEXANDER, from Forres, Moray, educated at King's College, Aberdeen, 1705, a minister who emigrated to Maryland in 1710, settled in St Paul's parish, Kent County. [EMA#63][ANQ.I.73][FPA#38]

WILLIAMSON, ALEXANDER, born 16 December 1731, a minister who emigrated to Maryland in 1756. [EMA#63][FPA#301/328]

WILLIAMSON, ANNA, was confirmed in Fortrose, Easter Ross, 1770. [EV#327]

WILLIAMSON, CHRISTOPHER, a cleric who emigrated to Maryland in 1711. [EMA#63]

WILLIAMSON, DONALD, was confirmed in Fortrose, 1770. [EV#327]

WILLIAMSON, JAMES, from Forres, Moray, educated at King's College, Aberdeen, a minister who emigrated to Maryland in 1713, settled in Shrewsbury parish, Kent County. [EMA#63][ANQ.I.73][FPA#32/38]

WILLIAMSON, JOHN, was confirmed in Fortrose, Easter Ross,1770. [EV#327]

WILLIAMSON, WILLIAM, educated at King's College, Aberdeen, a minister who emigrated to Jamaica in 1793, settled in St Thomas in the Vale. [FPA#136]

WILLIE, THOMAS, a Society for the Propagation of the Gospel schoolmaster in Barbados around 1727. [FPA#230]

WILLIE, WILLIAM, minister of Albemarle parish, Virginia, from 1740 until his death in 1776. [SCHR.14.143][FPA#191][WMQ.2.20.134]

WILLINGTON, MARGARET, was confirmed in Fortrose, 1770. [EV#327]

WILLISON, ..., a druggist and surgeon, and his wife .....Dempster, parents of David baptised in Forester's Wynd, Edinburgh, on 12 January 1757. Witnesses : Mrs Ramsay and her daughter; Samuel baptised in Craig's Close, Edinburgh, on 17 January 1760. Witnesses : Miss Dempster, Lady Dunnichen, Mrs Ramsay in Leith, and Mrs More. [DUAS.BrMsDC3/12]

WILLOX, JAMES, a minister in Raphan, a beneficiary under the will of Alexander Deuchar in Barbados, 1738 [NAS.CC8.8.100]

WILLS, JOHN, a tailor in Dundee, 1727. [ECD#24]

WILSON, ALEXANDER, and Ann Pirie, both in Fraserburgh, Aberdeenshire, : married there on 31 December 1796. [NAS.CH12.32.2]

WILSON, JAMES, stocking maker in Cowgate, Edinburgh, married Margaret, daughter of the late Robert Kay, a shipmaster in Leith, at the Yardheads of Leith on 27 November 1739. Witnesses : William Clarke uncle of the bride, Robert Fisher kinsman to the bridegroom, Mrs Laing and Mrs Clarke aunts of the bride, and Mrs Groat sister of the bride. [LER][NNQ.8.125]

WILSON, JANE, daughter of James Wilson and his wife Euphame Smith, was born 15 January and baptised on 19 January 1729 in St Andrews, Fife. [SER]

WILSON, LEWIS, was confirmed in Fortrose, Easter Ross, 1770. [EV#327]

WILSON, MARGARET, was confirmed in Fortrose, Easter Ross,1770. [EV#327]

WILSON, ROBERT, son of Robert Wilson and his wife Margaret Smith in Clochtow, Slains, Aberdeenshire, was baptised 20 October 1768. [CBER]

WILSON, ROBERT, son of James Wilson in Long Yester was born 22 May and baptised 29 May 1768 in Haddington, East Lothian. Witnesses : Charles Hay of Hops, Mr Williamson, and John Carfraes. [NAS.CH12.2.13]

WILSON, THOMAS, a merchant in Dundee, 1727. [ECD#23/24]

WILSON, WILLIAM, a writer in Edinburgh, a trustee of the Carrubers Close congregation in 1741;clerk to Alexander Lockhart, married Mrs Barbara, daughter of the late Patrick White a clergyman in Edinburgh, in South Leith on 20 August 1749. Witnesses : George Donald and Elizabeth Henderson. [LER][NNQ.8.125][JSC#84]

WILSON, WILLIAM, a merchant, married Elizabeth Susannah Lapsley, daughter of the late James Lapsley of North Woodside, on 24 April 1797 at St Andrew's Episcopal Church in Glasgow on 24 April 1797. Witnesses : Thomas Buchanan a merchant, Jonathan Wilson a tanner, and James Norris. [SA.X.23]

WILSON, Mrs, of the Perth Episcopalian Congregation, 1742. [TV.77.21][JWI]

WINGATE, JAMES, a minister in Forglen's Back Land, Edinburgh, 1746. [JSC#62]

Scots Episcopalians at Home and Abroad, 1689-1800

WINGATE, JOHN, born 1741, son of Thomas Wingate in Kincardine, educated at Glasgow University, minister of Dale, Virginia in 1771. [EMA#64] [FPA#310/330] [MAGU#71]

WINGATE, JOSEPH, a minister who emigrated to New England in 1763. [EMA#64]

WISHART, JOHN, a minister who emigrated to Virginia in 1764. [EMA#64][FPA#308/330]

WOOD, ALEXANDER, son of Dr Robert Wood and his wife Helen Rose, was born 3 February and baptised 4 February 1724 in St Andrews, Fife. [SER]

WOOD, ANDREW, born 1619, son of Reverend David Wood, minister in East Lothian, Bishop of the Isles 1678 to 1680, Bishop of Caithness from 1680 until 1688 when he was deposed, he died at Dunbar in 1695. [Keith#218]

WOOD, JAMES ALLARDYCE, married Jean, daughter of Rev. James McKenzie, in Lord Tweedale's Close, Edinburgh, 10 January 1751. [DUAS: BrMS3/Dc/12]

WOOD, JAMES, a tailor, and his wife Katherine ...., parents of Anne baptised in Toderick's Wynd, Edinburgh, on 19 October 1752. Witnesses : Elizabeth Irvine and William Watt; Katharine, baptised in Toderick's Wynd, Edinburgh, on 7 May 1755. Witnesses : David Tainsh and Lady Charlton; Joseph, baptised in Toderick's Wynd, on 23 March 1759. Witnesses : James Robertson, Mrs Brown and her son Peter. [DUAS.BrMsDC3/12]

WOOD, JEAN, was confirmed in Forfar, Angus, in 1770. [EF#26]

WOOD, RALPH, a soldier, and Helen Foster, after proclamation in the Kirk of St Quivox, : married in Ayr, 29 May 1794. [NAS.CH12.26.1]

WOOD, ROBERT, son of Dr Robert Wood and his wife Helen Rose, was born and baptised in St Andrews, Fife, on 19 February 1723. [SER]

WOOD, THOMAS, an Episcopal preacher, 1691. [NAS.CH1.2.1/90]

WYLLIE, JAMES, born 1780, died 1833. [St John's, Forfar, MI]

YEAMAN, JAMES, in Mains parish, father of Agnes, baptised 26 July 1723 in Dundee, and Robert, baptised 12 April 1726 in Dundee; in Dundee, 1727. [ECD#26][BNDBR]

YOUNG, DAVID, in Douin, father of David Young baptised 11 April 1731 at Lochlee, Angus. Witnesses : David Rose minister of Lethnott and Lochlee, and David Kinnear in Achlochie. [DUAS.BrMsDC3/174]

YOUNG, DAVID, son of John Young, a smith, was born 28 April and baptised 1 May 1768 in Haddington, East Lothian. Witnesses : David Perie and John Dickison. [NAS.CH12.2.13]

YOUNG, GEORGE, graduated MA from St Andrews in 1676, schoolmaster of Gask 1676 and of Auchterarder, minister of Strowan in 1685 until 1689 when deposed as a Jacobite. [F.4.281]

YOUNG, JAMES, an apothecary in Dundee, 1727. [ECD#23]

YOUNG, JAMES, clerk to the Chapel in Brechin, Angus, was married at Kinnaird's Mill to an un-named servant there, on 16 November 1798; father of Elizabeth baptised 19 October 1799. [NNQ.14.100/153]

YOUNG, JEAN, daughter of William Young the Sheriff Clerk, was baptised in Stonehaven, Kincardineshire, on 24 December 1760. [ST.ER]

YOUNG, THOMAS, in Dundee, 1727. [ECD#26]

YOUNG, Dr THOMAS, a physician in Edinburgh, a trustee of the Carruber's Close congregation, 1741. [JSC#83]

YOUNG, ROBERT, son of James Young in Miln of Cowie, was baptised in Stonehaven, Kincardineshire, 4 January 1756. [ST.ER]

YOUNG, THOMAS, of the Perth Episcopalian Congregation, 1742. [TV.77.21][JWI]

YOUNG, Mrs, of the Perth Episcopalian Congregation, 1742. [TV.77.21][JWI]

www.ingramcontent.com/pod-product-compliance
Lightning Source LLC
Chambersburg PA
CBHW061742270326
41928CB00011B/2343